PENGUIN HANDBOOKS
THE RUNNER'S HANDBOOK

Bob Glover is founder and president of Robert H. Glover and Associates, Inc., a fitness consulting firm. He is marketing director and chairman of the Board of Advisors for New York's prestigious fitness and dining center, the Atrium Club, and the former fitness director of New York City's West Side YMCA, where he developed and led one of the nation's largest fitness programs, with over 5,000 participants. He is director of educational programs for the 25,000-member New York Road Runners Club, advisory-board member of the 35,000-member American Running & Fitness Association, and fitness director of the Great Wall Run, an educational runner's tour of China. He is also founder and coach of several teams, including the Achilles Track Club for the physically disabled, and Atalanta, the elite women's team which has won several national championships in both the open and masters categories, including the New York Marathon four times and the Avon International Marathon five times. Glover has more than fifteen years experience coaching all levels of runners, but he derives his greatest satisfaction from helping the back-of-the-pack male and female runners increase their enjoyment of the sport. Over 50,000 of these athletes have participated in his classes, and thousands more have followed the training programs in his books.

Jack Shepherd graduated from Haverford College and Columbia University, and earned his Ph.D. at Boston University. As an author-journalist, he has covered assignments in forty-six of the fifty states, and in the Far East, Europe, the Caribbean, and Africa. As a foreign-policy specialist, he has worked for the Carnegie Endowment for International Peace in Washington, D.C. His articles have appeared in *Newsweek, Harper's, The Atlantic, Vermont Life, Saturday Review, The New York Times Magazine, Reader's Digest,* and other periodicals. Shepherd is the author or co-author of nine books, including the national best-seller *The Adams Chronicles.* After returning from an assignment in East Africa, he joined Bob Glover's running program, which, he soon decided, deserved to be the subject of a book.

Other Penguin Running Books:

The Runner's Handbook Training Diary
by Bob Glover and Jack Shepherd

The Competitive Runner's Handbook
by Bob Glover and Pete Schuder

The Injured Runner's Training Handbook
by Bob Glover and Dr. Murray Weisenfeld

THE RUNNER'S HANDBOOK

Revised Edition

BOB GLOVER *and* **JACK SHEPHERD**

PENGUIN BOOKS

PENGUIN BOOKS
Viking Penguin Inc., 40 West 23rd Street, New York, New York 10010, U.S.A.
Penguin Books Ltd, Harmondsworth, Middlesex, England
Penguin Books Australia Ltd, Ringwood, Victoria, Australia
Penguin Books Canada Limited, 2801 John Street,
Markham, Ontario, Canada L3R 1B4
Penguin Books (N.Z.) Ltd, 182–190 Wairau Road,
Auckland 10, New Zealand

First published in the United States of America in simultaneous hardcover and
paperback editions by The Viking Press and Penguin Books, with the subtitle
A Complete Fitness Guide for Men and Women on the Run, 1978
The Penguin edition reprinted 1978 (five times), 1981, 1982 (twice), 1983,
1984 (twice)
This revised and updated edition first published in Penguin Books 1985

Published simultaneously in Canada

LIBRARY OF CONGRESS CATALOGING IN PUBLICATION DATA
Glover, Bob.
    The runner's handbook.
    Bibliography: p.
    Includes index.
    1. Running—Training. 2. Running—Physiological aspects. I. Shepherd,
Jack. II. Title.
GV1061.5.G55 1985   796.4'26   84-26558
ISBN 0 14 046.713 0

A selection from this book appeared originally in the Summer 1977 issue of *Road
Runners Club N.Y. Association Newsletter.*

The authors acknowledge with thanks *The New England Journal of Medicine* for
permission to adapt material from an article that appeared in the January 20,
1977, issue, and Metropolitan Life Insurance Company for permission to reprint
the table appearing on page 290.

Printed in the United States of America by
R. R. Donnelley & Sons Company, Harrisonburg, Virginia
Set in Electra

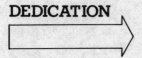

ACKNOWLEDGMENTS 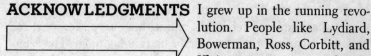 I grew up in the running revolution. People like Lydiard, Bowerman, Ross, Corbitt, and Kleinerman encouraged me and others to make Earth a runner's world. Later, Sheehan, Schuster, Ullyot, Henderson, Lebow, Kuscsik, Switzer, and many others spread the revolution.

I once saw Tom Fleming, a world-class long-distance runner, give a trophy he had just won to the man most responsible for encouraging his road racing efforts: New York Road Runners Club official Joe Kleinerman. I have few trophies to give away, but during my three decades of running I have made many friends, many of whom have helped with the original book and this revision; I can only reward them with the trophy of praise.

After he started attending my beginner's classes, Jack Shepherd suggested that we do the original *Runner's Handbook*. I'm glad he did, although I had no idea how much work it would be—it's worse than an uphill marathon. But, as with any race, we had a lot of help from other runners along the way.

We would like to thank several members of the medical profession for the time they spent gathering material for this book, and for reading the chapters as we completed them.

Dr. Hans Kraus, M.D., developed "The Y's Way to a Healthy Back" program and wrote the books *Backache, Stress and Tension* and *Sports Injuries*, which served as guidelines for the stretching and relaxation exercises in this book. Dr. Kraus is the founder of the President's Council on Physical Fitness and Sports. Over the years he has served as my "guru" in the area of physical fitness and has been a valued personal friend.

Dr. Richard Schuster, D.P.M., has been a pioneer in the field of sports podiatry. He developed orthotics for my feet that saved me from a crippling knee injury, and without his professional and personal encouragement I wouldn't be running today. His extensive reviews of the chapters on injuries and shoes aided the accuracy of this book.

Dr. Murray Weisenfeld, D.P.M., is the author of *The Runner's Repair Manual* and my co-author for *The Injured Runner's Training Handbook*. His extensive review of the injury and shoe chapters in the revision was much appreciated.

Dr. Edward Colt, M.D., a member of the Medical Committee of the New York Marathon, reviewed several key chapters of the original work and has always offered me professional help and encouragement.

Four medical doctors were extremely helpful in the early days of my career in physical fitness, and their ideas were incorporated into the pages of this book. Dr. George Sheehan is a cardiologist-runner-writer whose lectures and writings have opened up new paths for sports medicine in our running world; his advice to me has been of major value to this book. Dr. Edward Dwyer, head of cardiology at New York City's Roosevelt Hospital, worked with me at the West Side YMCA in the development of cardiac rehabilitation programs and taught me the basics of exercise-stress testing. Dr. Milton Brothers, the author of *Diabetes*, contributed his knowledge to this book as an athlete-doctor and as the chairman of my first medical committee at the West Side YMCA. Dr. Fred Grabo, chairman of the medical committee at the Rome, New York, YMCA, was instrumental in helping me follow sound medical practices in developing my first beginner's fitness program.

Several members of the National YMCA also helped develop this book and my program. Alexander Melleby, director of the National YMCA Healthy Back Program, co-author of *Jogging Away from Heart Disease* and *The Y's Way to a Healthy Back*, and one of the premier fitness experts in this country, introduced me to adult physical fitness programming and began guiding my career in 1971. As my supervisor for two years at the West Side YMCA in New York, Al led me down the road to fitness programming. Jack and I gratefully appreciate his review of much of this book.

Dr. Clayton Myers, Ph.D., author of *The Official YMCA Physical Fitness Handbook*, National YMCA fitness director, and developer of the "Y's Way to Physical Fitness" program, guided us in writing this book, and his friendship and direction were invaluable.

George Goyer gave me direction and inspiration in my career with the Rome, New York, Family Y. Dee Coughlin, my former associate at the Rome Y, was a great help in the women's chapter. Her friendship and support were always welcome. Robert Elia, executive director of the Enterprise, Alabama, YMCA, was my first employer when I returned, without direction or prospects, from Vietnam; he guided me into "people work" and showed me the satisfaction of helping others.

Other fitness experts pitched in. Dr. Richard Warner, Ed.D., served as adviser and class leader for my programs at the West Side YMCA. His review of the physiology in this book, and the review of Dr. Bernard Gutin, Ed.D., director of applied physiology at Teacher's College, Columbia University, were very beneficial. Much of my knowledge in the area of physical fitness comes from classroom lectures and personal discussions with Dr. Lawrence Golding, Ph.D., director of applied physiology at the University of Nevada, Las Vegas.

Pete Schuder, track coach at Columbia University and my co-author on *The Competitive Runner's Handbook*, contributed his knowledge of the technical aspects of running. Joe Henderson, writer and editor of running books and magazines, was extremely helpful throughout my career. Hundreds of members of the New York Road Runners Club have given aid and comfort to this work, including the club's president, Fred Lebow. Special thanks are due Barry Geisler, the National Road Runners Club age-group chairman, for working on the original chapter on running for children. Nina Kuscsik, R.N., a good running friend, a national-class marathoner, and a pioneer in the development of women's running, assisted with several parts of the original work, especially the women's chapter, and we are very much in her debt.

Ted Corbitt, R.P.T., a former Olympic marathoner and record-holder for ultra-marathon events, worked as the first president of the New York Road Runners Club, and got the running revolution off on the right foot. As a veteran runner and physical therapist, he was of great help in reviewing the injury, shoe, and "Mother Nature" chapters.

Mitch Maslin, owner and manager of New York's Athletic Attic Uptown and regular instructor for beginners in our New York Road Runners Club classes, extensively reviewed the revision of the shoes and clothing chapters.

I must also thank all the "guinea pigs" who have showed up for our New York Road Runners Club classes. More than 1,000 beginners have participated since 1975 and many are now pounds lighter and much happier—and have even completed several marathons. I am especially grateful to the dedicated, professional instructors who have taught our classes for beginners, advanced beginners, and intermediates: Lina Connors, Mike Cunney, Lisa Eben, Nadia Ghent, Linda Jannelli, Paula Morrell, Kathy Naughton, Patty Lee Parmalee, Ann Rugh, and Nancy Tighe.

The many members of six teams that I have founded and coached—Roman Runners (Rome, New York), West Side YMCA Runners Club, Greater New York AA, the Achilles Track

Club, and my present teams, the elite, Nike-sponsored women's racing team Atalanta and Team Atrium—have contributed to this book in many ways.

My initial work with the Rome YMCA, in adult physical fitness and running, was enhanced by the encouragement and hard work of Al Stringham, Carl Eilenberg, and the late Bill Coughlin, who was tragically killed by a hit-and-run driver while running in 1983. This trio was instrumental in the development of physical fitness in Rome, and the formation of the Roman Runners.

The many members of the Achilles Track Club, the running club for the physically handicapped, which I co-founded in 1983 with Richard Traum, must be thanked for their help in the development of this program, and for the chapter in this revision that focuses on their remarkable achievements.

John Eisner, my partner on the board of directors of the fitness consulting firm Robert H. Glover and Associates, Inc., contributed significantly to the development of this book as friend, runner, and adviser.

And what book would be complete without thanking one's family—my parents, Mr. and Mrs. H. Ross Glover of Dansville, New York, and my wife, Virginia, and son, Christopher—for their support and love.

CONTENTS

INTRODUCTION: DOWN THE ROAD TO FITNESS

Since 1975, when Jack Shepherd and I started working on the first edition of this book, and since 1978, when *The Runner's Handbook* made everybody's national best-seller list, running and runners have changed a lot. In fact, running has changed so much that we've revised this entire book!

The most fundamental change is numbers: more runners are running more and faster than ever before. American Sports Data (ASD) reports that there are some 12 million runners in the United States (other sources claim many more). Of these, 3 million are racers and 700,000 are marathoners. ASD also says that 1.2 million of us log more than 40 miles a week. The National Running Data Center recorded 440,000 individual performances in U.S. road races on certified courses in 1983. Also in 1983, *Running Times* listed 6,000 road races on its calendar—just half the number of races sent in for listing.

We are getting faster, and fitter. As this revised edition details, women have continued to lower their marathon times every year since 1975. Times for the 10K and half-marathon have also improved. All runners—not just the top competitors—have gotten better: The National Running Data Center shows that from 1975 to 1980 the number of finishers in races 15K and longer increased 805 percent!

Corporate fitness programs are also increasing. Ten years ago there were 25 members of the Association for Fitness in Business;

at this writing there are over 2,000. In 1975, the New York Road Runners Club moved their headquarters out of Fred Lebow's apartment—and into a closet in my office. They had 200 members. By 1984, they occupied their own four-story International Running Center just off Fifth Avenue, and had 25,000 members.

My own running classes reflect this growth. In January 1978 I started teaching classes for the NYRRC with 36 beginner runners. In 1984 we had more than 650 men and women registered for a single session, and the classes had to be divided into beginner, advanced beginner, intermediate, basic competitor, and advanced competitor groups. Between 1978 and 1984 more than 5,000 people of every age participated in these classes. The training programs I developed with my staff for these classes are part of this revised edition. (More advanced programs are included in *The Competitive Runner's Handbook*.)

Running has changed in more ways than just numbers. Psychologists, physiologists, exercise specialists, cardiologists—battalions of researchers, medical and other, have poked, probed, analyzed and measured all levels of runners. Their reports are updated and documented here, for their insights are increasingly beneficial. New information has become available about what to eat, how to train, how to avoid injuries, and what to wear. Major revisions have been made on chapters dealing with these topics, and on chapters concerned with running by women and children. These are all basic and valuable additions to running knowledge.

But some things never change. Our need to exercise—and not just promise Gallup Polls that we will—remains. Despite what we know, the general lack of fitness in American society, especially among our children, is still a problem. Moreover, there are whole categories of Americans, especially adolescents and blue-collar workers, who remain apart from America's movement toward fitness.

Despite the widespread activity and enthusiasm, one American out of two does not exercise at all. A 1980 U.S. Department of Health and Human Services study showed that by a "generous" estimate only 35 percent of us get enough "appropriate physical activity." Turn that around and you quickly see that "hypokinetic disease"—the disease of inactivity—is a fact of life for 65 percent of us. Most Americans do not exercise enough to run 100 yards at a slow pace without hard breathing and dangerous heart strain. Dr. Norb Sander says, "My patients need fitness more than they need medicine." Too many of us are victims of sedentary jobs, tension, inertia—and technological "progress."

In the 1930s, Dr. Paul Dudley White publicly disowned his automobile and started bicycling to work. People thought he was nuts. In the 1950s, he became President Dwight D. Eisenhower's physician, and when the President suffered his first heart attack, Dr. White had him back on the golf course within four weeks. Too few Americans are willing to get out of their cars, elevators, or other machines of ease, and start exercising. The medical results are well documented: Increased inactivity and obesity have led to an epidemic of heart disease, deaths from heart attack, strokes, and related illnesses. Heart attack is still the nation's number-one killer. But the death rate from heart disease is slowly decreasing, by 23 percent between 1968 and 1977. The death rate from strokes dropped 32 percent during the same period. New data now being tabulated shows continuing decreases among men and women who exercise vigorously for more than 140 minutes per week. Ulick O'Connor, the Irish poet, author, and playwright, put it this way: "When he popularized the motor car, Henry Ford could never have thought that he was unleashing bacilli that would strike down men in middle age like a medieval plague."

Too many of us are victims of the disease of inactivity. We are lazy and fat. When Yankee Stadium was remodeled in 1974, it contained 9,000 fewer seats than the old "House That Ruth Built." Why? The seats had to be widened from 18 inches to 22 inches to contain the expanding American posterior!

So, we begin by running for our lives: to control our weight, lower our blood pressure, slow the aging process, help prevent heart disease. It is generally agreed that exercise programs improve strength, stamina, coordination, flexibility. Running also gives an overall sense of well-being. Fred Meyer, a vice president of the Tyler Corporation in Dallas, says that "running long distances builds perseverance, and helps me solve business problems." It also helps us tolerate stress, and it may even prolong life, and offer protection against heart disease.

Research on running and runners has perhaps grown fastest in the category of health. What are the long-term benefits from running? How much running is beneficial? Can running prevent heart attack or heart disease? The answers to these and other running-related questions are still being sought, but research since 1978 offers some surprising and encouraging news, which we have included throughout this revised edition. Even the impact of running on your sex life is more fully known today, and so we have updated our last chapter.

Perhaps the best authorities about running are the men and women already on the road to fitness. They know that they feel and look better, and that their lives are being enriched and invigorated. Look at what happened to Jack Shepherd and me.

When Jack Shepherd, my co-author, entered my fitness office in September 1975, he looked like any other out-of-shape American. He had just finished writing *The Adams Chronicles*, a national best-seller, and was slightly overweight and very tense from months of sitting and typing. He talked nervously as he changed into shorts and sneakers for his fitness test. He wanted to begin a jogging program, he told me, because he thought he should have more exercise. He was, after all, thirty-seven years old; friends of his had already suffered and died from heart attacks.

I had heard this story thousands of times before from other men and women like Shepherd. He looked fit, or almost fit, and looked ready to run a mile or more. In fact, he was dangerously out of shape. He couldn't pass any of my flexibility tests. When I took his resting heart rate, it was 108, far above the normal range of 60 to 80 beats per minute for men. His blood pressure was measured at 160/90, also above normal, and I couldn't even test him on the bicycle ergometer because his heart rate would shoot up too fast.

Shepherd became a man of distinction: He was the first person to flunk my fitness test! Worse, when he mentioned it to his wife and friends, they laughed. How can anyone flunk a fitness test for a beginner's class?

Yet Shepherd exemplified the average middle-aged American man (or woman). He wasn't aware of how out of shape he had gotten, but he knew he couldn't run the length of a city block, or climb a flight of stairs, without becoming breathless. He was the epitome of Dr. Thomas K. Cureton's warning, "The average middle-age man in this country is close to death. He is only one emotional shock or one sudden exertion away from a serious heart attack—this nation's leading cause of death."

Obviously, Shepherd is still with us—and, I might add, full of vigor and bite. What did we do? First, I sent him to his doctor, who gave him a stress test and a 24-hour out-patient, ambulatory electrocardiogram (EKG). A minor heart condition was discovered, and a medical conclusion similar to mine was reached: Shepherd was grossly out of shape. Start exercising!

In December 1975, he entered my beginner's fitness class at the Y. For the next eight weeks, Shepherd and the men and women in his class took my beginner's program detailed in Chapter 2. At first, like many other sedentary Americans, Shepherd couldn't run for 20 consecutive minutes. So he ran 2 minutes, walked 2, ran 2, walked 2 during that time period. After eight weeks, however, he was out of the gym and in Central Park, running a mile and then 2 miles non-stop. By the end of six months, he was up to 5 miles. His resting heart rate was down to 75 beats per minute; his blood pressure had also dropped to normal. By

1984, Shepherd had run and completed two New York City Marathons, and had discovered that his favorite racing distance is the half-marathon, which he runs along the Connecticut River from New Hampshire into Vermont.

The exercise method I prefer is running. I was hooked on it as a child. In 1963, while a junior in high school, I went out for track, ran the half mile, and won fifth place in the Livingston County, New York, Championships. The next year I became a 2-mile runner and an instant "hero"—the "marathon man" of the team and a county champion. But in college, I injured both knees, and doctors told me I would never play sports again. I never realized how much I loved to run until I couldn't. So, I cheated: I played a little basketball and baseball in college, and later in Vietnam with the U.S. Army. But I missed running. When I started working as the physical fitness director of the Rome, New York, YMCA in 1971, the Y didn't have any joggers at all. Running was just becoming the sport of the seventies.

In the 1960s, a movement led by Arthur Lydiard, Bill Bowerman and Dr. Kenneth Cooper promoted running as a health-building activity. A new term made the rounds: "aerobic fitness." Even so, runners were few and far between; whenever one passed another they would wave and smile. In some parts of the country, runners who ventured out in flimsy shorts were laughed at, or worse. A few had cigarettes tossed at them, or bottles. Some were chased by cars, or shot at.

In Rome, I was quickly challenged by Carl Eilenberg, a local radio announcer, to run/walk 20 miles in a Walkathon for YMCA Youth, which we co-chaired. Carl announced on the air that if we both didn't make it, we couldn't collect the pledge money. More than $1,000 was "bet" against us. Eilenberg, a former fat man, and me, a cripple, didn't look like we could complete 100 yards, but we started and finished the ordeal. (My time remains a closely guarded secret.) I admit, however, that I was beaten by a forty-two-year-old jogger, but at least I was running again.

In 1972 I saw Frank Shorter win the Olympic Marathon on TV. I knew I had to start long-distance running again. But I didn't want to start it quite this way: I visited Mike Wiley, a former hurdler, in his Kansas University apartment, and we drank beer all night with a group of other runners. There was a marathon the next day, and as the beer went down the challenges went up. More beer, more challenges; when dawn shone I agreed (as I remember) to run. Anyway, a few hours later I found myself on the starting line, a little furry around the tongue. I actually finished—perhaps due to the "foresight" of carbohydrate (beer) loading—and returned to Rome determined to train for and complete the Boston Marathon.

That's when Al Stringham, a co-founder with me of the Roman Runners, introduced me to two important things: regular long runs, and *Runner's World* magazine. *Runner's World* became my coach; Joe Henderson, its editor, my inspiration; and Dr. George Sheehan, a cardiologist and its medical editor (now medical editor of *The Runner* magazine), my life saver. Dr. Sheehan's articles about podiatrist Richard Schuster's work with shoe inserts led to a great discovery: My knee pain didn't mean that I needed surgery. I merely needed proper shoe inserts. It worked, and I was off on a running path that would carry me through more than 30 marathons by 1980.

So were a lot of Americans. In the early 1970s, running and fitness classes were promoted to help prevent heart attacks. A new term swept the country: "cardiovascular fitness." I started a runners' club in Rome, New York, a youth track program, group workouts—and cardiovascular-fitness programs. I was also sensing a change in my personality: As I ran more, reaching toward 10 miles a day, I was becoming less competitive and more contemplative. I was seeing a new world around me.

In 1975, when I became fitness director of the largest YMCA (then 12,000 members) in America—on New York City's West Side—I was faced with classes still involved with the sixties concept of fitness. "Calisthenics drills" with rapid movement were being taught and so were lots of muscle-strengthening exercises. Running meant a five-minute burst around the gym; relaxation and stretching exercises were ignored. Few women ventured into the classes.

Al Melleby, my supervisor at the Y, brought me in as a runner to emphasize the importance of running and fitness. I slowed everybody down, wrote a manual for the instructors, started fitness and stress testing. Within one-and-a-half years I had tested more than 1,000 men and women, and gotten 2,000 started in beginner's, intermediate, or advanced running classes. Even Jack Shepherd joined.

This book, therefore, in its original version and this revision, combines the knowledge and experiences of an out-of-shape, middle-aged American who in three years went from zero to 26.2 miles using this program, with that of a high-school and college athlete who has run over 30 marathons and coaches national-class runners. The early chapters follow the same order that your running life will take: from beginner to competitor. The remaining chapters are filled with material that we both think will interest and help you. The basic theme of the book remains the same, of course: It's a *handbook*, designed to get you exercising down the road to fitness and to keep you there.

But what do I mean by exercise? Simply stated, three basic things: Change your clothes, sweat, and shower. Let's agree from the start that we are going sweat. You may even get to like it. You may recognize it for what it is: a healthy sign of an exercising body. The sweat will come from running, which is the basis of my exercise program. We are going to run slow, and far, but don't panic, because it will be easy. We will run because I agree with the doctors on the President's Council on Physical Fitness and Sports who rated fourteen popular forms of exercise and evaluated them in terms of health benefits. Running, bicycling, and swimming came out first, second, and third. I would also add vigorous walking. These are the rhythmic exercises that use the major muscles repeatedly. The other kinds are the power exercises, such as weight lifting and isometrics, which require short, rapid, forceful movements and put stress on the heart for short periods. The stress on the muscle bundles during contractions tends to impede circulation rather than aid it. On the other hand, running involves vigorous contraction and relaxation of the large muscles of the legs and trunk. Sustained for a period of time, this kind of exercise will raise your body temperature, increase your heart rate, and induce sweating. The rewards will be a greater ability to consume oxygen during strenuous exertion, a lower resting heart rate, less fatigue-inducing lactic acid produced by your skeletal muscles, reduced blood pressure, and more efficient heart and lung action.

While the doctors research and debate the relative benefits of exercise, we are going to run. At first, if you are just beginning, you may find it rough going. Then, after a while, you will feel better—and better. You may even become addicted and want to run every day, especially if you discover meditative running and its euphoria. The way I see it, if I can get Jack Shepherd running and in shape, I can get anyone to run—even you.

1 THREE BASIC QUESTIONS: HOW FAR? HOW FAST? HOW OFTEN?

The most common questions runners ask are: How far should I run? How fast should I run? How often should I run? The answers comprise the ingredients of a successful running program, whether you are a beginner just lacing up your shoes for the first time, or a veteran of several races.

HOW FAR?

For the beginner, how far you should run is measured in time, not distance. The minimum length of time for your workout, determined by studies conducted by exercise physiologists, is 20 minutes. This means that after your warm-up, and before your cool-down, you should exercise briskly enough for 20 consecutive minutes to bring your heart rate into your training range (see chart, page 7). This does not mean that you start out running for a full 20 minutes. Rather, you start by walking briskly, alternating with slow running if you can; gradually build up to running for the entire 20 minutes nonstop.

If you go out and run around the block and stop, or even run a mile in 10 minutes and stop, you aren't exercising long enough to improve and condition your cardiovascular system. Even if you run for four or five minutes, but then sit down or walk slowly and then run again, you are not conditioning yourself properly. The idea is to move briskly, by walking or running, for the entire 20-minute period.

Start by walking briskly, and gradually ease into running for the entire 20 minutes. At first, you will walk more than you run, but after a period of training you will be running more than walking. After you reach a consistent 20-minute run, you should gradually increase that run to 30 minutes. At this point in your training, you will run for 20 to 30 minutes during each of your workouts. After you build up to runs that last longer than 30 minutes, you may want to start alternating long runs and short runs. An advanced runner's shortest runs will still last for at least 30 minutes.

Once you are averaging 30 minutes of nonstop running for at least five days a week and are starting to ease into longer runs, you may wish to start counting daily and weekly mileage instead of minutes run. Most runners eventually switch to counting mileage, since all their friends do and all races and training for races are measured in miles run. Thus, training programs, including those in this book, are written in mileage. I will therefore speak in terms of running for time for the beginner, advanced beginner, and intermediate runner, then switch to mileage running for the beginner racer and beginner marathoner.

HOW FAST?

How fast you run should not be measured by speed but by how your heart responds to exercise (training heart rate). You want to run slowly enough to be comfortable, but fast enough to gain fitness. The beginner alternates brisk walking with slow running. The key here is to exercise *aerobically* for at least 20 minutes.

Aerobic exercise. This is the pulse-rated system of exercise developed by exercise physiologists, and supported by the American Heart Association and leading fitness experts. The aerobic theory was popularized in the 1960s by Dr. Kenneth Cooper, author of several books on the subject.

Aerobics means "promoting the supply and use of oxygen." Dr. Cooper defined as aerobic such exercises as walking, running, biking, and swimming—his "Big Four" of aerobic exercise. These activities, performed at a vigorous level over specific times, burn calories and strengthen your cardiovascular system.

The basic principle of aerobics is that your body must exercise at a rate that demands large amounts of oxygen for a sustained period of at least 20 minutes, three times a week. The exercise must also involve continuous movement at a brisk pace, and yet be moderate enough not to overtax your heart and muscles.

Most fitness workouts are not aerobic. Pumping iron will tone your muscles and improve your strength, but unless done rapidly with light weights for at least 20 minutes, it will not condition your heart and lungs. Tennis, handball, squash, touch football, softball, basketball, and other stop-go sports may be aerobic in spots, but they encourage only bursts of activity, not the sustained workout of cardiovascular conditioning. Bowling, paddleball, doubles tennis, and golf are more socializing than exercising. Worse, they create the illusion of being fit.

Don't be dismayed. There are still plenty of aerobic exercises to choose from, even for the physically disabled. Running, swimming, biking, walking, cross-country skiing, hiking, ice and roller skating, continuous snowshoeing, rowing, even bench-stepping and some forms of vigorous dancing are all aerobic. So, too, is sex—if you can sustain the aerobic training level for at least 20 minutes, three times a week!

The basic reasoning behind such exercising is simple: The more oxygen we supply our bodies, and the more efficiently our bodies use this oxygen, the more physically fit we become. We breathe in oxygen from the atmosphere and our lungs supply our blood with it. Our hearts pump this life-supporting oxygen-enriched blood to our bodies' tissues, where it combines with fuel to produce energy. The blood then carries carbon dioxide and other waste products to the lungs for release back into the atmosphere.

If your body is doing very little work, it is "deconditioned" and cannot perform this cycle well. As Dr. Thomas Cureton, Ph.D., says: "The human body is the only machine that functions better and more healthfully the more it is put to use." By stressing the body with vigorous exercise, we improve the efficiency of the oxygen-transport system: the lungs and heart become stronger, and the heart beats less but pumps with greater strength; the blood carries more oxygen; the blood vessels increase in number; the peripheral circulatory system increases in efficiency; the cells "pick up" oxygen more easily.

But how fast should we run? Dr. Cooper awards aerobic points for increasing speeds run over a fixed distance. I disagree with this method. I believe that aerobic exercises should be performed at a "steady state" heart rate for at least 20 to 30 minutes. You should follow two simple guidelines in controlling your pace:

- You should run at an even pace during which your heart rate levels off at a "steady state" well within your training heart range.
- You should run at a pace that allows you to pass the "talk test."

If you run too fast, you become breathless and your muscles may tighten, perhaps causing injury. Only experienced runners train and race above their training heart-rate range and at a pace where they can't talk comfortably. This is called exercising "anaerobically" or going into "oxygen debt": at this pace, these runners cannot meet their bodies' demands for oxygen, and they have to borrow chemically from their bodies, causing a buildup of lactic acid in their muscles.

As a beginner runner, you should do all of your running aerobically: run within your training heart-rate range and at a pace that allows you to talk comfortably.

The Training Heart-Rate System
You should run by following the best pacer you have—your heart. Many veteran runners can easily tell, by how they feel,

when their heart rate is within their training range. This is perceived exertion, and you may develop it as you train. Beginner runners, however, will need to check their pulse (heart rate) regularly to monitor accurately the intensity of their workouts. This keeps you from running too fast.

Your pulse, or heart rate, is the number of times your heart beats per minute. The faster it beats, the harder you are working. The slower it beats when you are under stress, the better shape you are in. For example, before training, your heart rate may go to 140 beats per minute when you run at a pace of 10 minutes per mile. After perhaps two months of training, it may rise to only 120 beats per minute at the same speed. This is one indication of improvement in your cardiovascular system from a consistent running program.

You can count your heartbeat at several places on your body: over the left side of the chest, at about the middle of your upturned wrist, at the carotid artery just in front of the large vertical muscle along the sides of your neck, or at any convenient place where you feel a pulse. The most common method is to gently press your wrist or neck with the tips of your first two fingers. Don't use your thumb and don't press too hard. Excessive pressure at the carotid artery can be dangerous and may slow the heart rate by three or four beats per minute.

When you feel a pulse, count the number for 10 seconds, then multiply it by six. That will give you your heart rate per minute. (For example, if you count 12 beats in 10 seconds and multiply by six, that will give you a heart rate of 72 beats per minute.) This enables you to determine your resting heart rate easily.

Obtaining your exercise heart rate can be more difficult. Take your pulse immediately after stopping. (This may be for a pulse check break during your run or at the conclusion of your run.) If you don't, your heart rate drops too quickly to give you an accurate estimate. If you take the pulse immediately—you don't have to jog in place to keep your heart rate up—you should get a close reading of your exercise heart rate. Note that counting your heart beats for 15 seconds (and multiplying by four) sometimes gives a lower rate.

Four types of heart rates are important in developing a safe exercise training program.

1. Resting Heart Rate (Base Pulse)   This is your heart rate when you first wake up in the morning, or when you are very relaxed during the day. The average resting heart rate for men is 60 to 80 beats per minute; for women, the average is 70 to 90 beats per minute. A well-conditioned person's heart rate may be around 60 or below; the serious runner often has a resting heart rate in the 40-to-50-beats-per-minute range.

This base pulse is helpful in several ways. First, most people chart their resting heart rates over the course of months or years as a measure of how they are progressing. Generally, as you get in better shape, your resting heart rate lowers. Second, the pulse rate may serve as a warning signal of overtraining. A higher than usual morning resting heart rate may indicate that you are training too hard, not sleeping well or long enough, or are over-stressed. You should take a day off from running, or exercise less until the rate returns to normal.

2. Maximum Heart Rate   This rate is at or near the level of exhaustion, where the heart "peaks out" and cannot satisfy your body's demand for oxygen or beat much faster. You should *estimate* your maximum heart rate by subtracting your age from 220. *This is not a goal.* It is merely a figure from which you can obtain your training heart-rate range. (Your exact maximum heart rate can only be obtained by taking a stress test, supervised by a physician.)

3. Training (Exercise) Heart Rate   Each of us has a specific range—between two heart rates—in which we should achieve sufficient and safe cardiovascular training. This "target zone" or training range falls between two numbers: the minimal target of 70 percent of your maximum heart rate and the cut-off figure of

85 percent of your maximum heart rate. (The 85 percent figure is the approximate border between aerobic and anaerobic conditions.)

Exercising at a heart rate below the lower of the two numbers will not provide much conditioning for your cardiovascular system. Exercising at a heart rate above the higher number will cause a great deal of extra effort (and agony) and potential heart strain or musculoskeletal injury. It will not improve your cardiovascular conditioning because you will not be able to sustain it long enough for the conditioning to take place.

To find your approximate training heart-rate range, subtract your age from 220. Your minimum training heart rate is 70 percent of this number, and your maximum (slowdown) rate is 85 percent. For you runners counting on your fingers and toes, I have included a chart.

HEART-RATE CHART

The following chart designates heart-rate targets for various age groups:

Age	Target HR (70%)	Cut-off HR (85%)
20–25	140	167
26–30	134	163
31–35	131	159
36–40	127	155
41–45	124	150
46–50	120	146
51–55	117	142
56–60	113	138
61–65	110	133
66–70	106	129

Training Range

The pulse rates are based on a predicted maximum, and thus some error is possible. One runner may be able to exceed his or her cut-off rate without "breathing hard," or he or she may feel tired at a lower level of exertion. The "talk test" is a good monitoring device. If you are running so fast that you cannot converse with someone, slow down! Exercise should be fun and beneficial, not exhausting. The beginner runner should run at the lower end of the training range; you do not gain more by running at the top end of the range.

This system helps you determine how fast you should run. During your run, if you are a beginner, occasionally stop and take your pulse. Then continue your exercise. If you are below the training heart-rate range (the 70 percent figure), pick up your pace a little. If you are at or above the 85 percent figure, walk until your heart rate comes back into the training range.

The key is to keep your heart rate between 70 and 85 percent of your maximum heart rate for 20 to 30 consecutive minutes. Your goal is to hold your heart rate in a "steady state" near the 70 percent figure where your body handles the workout easily yet gets aerobic conditioning. Your heart rate will increase as you run uphill, increase your speed, run in heat and humidity, or grow tired. At this point you should slow down or walk briskly to keep your heart rate in that 70–85 percent range.

By running and walking, you can control your heart rate and your conditioning. It should be clear that running hard for a few minutes and then walking slowly for a few minutes will not achieve the "steady state" goal or the conditioning effect. Run enough to keep your heart rate up in that training range, and walk enough to keep the rate down. Gradually build to a 20-to-30-minute run with your heart humming along at about 70 percent of maximum.

For the first few weeks of your training, check your heart rate frequently—at least twice during each workout and at the conclusion before your cool-down. You will find that after a month or so you can run farther, faster, and with less effort at the same heart rate or less. As you get in better shape, and learn the "feel" of running in your training heart-rate range, you may only need to check it halfway through your run and at the end. You may progress to checking it at the end of your workouts, and then only once in a while.

4. *Recovery Heart Rate* The cool-down, described in the next chapter, is essential after all exercise. A leisurely five-minute walk after exercising should bring your heart rate below 120 beats per minute; below 110 for those over age 50. That's your goal. If your heart rate doesn't drop that much during the five-minute walk, keep walking slowly. After 15 to 20 minutes of slow walking and stretching, your heart rate should be below 100 beats per minute, or within 20 beats of your pre-warm-up resting heart rate. If it isn't, you may have run too fast or your cool-down wasn't done properly.

The "Talk Test" System

This is part of the training heart-rate system described above. In that system, you exercise to get your heart rate into your training range (above 70 percent of maximum), but not above 85 percent of maximum. You should alternate slow running and brisk walking for 20 to 30 minutes to reach this training level.

The "talk-test" system is basically the same system, except instead of taking your pulse you simply "listen to your body." This means that you run according to how you feel. You should be able to talk, or hum if you're alone. If not, you are running too fast. Listen to your body. If it yells that you are getting breathless, feeling overheated or uncomfortable, or that your legs are tiring, slow down and walk briskly until you feel ready to run again. Some runners can run above their training range and still hum or talk. Others feel fatigued or breathless even below that range. The bottom line here is simply: Listen to your body. If you feel tired, ignore the heart-rate numbers and cut back.

Running should be fun and beneficial, not a duty and exhausting. Run as slowly as you wish so that you are able to talk comfortably. Alternate this running with brisk walking until you can run nonstop for the entire 20 to 30 minutes. After you develop a feel for that conversational pace, forget about measuring your heart rate and just go by how you feel. You might check your pulse occasionally to be sure that you are not pushing too hard on your runs. Otherwise, listen to your body—and go with the flow.

One other thing: Don't be too competitive with yourself. If you combine distance with time as goals, you will be racing against yourself and overstraining. The most common mistake runners make is that they run too fast. It is better to run slow and long. Remember: To graduate from my beginner's running class you must be able to run for 20 consecutive minutes nonstop—smiling all the while! We give no rewards for how fast you run, only for hanging in there for 20 minutes. Don't compare yourself to anyone else. Run only to improve yourself. Run only against the old, out-of-shape you.

HOW OFTEN?

You must perform some form of aerobic exercise at least three times a week to gain any conditioning, but don't run three days in a row and then take the rest of the week off. Spread the exercise out over the entire week. This usually means every other day.

Most beginners easily find time to exercise on the weekend, but have trouble getting out during the week. Take Monday and Friday off, run on the weekend, and schedule yourself at least one more run in midweek. Some so-called experts argue that you must run every day to build a habit you won't break: it's too easy to take more days off if you give in and take one, they say. This is nonsense! I feel, and studies back me up, that your body needs at least one, and perhaps two, days off a week. The average beginner runner should run four days a week, and then gradually move up to five, and later, if he or she wishes, to six. Running every day is not recommended unless you are logging more than 60 miles a week. Remember these points:

- Run *far* enough to cover 20 to 30 minutes.
- Run *fast* enough and *slow* enough to enable you to talk while you run and also keep your heart rate between 70 and 85 percent of your estimated maximum heart rate—your training range.
- Run *often* enough to achieve a minimum level of fitness— at least three times a week.

2 THE WARM-UP AND COOL-DOWN

Every workout should follow the 1-2-3 approach: warm-up, run, cool-down. A proper warm-up and cool-down are essential for all runners. The proper routine, with relaxation, stretching, and easy running, is important. A balanced program of stretching tight muscles and strengthening opposing muscles should be followed to minimize injury. Such a program is wise since running strengthens the muscles along the backs of your legs and back, making them less flexible than the opposing, or antigravity, muscles along the front of your body.

Our warm-up and cool-down routines will help you prepare for and recover from each run in three ways:

1. These exercises will help you make the important transitions from one activity to another. The relaxation exercises calm you and prevent your carrying tension with you on the run. The cool-down relaxation leaves your run behind and makes you feel surprisingly fresher. These routines help move your mind and body from your hectic life into running and calmly back again.

2. Walking and running at the start of your exercise gradually help your lungs and heart respond to exercise. Following your runs, your cool-down slows your heart rate and allows blood to return from your muscles to your heart and other vital organs.

3. Stretching will relieve muscle tension. This, in turn, in-

creases your athletic ability, fluidity in running, and even lengthens your stride.

The first requirement for increasing your flexibility is learning to relax. A few minutes of relaxing and stretching releases tension and stretches and conditions muscles and connecting tissues. A muscle works best when at its maximum length.

Remember: Do only static stretches. This is slow, rhythmic movement, stopping and holding at the point of first discomfort. Never "bounce" when doing your stretching exercises.

Always perform about 10 to 15 minutes of static stretching exercises before vigorous activity. The time you spend will save time you might lose to injury if you don't stretch. At least 10 minutes of stretching and relaxation exercises should be done after your workouts to prevent muscle tightness. And do the exercises during the day, while on the phone, waiting for the bus, or standing next to the Xerox machine. It all adds up to increased flexibility and a more fit body.

GUIDELINES FOR STRETCHING

- Don't force it. Easy stretching is best.
- Don't bounce or swing your body against a fixed joint—like forcing a toe-touch with knees locked.
- Avoid overstretching any muscles.
- Don't stretch injured muscles. Stick to easy limbering movements until the muscle is healed and ready to be stretched.
- Don't overstretch after a hard race or workout.
- Avoid exercises that might aggravate a preexisting condition, especially in the knees or back.
- Ease into each stretching routine. Advance from one level of stretching to a more advanced level slowly, as you did with your running.
- Breathe properly. Do belly breathing while stretching, just as you do when running. Take a deep abdominal breath and

let it out slowly as you reach forward with your stretch.

- Warm the muscles. A muscle can be stretched safely only when it is relaxed and warmed up. Do some relaxation exercises and some relaxation and gentle stretches before starting slowly on your run. End with more stretches after you run.
- Stretch so you include all major joint movements.
- Stretch specific areas: hamstrings, calves, Achilles tendons.
- Stretch a lot to continue being flexible as you grow older. Stretch during the day even when not exercising.
- Stretch very carefully before morning workouts. Try limbering up slowly, and then walking, before running. A hot bath or shower before your workout will help. Stretch slowly and thoroughly after your run.
- Warm up indoors in cold weather. Here, too, a bath or shower beforehand will help loosen muscles tightened overnight. Some runners warm up with stretches followed by a short, easy workout on a stationary bicycle.
- Continue your stretching routine in warm weather. Just because you are warm, or hot, does not mean you are stretched and ready.
- Don't hurry. Take your time. Stretch step-by-step, and thoroughly. Use the same basic routine every day so you feel comfortable with it. Know it, and stay with it.
- Never cut short your stretching to join friends running by or to get in an extra mile.
- Add to your stretching routine exercises for other parts of your body: bent knee sit-ups for your abdominals; push-ups for your upper body and arms. You may add special exercises to your routine for specific strengthening or stretching: leg extensions for your quadriceps, for example, or additional stretches for your groin area (see Chapter 8).

Remember: when a muscle is bounced or jerked into extension, it tends to "fight back" and to shorten. When the muscle is slowly stretched and held, it relaxes and lengthens. Reach out easily and hold; do not tug and pull. Your relaxed, lengthened muscles are less prone to injury and recover sooner from stress than unstretched muscles. Reach out easily to the point of first mild pulling sensation, hold for a count of ten, and slowly return. Then relax for a count of ten before repeating.

Here is a basic sample program to follow for your warm-up and cool-down. To add variety or specialized stretching exercises for specific problems, see *Stretching* by Bob Anderson, and also Chapter 8.

THE WARM-UP

This consists of three steps: relaxation exercises; stretching and strengthening exercises; and the cardiorespiratory buildup. You begin with relaxation exercises to decrease muscle tension, especially in your back, and to warm up muscles that are tense and difficult to stretch.

Here is a sample 15-minute warm-up routine.

Start by lying on the floor with your knees bent. (Always have your knees bent, feet flat on the floor, when lying on your back, to relieve pressure on the lower back.) Do the following exercises in order.

Relaxation Exercises
1. *Belly Breathing* Close your eyes. Take a deep breath. Concentrate on letting your stomach rise as you breathe in. Let go slowly and breathe out. To be certain that you are breathing properly, place your hands on your stomach. They will rise as you inhale.

2. *Head Roll* Same position. Roll your head slowly to one side, relax and go limp. Roll your head slowly back to the center, and then to the other side. Relax and go limp. Repeat three rolls, with right to left and left to right equaling one roll.

3. *Shoulder Shrug* Same position. Relax, and as you take a deep breath, slide your shoulders up toward your ears and hold

that position for a few seconds. Exhale, dropping your shoulders limply to a relaxed position. Repeat two more times.

4. *Arm Limbering*   Same position. Raise your right arm ten inches off the floor, clench the fist tightly for ten seconds, then let the arm drop limply to the floor. Repeat with your left arm.

5. *Leg Limbering*   Same position. Knees bent. Slowly slide one leg forward until it is stretched flat on the floor, and let it go limp. Raise the leg ten inches off the floor, and tighten all the leg muscles for five to ten seconds. Let the leg drop and relax, and slowly return it to the bent position. Repeat with the opposite leg.

Lying Down Stretches

1. *Double Knee Flex*   Same position. Pull both knees to your chest as far as you can without raising your hips. Then hug your knees with your arms, and bring your head to your knees. Let go, bring your arms back down to your sides. Lower your legs slowly to the flexed position with feet on floor. Repeat at least three times, up to twenty.

2. *Double Knee Roll*   Same position—arms outstretched, palms down. Roll both knees together to one side until the outside knee touches the floor. At the same time, turn your head to the opposite direction, and hold. Remain in this position for a few seconds. Then roll to the opposite side. Do one complete set three times.

3. *Lying Hamstring/Calf Stretch*   Same position. Bring one knee to your chest and slowly straighten the leg toward the ceiling, pointing the toe (hamstring stretch). Slowly lower the leg to the floor and relax. Return to the bent-knee position. Alternate legs, and repeat for a total of two full sets. Then repeat the process, pointing the heel toward the ceiling (calf stretch), for a total of two full sets.

4. *Back Arch*   Same position, but with feet as close to buttocks as possible with heels on floor. Grasp your heels with your hands, and as you take a deep breath, arch your back, lifting your bottom off the floor but keeping your heels flat and shoulders level. Hold; exhale as you return. Repeat twice.

5. *Cobra* Lie on your stomach, arms at your side. Arch your back and look toward the ceiling. Hold, relax, and repeat.

Sitting Stretches

1. *Ankle Rolls* Sit cross-legged. Grasp right foot with both hands and rotate ankle. Reverse direction. Repeat with left ankle.

2. *Groin Stretch* Same position. Place the soles of your feet together. Push down on your knees. Gently bend your head toward your feet. Hold the position with head down for a few seconds. Sit up; repeat two more times.

3. *Sitting Hamstring, Calf, and Back Stretch* Sit with legs straight and spread, both hands overhead. Inhale, and then exhale slowly, and slide your arms along your left leg toward your left toe (keep the back of your knee flat against the floor). Reach as far as you can comfortably, and hold for a ten-count. Inhaling, bring arms back overhead; sit up straight. Exhale as your arms reach toward your right toe, and hold at the point of first discomfort. Don't worry if you can't reach your toes. Repeat twice for each leg.

4. *Sitting Quadriceps Stretch* Tuck your legs under you, sit on them, and lean back on your hands. Push your hips gently forward. Hold to a count of ten. Repeat two more times.

5. *Hip Stretcher* Sit with your legs straight out. Bend your left leg across the right and hug it with your arms, knee to chest. Hold; count ten; repeat with your other leg. Repeat twice with each leg.

Standing Stretches

1. *Total Body Stretch* Stand with legs apart, arms extended toward the ceiling. Grab air with your right hand, then your left, alternating as you rise on your toes. Do this for ten seconds, then let your upper body slowly bend forward at the hips, breathing out, and hang loosely as you slightly flex your knees. Slowly rise to a standing position as you inhale.

2. *The Wall Push-Up*   Stand about three feet from a wall, tree, or lamppost. Place your hands on the wall, keeping your hips and back straight, heels firmly on the ground. Now slowly allow your straight body to lean close to the wall. Drop your forearms toward the wall so that you touch it with your hands and elbows. Keeping your back straight and heels flat, now tuck your hips in toward the wall. Then straighten your arms and push your body back to the starting position. Repeat twice. Hold to a ten-count.

Next, stand close to the wall, feet together, hands on the wall. Bend at the knees, keeping your feet flat on the ground. (This is good for your Achilles tendon.) Hold for a ten-count. Repeat two more times.

3. *Standing Quadriceps Stretch*   Lean against the wall with your right hand. Reach behind you with your left hand and grasp the top of your right foot. Gently pull your heel toward your buttocks. Hold for a count of ten. Do twice with each leg.

4. *Upper Back, Arm, and Hamstring Stretch*   Stand with legs apart, hands clasped behind your back. Bend forward, bringing your arms overhead, tucking your chin into your chest. Hold for ten seconds. Slowly rise back to a standing position.

5. *Side Stretches*   Stand with legs apart, right hand on the side of your right leg, left hand overhead. Bend to the right at the waist, also stretching overhead arm to the right. Look up to outstretched hand. Hold for ten seconds, and alternate stretch to the other side. Repeat each side one more time.

Strengthening Exercises

1. *Push-ups*   Lie on the floor on your stomach. Push your body off the floor with your hands, so that you rise with your back straight and only your hands and toes touch. Form is important. Do five and work up to 15 or so with good form. Keep your back straight, fanny high, and lower yourself so that you touch only your chest to the floor. Then push back up.

2. *Sit-ups* Lie on your back, knees flexed. Hook your toes under the sofa, bed, or other stable object, or have someone hold your feet. Put your hands behind your head, "roll up" smoothly to a sitting position with your head close to your knees. Breathe out as you roll up. Now, roll back smoothly, breathing in. Do this slowly, carefully; do not arch your back or strain for one extra sit-up. Start with 5 and work gradually up to as many as you can comfortably do with good form. Good for abdominal muscles.

A special word is needed about sit-ups. One of the major causes of back pain is not "weak back muscles," but weak stomach muscles. If your abdominal muscles can't properly carry their workload, then your back muscles may overstress, resulting in back pain.

Sit-ups, properly done, are an excellent way to keep abdominal muscles in tone. Yet most Americans do not perform them correctly. Our coaches and drill instructors have for years emphasized very fast, multi-repetition, straight-legged sit-ups that are not only incorrect, but also harmful to your back. Straight-legged sit-ups use both the abdominal and hip-flexor muscles. Many people can do them but cannot do sit-ups with knees bent. Their stronger leg muscles compensate for their weak abdominal muscles.

Always do sit-ups with your knees bent. That takes the pressure off your lower back and maximizes the use of your abdominal muscles. Sit-ups should not be done in a fast or jerky motion. Arching the back or bouncing off the floor for high-speed sit-ups puts tremendous strain on your back. Instead, "roll up" smoothly, as suggested above, breathing out as you come up. Roll slowly down. "Gutting it out" for a few fast sit-ups, or a few extra, is inadvisable. The result may be a strained back. Instead of pushing for a few more sit-ups, do some other abdominal exercises and return for another set of sit-ups later.

The stomach muscles should be relaxed between each sit-up, even for a brief second. A long series of abdominal work may be dangerous; as your muscles get tired, you tend to arch your back or jerk yourself up to compensate. The result may be a back injury. Space your abdominal exercises throughout your workout. More important, do only as many sit-ups in one set as you can with proper form. Gradually add more as you become stronger.

Some beginners cannot do sit-ups with their hands behind their heads. If this is the case, you can work into proper sit-up form by a series of progressive steps. Try each step until it becomes too easy, and then move to the next. First, lie on your back, raise your knees with your feet flat on the floor. With your arms at your sides, raise your head, chest, and arms off the ground in a half sit-up. Do several of these. The next step requires that you

SAMPLE 15-MINUTE
WARM-UP AND COOL-DOWN ROUTINES

Relaxation Exercises
1. Belly Breathing
2. Head Roll
3. Shoulder Shrug
4. Arm Limbering
5. Leg Limbering

Lying-Down Stretches
1. Double Knee Flex
2. Double Knee Roll
3. Lying Hamstring/Calf Stretch
4. Back Arch
5. Cobra

Sitting Stretches
1. Ankle Rolls
2. Groin Stretch
3. Sitting Hamstring, Calf, and Back Stretch
4. Sitting Quadriceps Stretch
5. Hip Stretcher

Standing Stretches
1. Total Body Stretch
2. The Wall Push-up
3. Standing Quadriceps Stretch
4. Upper Back, Arm, and Hamstring Stretch
5. Side Stretches

Strengthening
1. Push-ups
2. Sit-ups

Note: For the cool-down routine, do the exercises in reverse order, from standing stretches to relaxation, ending with belly breathing. Then close your eyes and rest for two minutes.

keep your arms at your sides but roll slowly into a full sit-up. After you can do these easily, try folding your arms across your chest, and rolling slowly into a full sit-up. After doing the above for several weeks, place your hands behind your head, elbows extended, and roll into a full sit-up. This is the proper form. Remember to keep your knees bent, roll into the sitting position without jerking, and breathe out as you come up.

The Cardiorespiratory Warm-up

After stretching, begin a five-minute brisk walk. Pick up your pace as you approach the start of your run. Or, instead of a brisk walk, start with a five-minute slow jog and ease into your training pace.

Don't go from your stretching, warm-up phase into running without some transition. Allow your pulse to increase gradually, and then settle into your training range.

THE COOL-DOWN

This is the warm-up in reverse. It includes cardiorespiratory cool-down, stretching, relaxation exercises. Runners who skip the cool-down phase are often injured because they haven't stretched and relaxed their muscles after a run.

After your run, walk for about five minutes. Then, do the same stretching routine that you did for your warm-up, except in reverse. You may skip a few stretches to make the routine fit into ten minutes. Don't do any push-ups or sit-ups.

The purpose of the cool-down is to return your body to its pre-exercise level. This insures the return of normal blood flow from your extremities to the heart, and helps prevent muscle tightness. It is important to slow your heart rate; your recovery pulse should be under 100 beats per minute at the conclusion of your cool-down routine.

Try this series to help you relax and cool down at the end of your workout:

On your back, flex your knees. Let one leg slide slowly

forward, and drop to the floor. Raise the leg 10 inches off the floor and tighten. Hold for 10 seconds. Drop it, relax, return the leg to its flexed position. Repeat with your other leg.

Now, push the small of your back into the floor. Hold for 10 seconds, then let go. Raise one arm high into the air, and tighten the fist. Hold for 10 seconds, then let it relax. Repeat with the other arm and fist.

Tighten the muscles in your face. Really make a contortion. Hold for 10 seconds, then relax.

Repeat the belly breathing exercises. Now, lie with your knees flexed, eyes closed. Allow your body to go limp. Think good, clean thoughts. Tell yourself that you feel very heavy, very loose. (I said *clean* thoughts!) Rest for 30 seconds to one minute.

Slowly, get up, rising to your hands, then knees, then one leg, then both legs but bent over, then slowly erect. Check your pulse after your cool-down, walk; keep walking slowly, like a racehorse after a race, until your pulse reaches 100 beats per minute or less. Stretch, shower, and get on with the rest of your life.

3 GETTING STARTED: THE RUN-EASY METHOD

You may want to read Chapter 4 before you read this chapter. Why? This chapter is filled with good advice about getting started, and staying on the road to fitness. It is appropriate for all runners, beginner to intermediate. But first, you may want to decide which level of runner you are: beginner, advanced beginner, intermediate. Not that it truly matters, yet. These tips apply to everyone, including the authors. No matter how much running you do, you will want to review this chapter regularly, because we are going to yank the covers off all your excuses, whimpers, and whines about getting started, and get you on the road and keep you there.

First, remember one thing: I've heard every excuse that exists about not running. (If you think you've got a foolproof one, mail it to me.) I've heard 'em all:

"I don't have time."

"I've never been much of an athlete."

"Running is sooooooo boring. I feel like a gerbil on a treadmill."

But let's get started. There are five important steps to becoming a runner:

1. Make a commitment.
2. Check with your doctor.
3. Get good running shoes.
4. Make a schedule and start a sensible training program.
5. Stay with it.

COMMITMENT

Be committed to your fitness program. This is important because lack of commitment and motivation are the primary reasons why one out of five people don't exercise. Why should you start running? There are many reasons why running is good for you. However, running may not be the right activity for you. You need to exercise aerobically at least three times a week for at least 20 minutes in order to achieve a minimum level of fitness. So, if you prefer to swim, bike, or walk briskly, do it! Of course, you can enjoy a variety of aerobic exercises by alternating running with other activities. I feel running is the best way to get in shape and keep in shape since you don't have to find a pool or buy a bike to work out. Just put on your shoes and head out the door. You can exercise alone, or run and chat with others. Running isn't the only answer to fitness, but it is an excellent choice for most men and women who wish to get in shape.

Running helps you lose weight and firm up your muscles. It relieves stress, helps control your blood pressure, and minimizes your chance of developing heart disease. It can be effective in helping you overcome bad habits such as smoking. All of these reasons for exercising are based on what you *have* to do to keep physically and mentally healthy. If you only exercise because you have to, you won't enjoy it fully. I know people who run despite the fact that they hate every step. They run because they know it is good for them.

If you hate running, try another aerobic activity. Often, when you don't enjoy running it is because you are not doing it correctly. By slowing the pace down so you can converse, or alternating running with walking and progressing slowly, or changing the time of day that you run or where you run, or meeting others to run with, you may learn to enjoy running. Most of us, however, enjoy running once we overcome the initial obstacles we face as beginners: our out-of-shape bodies and a too-hurried daily schedule. Some individuals, such as the very overweight or those troubled by injuries that are aggravated by running, may be better off to switch to a non-weight-bearing activity such as biking or swimming.

Since it probably took you years to get out of shape, make a commitment to give yourself two or three months to get back into shape. You should commit yourself to exercise at least three times a week and be prepared to struggle, if need be, through the early stages until definite results are achieved. If overweight, you should also make a commitment to lower your caloric intake. When you start exercising, you'll want to maintain a balance between your fitness program, career, and social responsibilities. There is no need to become a fanatic about running—what is important is to work fitness into your life.

But make the first step on the road to fitness: commitment.

CHECK WITH YOUR DOCTOR

If you have been sedentary, or you are over forty years old, or overweight, or there is a family history of cardiovascular illness, you should consult your physician before starting any exercise program. He or she may request that you take an exercise stress test to check out your heart before you get started. If muscular or skeletal problems develop after starting to exercise and don't go away with rest, see an experienced sports-medicine authority. Don't try to keep running despite an injury—you will just make it worse. By starting with a conservative training program, and by "listening to your body" for warning signs (pain), you will greatly reduce injuries. Beginners often try to do too much too soon.

SHOES

The only major equipment you need is a good pair of running shoes. Although you could get by the first few sessions with an old pair of tennis shoes or a cheap pair of running shoes, it would be wise to make the commitment to start safely by investing in a quality running shoe. See Chapter 15 for guidelines for choosing your first pair of running shoes.

SCHEDULE AND FOLLOW A SENSIBLE TRAINING PROGRAM

You need to run at least three times a week, approximately every other day. Each workout, including warm-up and cool-down, will only take an hour. Make your exercise hour "sacred" and free from interference. Pick the best time of day for you, and stick to it. Never put off exercising because you are feeling too harried or too busy. That's when you need exercise most.

I am only asking you to set aside three hours a week at the start. But you may complain, "I don't have the time." You do. In fact, you can easily find three hours out of the 168 hours every week. Here's how:

Make a firm commitment that you will set aside one hour every other day for exercise. That's roughly one hour from every 48. You're sleeping 16 hours out of those 48, and working 16 hours. That still leaves 16 hours for other things, and one of those hours could be set aside for exercise. On a weekly basis, three hours out of 168 hours in every week takes only 1/56th of your time for exercise. Best of all, what you do with the remaining 55/56ths will be enhanced and invigorated by what you do in that time.

Next, make a schedule. Even though I hate them, in the beginning they can help. Block in your work hours and sleep hours. Allow time for eating and commuting to work. Now stop. Your next priority is to find those three hours of exercise. Block out three hours—one every other day, or every 48 hours—for your exercise program.

Find the time that's best for you. Some runners prefer the early morning, when the day is fresh. It's great—they tell us—to wake up and start running. Sudden house guests or business meetings won't interrupt you, and watching the sunrise can be lovely. In the summer, you miss the unpleasant heat of the day. Others, like myself, prefer midday. Noontime runs are favorites of businessmen and businesswomen. I frequently have noontime meetings on the run. Why not burn calories and ideas at the same time instead of stuffing booze and food into yourself? Many runners are substituting a run for those large and unnecessary lunches that make you sleepy all afternoon. You'll find that a run will invigorate you, and low-calorie foods like yogurt, fruit salads, and juices will taste terrific after a workout. You're beating caloric counts at both ends. Shepherd claims that his old joints won't turn until midafternoon. He runs in the cool of the evening. Most runners prefer this time, when they can release the tensions of the day, and separate the work world from the leisure or home world.

Your schedule should be flexible. Yet you will also have to find a time that fits your lifestyle, and *stick to it!* Be firm. Set a priority. I usually run at noon, four times a week, and then in the evening with our team one evening per week. I also run every Saturday and Sunday morning. Most of my business meetings and social outings are scheduled around these times (or rather around babysitting for Christopher and these times).

Follow your schedule: Monday, Wednesday, and Friday; sunrise, noon, or evening. Put it in your appointment book. Make a date with yourself. Bill Horowitz, my running dentist, says, "I schedule an appointment for myself each day just as patients schedule themselves to see me. I run when scheduled, come 'Hell or high water.' " You do, however, have to be somewhat flexible. If I know I can't run in the day because of a business trip, I may get up early and do a short run in the morning, for example.

It is extremely important to follow a sensible training program. *Do not* follow programs made up by friends who happen to run or track coaches who are only experienced at coaching elite runners. You must follow a very conservative program to gently ease you into running. The key is learning how to run enough, but not too much. As a beginner, more is not better. If you try to run too fast, too often, or too long—you are likely to become injured, exhausted, or frustrated. The methods I use for cautiously, systematically guiding beginners to minimal levels of fitness have been tested successfully on thousands of out-of-shape men and women of all sizes, ages, and fitness levels. Follow the programs outlined in this chapter to ease your body through the stages of a beginner runner.

Give your running program a chance.

STICK WITH IT

You must get out there at least three times a week for at least six to eight weeks before you have really conquered the sport. Once you get past that stage, stick with it. It has been my experience that there is a 50 percent dropout rate in the first eight weeks. Why?

Starting a program alone can be very demanding. You need the support of others. Enroll in a beginner's running program at your local Y or get a few friends to start with you. Our classes at the New York Road Runners Club get 20 to 50 beginners with each session. The fact that they have to show up once a week to run with their new friends encourages them to get out at least two more times during the week for "homework" runs in order to be able to keep up with the progress of their classmates. You will be more motivated to stick it out if you're committed to keeping up with the gradual progress of a class.

Or, try meeting a friend twice a week to get you off on the right foot. You will have a running partner, and you will motivate each other.

Beginners try to do too much too soon. Follow a sensible training program such as the ones that follow in this chapter. If you try to run too much too soon you are likely to get injured or frustrated. I prefer that beginners start with a very conservative program of run one minute, walk one minute, and add one minute of continuous running each week. Most can run more than one minute at a time from the start. But if you run as far as you can from the first day you may injure yourself. And it will be difficult to improve upon your performance for a while. You may reach a point where you won't be able to continue improving, or will not even be able to match your performance from the previous days. It is better to see progress—very gradually—each week as you gently, safely build up to being able to run for 20 minutes nonstop.

Many runners—but not all—need a coach. A coach, or group instructor, can keep you on the road to fitness. The coach can answer your questions and help you adjust your training to minimize injury and maximize enjoyment. If you don't have a coach, use a spouse or friend as a cheerleader. It is a cheerleader's job to help you become a graduate of your beginner running program by being available to listen to you brag and complain about your daily running and offer cheerful encouragement. Beware! Don't let a spouse or friend who is not experienced at coaching beginners become your coach. Use them as motivational cheerleaders, not running experts, or they could innocently lead you astray.

You need some type of follow-up system or tangible goal to help insure your success. Some of my beginner program instructors call students if they miss two classes in a row. In these classes, over 85 percent of students graduate. This is a very high percentage. Make a running friend responsible for calling you regularly to keep you committed.

Keep track of your running in a daily diary. If you have to write in your diary, you will be less likely to skip several runs in a row. You would mess up your careful bookkeeping with all those blank spaces. Another technique that I have used in my beginner's classes is the graduation certificate. All students who attended at least 80 percent of classes and were able to run for 20 to 30 minutes, nonstop, and smile at the same time were awarded a graduation certificate. Have that running friend promise to give you one when you "graduate," or take you out to dinner. It is very important to have some system of following up on your running progress and a tangible goal.

Start in a good season—the spring or fall, if possible. Many beginners give up because of bad weather in the winter or summer. Of course it is better to start than not, but you are more likely to force yourself out the door when you don't have to face cold, heat, or darkness. Be flexible. If it is too hot, swim instead that day. If it is cold and rainy, ride a stationary bicycle indoors. Don't let the weather stop you.

Keep your running schedule flexible. If you try to run at sunrise and hate it, you won't succeed. If you try to rush through a workout on a short lunch hour or hurry home after work to fit it in before another appointment, you won't succeed. You must make the time to run when it will be convenient for your enjoyment.

Why do runners become ex-runners? Psychologist Lynn McCutcheon, author of *Psychology for Runners*, conducted a survey and found that the five main reasons for stopping were:

1. Time constraints (efficient scheduling is necessary);
2. Bad weather (be prepared to dress for the weather, or work out indoors on an indoor track, pool, or bike);
3. Preference for another type of exercise (this is fine as long as it is an aerobic alternative);
4. Inability to stick with a schedule (progress slowly, move back a few steps, and start over if necessary);
5. Lack of running partners to keep company (try enrolling in a class, joining a running club, traveling to local parks or tracks where lots of others run, making appointments with friends on a regular basis).

Of the 56 dropout cases in McCutcheon's survey, however, half said they intended to return to running.

Other major reasons for dropping out are illness (back off and start all over from the beginning when you feel healthy again) and injury (try an alternative exercise such as swimming or hiking until you can run again).

Running may not necessarily be fun for you at the start. Once your body adjusts to the work and you begin to feel the benefits and energy, you will be more committed to sticking it out. It takes four or five months of running to become truly committed. You need to build up to running for at least 30 to 45 minutes at a time to get some of the psychological highs associated with running. Even though you successfully make it through the beginner's stage, you still haven't totally conquered running until you make it a part of your life for several years.

Others drop out after running for six months to a year. They've conquered the challenge of getting in shape and then have little motivation to continue. For some, the next challenge is racing. By running a few races now and then—more for the challenge of improving yourself than for competing against others—you provide new goals to keep you going during your daily runs. Also, you meet many new running friends and get "recharged" by running in a race with hundreds or thousands of others enjoying the spirit of exercising.

Here are some tips to keep you going:

- Persist. It may not be fun. It may hurt. Your body may scream: "Why did I let Glover talk me into this?" But most runners will tell you that the first mile or two are the worst. Once you're out beyond that, the run gets to be fun.
- Set that schedule. Three times a week. An hour each time. Put it on your calendar.
- Keep a diary. Record your mileage daily, weekly, monthly, yearly. This record will motivate you, and make you consistent.
- Go to a race. Run with others. Hang around runners. Join a running club that does not stress competition, but enjoyment.
- Be patient. You won't notice results right away. But you will notice them. Give yourself a chance.
- Reinforce your commitment. Buy a new pair of running

shoes. Join a fitness class.
- Prepare your body for every workout by properly warming up and cooling down.

As you get underway, try to encourage a friend to start. The two of you will support each other when the weather turns bad, or when excuses blow in the wind. Beware of "quitter's disease," which discourages many men and women. You may find yourself obsessed with forcing out that extra mile "at all costs." Avoid these traps, or running will become just another duty, like mowing the lawn. Soon you'll hate it, and embrace any excuse to give it up.

Beginners, after the first four weeks, should set two goals: finishing four more weeks, and searching for that feeling of "I want to run." It may also be a good time to subscribe to a runner's magazine, such as *Runner's World* or *Running Times* or *The Runner*. Read books about running.

Search for growth in yourself, and variety in your running route. Run your old course in the opposite direction. Explore a trail through the woods, or when you're in a new city, explore parts of it. Run with new people.

As you emerge along the beginner's path, you will find new horizons to explore.

COACH GLOVER'S RUNNING PROGRAM: THE RUN-EASY METHOD

Most books on running preach systems. The common theory is that we must be programmed to follow a rigid, systematic schedule that tells us in advance what we will do every day for eight to twelve weeks. But I hate schedules. I find them too rigid and scientific. Running embodies a special freedom: a freedom from the computerized world, a return to nature. My basic plan for running revolves around people and such unscientific principles as feelings and body language. I believe that running should be easy, simple, fun. Running at an easy pace, you'll find that your body will gently move into a new life with a minimum of discomfort.

The American Running & Fitness Association says, "Run Gently." Joe Henderson popularized the phrase "LSD" (Long Slow Distance). "Train, don't strain" was Oregon coach Bill Bowerman's Golden Rule. "The Run-Easy Method" is just another name for the same principle. We are all saying, "Throw away the stopwatch and listen to your body instead."

Pace is the most important and difficult part of running to learn. Too often we are in a hurry. But we can't rush to get into shape and we shouldn't run in a hurry. Instead, running should relieve the pressures of our hurried pace. Of course, you can run so that time counts—the first 20 minutes for the beginner runner—but not distance. My point here is simply: Get out of the distance hang-up, where runners greet each other with "How far did ya run?" You can run for distance if you like, but if you combine distance with time the result is competition, the desire to hurry. This brings the hectic pace of your workaday life to the leisurely pace of running. I insist that you run easy. To do otherwise is to encounter not fitness, but often injury and frustration.

Remember, the only person you compete against during your workouts is the old, "out-of-shape" you—no one else. Let other runners brag about their running mileage or times. You should exercise at your own speed. When you run—and I'll emphasize this again and again—run at a pace that enables you to talk with someone. Exercise aerobically for at least 20 continuous minutes at least three times a week. Consistency and endurance—not speed—are the key.

Run for fun. As your muscles firm and stretch, as you relax, eat, and sleep better, meet new friends and discover that running can be graceful and fun, you'll understand what Joe Henderson meant when he wrote in *The Long-Run Solution,* "Running only to exercise the muscles is like eating only to exercise the jaws, or having sex only to train the pelvis."

Okay, let's get started. Remember, Jack Shepherd was in bad

shape when I got him into my beginner's fitness class. He has traveled down the road to fitness, and you can do it, too. Be determined—but also be patient. Muscles and wind won't return in two weeks, but they will return.

4 TRAINING PROGRAM: THE BEGINNER, THE ADVANCED BEGINNER, THE INTERMEDIATE RUNNER

A *beginner* runner is someone who cannot run for 20 consecutive minutes at a steady comfortable pace. An *advanced beginner* runner is someone who can run at least five consecutive minutes and can run for 20 minutes with only a few walk breaks. An *intermediate* runner can run for 30 minutes nonstop at a comfortable pace, and runs at least three times a week.

You should select the category of runner that best describes you. Don't inflate your value: You want to select the best training program for you at your present level, and then work up from there.

It's okay to be a beginner runner. In fact, it may be an advantage to start at this level and progress steadily. Don't be embarrassed. All of us have started as beginners sometime in our lives. In just a few short weeks, following the program in this chapter, you will have graduated and become a full-fledged runner!

Remember the five key steps to becoming a runner: commitment, a medical check-up, shoes, a schedule, and persistence. Make your running schedule, and fit these programs to your level of running and your schedule. Beginner runners should reread the previous chapter and incorporate into their lives the keys to getting started. All runners should reread the previous chapter and memorize the tips to keep you going.

Remember, as emphasized in Chapter 2, that *every* exercise program consists of three important steps: warm-up, run, cool-down. Design for yourself from this book, and follow every day, a practical warm-up and cool-down routine. Remember, too, ol' Coach Glover's "Run-Easy Method." The runners who quit or get injured are always those who think they can beat the system; they don't warm up, they train too fast or too much for their level, they never cool down. These are the same people who go through life taking a fast bite of everything, and tasting nothing. Relax. Be patient.

BEGINNER RUNNER

If you are just beginning, start first with *walking*. Older or overweight persons, anyone with joint problems, or someone who has been inactive for a long time, should start with a walking program. *Walk before you run.* Think of it as a preconditioning program. Some of you may find that walking is sufficient exercise in itself. My father can't run due to an old World War II injury. He walks briskly for an hour or more several times a week.

Start with a fast walk for 20 to 30 minutes. Slow down if you find yourself short of breath. Don't stop. Keep moving. By pumping your arms as you walk, and really stepping out, you can increase your heart rate to a level nearly equivalent to a slow run. Also, by walking vigorously uphill, you can add to the rigor of your walking workouts.

Once you can walk briskly for 30 minutes, you can start interspersing some easy running into your walking. By slowly exchanging running for walking, over several weeks, you will gradually progress to nonstop running.

Three Methods for Beginner Runners

I use three methods for starting beginner runners. These are conservative, progressive programs based on the principles discussed in Chapter 1. These methods work on your exercise heart rate, running at a conversational speed, and training for 20 to 30 minutes three days a week.

The first two methods allow more freedom to select how far you run before taking a walk break, and more flexibility for increasing your run-walk ratio. The third method is structured and has emerged during the last five years from techniques I developed training some 10,000 runners face-to-face. I found that many runners need the discipline and motivation of a precise, structured program. This third method is the one I suggest.

Method 1: The 20-Minute Run-Easy Program   First, warm up with your stretching routine. Then, walk for five to 10 minutes, and alternate walking with running for another 20 minutes. Start your running slowly, taking walk breaks at a fast pace whenever your body needs to slow down. The signal for this may be shortness of breath, weakness in the legs, and so forth.

Be conservative. Take several walk breaks during your run: approximately every one to five minutes, depending on the level of your conditioning. Resume running when your body feels ready, perhaps after about one minute of walking. Don't stop moving. Don't simply quit and sit down.

The goal is to alternate brisk walking and slow running (but running so that your heart rate stays within your training range). Walking too slowly may lower your heart rate out of your aerobic training range; running too fast may raise your heart rate over the training range.

Follow this routine—without stopping (except to monitor your pulse)—for 20 minutes. Gradually, over a period of several weeks, shift the ratio of walk-run so you are progressively running more and walking less. The goal is to run the full 20 minutes nonstop, and at a conversation pace.

Don't try to run a specific distance at first (like a mile), or see how far you can run. This will put too much pressure on you, and may injure you. Since you are exercising within a *time* measurement—20 minutes—it doesn't matter how much *distance* you cover. Your goal is to keep your heart rate in that exercise training range for a specific period of time. Distance doesn't matter.

Don't be concerned if a friend goes farther or faster than you for the 20 minutes. If you are both working on your training heart rates, you will have gained equal benefit. Most important, you are not competing with anyone—except that old, previously out-of-shape you. That's someone you improve on every time you go out the door.

How many minutes you can run at one time, and how long it takes you to build to 20 minutes of continuous running, will depend on many factors: your age, previous athletic experience, body weight, weather conditions, and so forth. Most beginners will take eight to 10 weeks to run 20 continuous minutes. Be patient.

Method 2: The 1½ Mile Run-Easy Method   This method is the same as the previous one, with a minor difference: Instead of alternating running and walking for *time* (20 minutes), you alternate running and walking for *distance*. In this method, that distance approximates 20 to 30 minutes in time.

I have incorporated this method into my training programs because some runners prefer a physical, tangible goal. They can see a distance; they cannot seem to "see" or feel time. For example, there is a cinder track around the reservoir in New York City's Central Park which is a popular running path. The 1½-mile distance around it is an excellent goal for Beginner runners. They start by alternating walking and running and complete a loop that way. Gradually, they replace the walking with running, always completing one loop of the reservoir. The day they run the 1½-mile distance nonstop, you can hear their whoops of joy throughout the park.

You may prefer a system of distance instead of time. Here are some suggestions:

- Walk/run a measured loop in a local park.
- Walk/run from your house to a friend's.

- Walk/run a specific number of laps of a local high school or college track.
- Walk/run a measured loop, or an out-back course in your neighborhood.
- Walk/run home from work.

Caution: Do not combine time with distance yet. Either run 20 to 30 minutes, or run a distance that approximates that time (perhaps 1½ to two miles). If you start timing your runs each day to see how fast you are running, you will be racing yourself. This will result in additional pressure to start running faster than conversation pace or to run too long before taking walk breaks.

Method 3: The New York Road Runners Club Run-Easy Program   Let me repeat: I hate schedules. I do argue, however, that many beginner runners benefit from a structured program, and the program I have developed from our New York Road Runners Club classes is now widely used to help thousands of new runners. It's ridiculously easy. We start out running only one minute at a time!

True, most of you can run more than that at first. But we start running for just one minute. Very gradually, we increase that amount to running 20 minutes without stopping—a level that comes after 10 weeks.

Such a program cuts to almost zero your chances of injury—or discouragement. Each week you improve with this program. And less is more: By running less than you can each week, you make it easier to run more week after week.

The following schedule should be run at least three times per week. All running should be done at conversation pace, and all walking should be done briskly. Of course, a proper warm-up and cool-down are required.

This program starts conservatively. You can even fall a little behind schedule and still get back on easily. Once you reach the halfway mark, however, you will find it difficult to keep up unless you run faithfully at least three, and preferably five, times a week.

If you can't keep up, or lose time from illness or injury, don't panic. Stay at the level you can handle (or go back a level) until you are ready to move up. This may mean that it will take 12 or 15 or more weeks to build up to running 20 minutes nonstop. Don't worry. Don't hurry. Just remember how many years it took you to get out of shape; take your time getting back into it. Your goal is running 20 minutes nonstop—smiling and talking all the way. It doesn't matter if you take six weeks or four months to reach that goal.

If you find that the program is too easy, simply adjust by moving up to a level that is more difficult for you, and continuing from there. *Warning:* It is better to be cautious than to be *macho*

TEN-WEEK BEGINNER'S RUNNING PROGRAM

Week #	Run-Walk Ratio (20-Minute Total)	Total Run Time
1	Run 1 minute, walk 2 minutes—do 6 sets, followed by running 1 minute	7 min
2	Run 1 minute, walk 1 minute—do 10 sets	10 min
3	Run 2 minutes, walk 1 minute—do 6 sets, followed by running 2 minutes	14 min
4	Run 3 minutes, walk 1 minute—do 5 sets	15 min
5	Run 4 minutes, walk 1 minute—do 4 sets	16 min
6	Run 5 minutes, walk 1 minute—do 3 sets, followed by running 2 minutes	17 min
7	Run 6 minutes, walk 1 minute—do 3 sets	18 min
8	Run 8 minutes, walk 1 minute—do 2 sets, followed by running 2 minutes	18 min
9	Run 10 minutes, walk 1 minute—do 2 sets	20 min
10	Run 20 minutes nonstop	20 min

and try to go too far too fast. Runners who go too far too fast end up being sedentary whiners!

After completing one of these three programs, you will be running 20 minutes at a time nonstop. Congratulations! You have gone from running one minute to running 20. You may now graduate from my beginner runner program, with honors! You're ready for the next step.

ADVANCED BEGINNER

Sometimes, young men and women former athletes or even creaky duffers like Shepherd who keep themselves together can start with the advanced beginner program. Be cautious! It's better to start at too low a level, and work up, than to start too high and drop out. If you get injured or fatigued, or you cannot progress on a gradually increasing plane, you may not make it. Let common sense and caution guide you, not your ego or your competitive friends.

If you are running at least five consecutive minutes, and can run for a total of 20 minutes with a few walk breaks in between, you are an advanced beginner. This may mean that you started with the beginner program, and found that you could progress quickly. Or, you have been doing some running, or a lot of brisk walking, or are still athletic—can turn sideways naked in front of a mirror without groaning at your pot—and feel comfortable starting at this higher level. I cannot stress too much: Do not start at this level to inflate your ego. You will deflate all too soon.

There are several programs you might follow at this level. You might select any of the three methods in the beginner runner section. Instead of starting at week one, however, try starting at week six; this works especially well with the Road Runners method. Or you might start running five to 10 minutes at a time, with a short walk break in the middle, for a total of 20 minutes. That is: five-minute run, walk, five-minute run, walk, for 20 minutes.

After you can run for 20 minutes, nonstop, you are still an advanced beginner. Stay at this level, and run for 20 minutes each time, three to five times a week, for three to four weeks. Then, if you wish, progress to 30 minutes of nonstop running by following this four-week program:

Week	Run
1	22 minutes nonstop, at least 3 to 5 times per week
2	25
3	27
4	30

When you reach 30 minutes, three to five times a week, pause. Hold your running at this level for *at least* three to four weeks. What's the point of rushing now? You are progressing well, and you don't want to risk injury, fatigue, or boredom.

INTERMEDIATE

You reach this level of running when you can run at least 30 minutes nonstop at a comfortable pace for at least three to five times a week. Now you are ready, if you wish, to start adding a few runs that are longer than 30 minutes, and to switch to counting miles instead of minutes.

Go easy here. This is a serious and important transition. You are becoming the runner you have dreamed of, and are capable of looking forward to 10Ks, marathons, or just lovely, long, weekend runs. At this level, the next two chapters have special significance for you.

Keep your easy days at 30 minutes per run (about two to three miles). Add one or two days per week of longer runs (four to six miles). Here is a typical four-week progression:

Week	Mon.	Tues.	Wed.	Thurs.	Fri.	Sat.	Sun.	Total
1	2	3	2	2	Off	4	2	15
2	2	3	2	3	Off	4	3	17
3	2	4	2	3	Off	5	3	19
4	3	4	3	3	Off	5	3	21

Never increase your mileage by more than ten percent from one week to the next. This is a basic rule for *all* runners at *every* level. Also, buffer longer runs, which are stressful, with shorter, easy days. After reaching 15 to 20 miles per week on a regular basis, you may want to prepare for your first race (see Chapter 5) or even your first marathon (see Chapter 6). In our New York Road Runners classes, we start easing the intermediate runner into gentle speed work to improve running form, the ability to run up hills, and race times.

Remember: Once you reach the intermediate level, and can run for 30 minutes at least three times a week, you do not need to progress any further. You have achieved the level of fitness, and only need to hold there. Many runners do advance—largely because the challenge is there and they want to be in excellent shape. But at the intermediate level, you can sightsee on runs in any city you visit, work out with friends, join a running club and its workouts, or just enjoy the running experience.

5 THE BEGINNER RACER

Racing isn't for everyone. But I think every runner should try competition of one sort or another. For one thing, the era of the "fun racer"—the average runner—has emerged. The competition is not to win, but to better personal goals. After all, in most races today there are hundreds, perhaps thousands of entrants, but only a few top athletes.

The rest of us battle not against them, but against ourselves. And we win by meeting realistic goals, such as simply finishing the race. Leslie Buckland, a New York Road Runner, was so moved by "winning" the 1976 New York City Marathon that he produced a motivational film about it for salesmen, titled "Any Number Can Win." In it a competitive salesman-runner notes elatedly, "I won! Some other guy named Rodgers thinks he won. But I did. He was in a different race."

For the beginner competitor, the main thing is to get out there, pin your number on correctly, start slowly, and finish smiling. Many more runners are entering races every year. Why race?

- It gives your running life a goal, a focus. Circle the race date on your running calendar, and train for that day.
- You make friends. Races are large social gatherings—parties in running shorts—that give you the opportunity to meet other runners. You can also exchange training tips and running experiences.
- You can test yourself. Racing lets you measure your

progress. It also gives you a great sense of achievement: you set a goal (to enter a race) and accomplish it. You will see your racing times improve, feel better physically and mentally, stay in competitive form, and enjoy the special camaraderie that goes on before, during, and after a race.

I love converting runners to racers. Why? It can be the best test of your fitness and discipline, even though it also contradicts much of the advice given earlier to the beginner runner. It can cause both physical and mental breakdowns in fitness. It can lead to frustration. It works against the theories of "talk test" and "be sociable." Only a fool wants to destroy himself during a race. But we are all fools to varying degrees. The race excites because it makes us play the edges, realize boundaries, follow common sense. We overcome pain, and that's exhilarating. And we discover an honest flirtation with danger that must be respected.

We suffer individual hardships together in races. We respect a whole range of competitors. We test ourselves against ourselves and against the elements and, if we wish, against each other. The competitive runner wins by sharing his or her unique personal experience.

Once, while I was lecturing, someone asked me if I really enjoyed the actual race itself. For the first time I realized how much I *hate* the race. This unique love-hate relationship with running begins weeks, even months before a big race, when my optimism is high. As race day approaches I get pessimistic and invariably develop all sorts of aches, pains, and other excuses. The last few hours before the race are very bad ones for me. My confidence fades. But during the race, almost at the starter's gun, a new surge of confidence pumps my blood and drives me onward! How do I feel during the race? I hate it. I want to quit over and over. But I love it, too. The challenge of defeating fatigue, of reaching beyond my potential keeps me going forward. When I finish, I hate it. I invariably throw up. I often rival Doc Sheehan for moaning and groaning and praying to be saved from the grasp of the

Demon Pain. Fortunately, all this fades with my first postrace beer. After the second, I'm ready to say I loved the race. Then analyzing it, I know I could have run faster "if I had made my move sooner." Or, another favorite line told to the person you beat in a stretch run, "I was only using the race as a workout." The sense of accomplishment, the telling of stories—"Wow, what did you think of that bleep-bleeping hill?"—binds the young and old, fast and slow. I hate races. I love races.

Despite this, competitive running is fun. I tell myself that a lot. And converting new runners to competitive running is even more fun—who else can I beat as I grow old? It's a chance to run with dozens or maybe thousands of other runners over the same course. If you finish well—in some races if you finish at all—you will be awarded a medal or certificate, and that will give your self-confidence a real boost.

ON YOUR MARK: SELECTING YOUR FIRST RACE

If you are running at the intermediate level or better, you're ready. That is, you're running for 20 to 30 minutes at a time, three to five times a week.

Pick a race. The distance should be long enough to challenge you, but short enough to be completed without pain. I recommend a distance between two miles and 5K (3.1 miles), but not more than 10K (6.2 miles), which is a popular race distance. Choose a local race; traveling adds to your excitement and stress, and you want something low-key like a "fun run" or a mass-participation event filled with runners of every level. Today, the "fun runners" at the back of the pack far outnumber the competitive racers at the front. Let them blow out the course while you concentrate on finishing. Stay away from hilly races, and don't race on hot days. Women may prefer women-only races at first.

GET SET: TRAINING FOR YOUR FIRST RACE

The first step is to train your mind. Pick a race, train toward that date, condition yourself slowly and regularly by following the fundamental guidelines in this book.

Develop a base of endurance for racing. Pace your workouts to get the feeling of running at a steady clip. Do not concern yourself with speed work or the various phases of training used by more experienced racers. Concentrate on building your endurance to the point where you can run and finish a race comfortably, tapering off as you approach the race date.

To finish in comfort, you will need to set a minimum amount of mileage and run long runs spread out over several weeks. My basic guideline is this: your weekly mileage should be at least two or three times the race distance (I prefer three). You should be running this mileage consistently for six to eight weeks before the race itself. You should also complete at least three longer runs, covering at least two-thirds of the race distance, prior to the week before the race. Never try to cram this mileage into your schedule during the last few weeks before any race.

Build gradually. If you plan to run a 5K race, for example, you should be running at least 6 to 9 miles a week, with long runs of at least 2 or 3 miles. For a 10K (6.2 miles), you should be logging 12 to 18 miles per week, with your minimum long runs in the 4- to 6-mile range.

Remember the hard-easy system. Alternate your conversational endurance runs—long, short, medium. If the race route includes hills, run up and down a few before race day. A few days before the race, however, take it easy. No amount of additional training will help you then.

The charts on page 48 are models for your first race. I suggest that you race shorter distances, perhaps 5K, before your first 10K run. Many runners, however, prefer the 10K distance since it is a popular and frequently run race.

Look what Mary Rodriguez, then a fifty-five-year-old secretary, was able to do. She started running for her health, after attending my New York Road Runners Club beginner's running

EIGHT-WEEK TRAINING
PROGRAM FOR YOUR FIRST RACE
(5K—4 MILES)

Week	Mon.	Tues.	Wed.	Thurs.	Fri.	Sat.	Sun.	Total Mileage
1	Off	2	2	2	Off	2	Off	8
2	Off	2	2	2	Off	2	2	10
3	Off	2	2	2	Off	2	2	10
4	Off	2	3	2	Off	2	3	12
5	Off	2	3	2	Off	2	3	12
6	Off	2	3	2	Off	2	3	12
7	Off	2	3	2	Off	2	3	12
8	Off	2	2	2	Off	2	Race (5K— 4 miles)	8 + race

clinic in March 1977. Inspired, she ran for the first time and couldn't make it around a quarter-mile track. She showed up at a Saturday morning workout in Central Park, and walked-jogged-walked with me for an entire loop of the reservoir (1.5 miles). A few weeks later she completed the loop running nonstop, and her husband greeted her with a smile and kiss at the finish.

Mary then decided to aim for the women's Mini-Marathon in

EIGHT-WEEK TRAINING
PROGRAM FOR YOUR FIRST RACE
(10K)

Week	Mon.	Tues.	Wed.	Thurs.	Fri.	Sat.	Sun.	Total Mileage
1	Off	2	3	3	Off	2	4	14
2	Off	2	3	3	Off	2	4	14
3	Off	3	3	3	Off	2	5	16
4	Off	3	4	3	Off	3	5	18
5	Off	3	4	4	Off	3	4	18
6	Off	3	4	3	Off	3	5	18
7	Off	3	4	3	Off	2	4	16
8	Off	4	2	2	Off	2	Race (10K)	10 + race

June, in New York. She worked out three times a week running 2 miles on a track, and on Sundays, she jogged 2 miles in a local park. On Saturdays she was all mine! She and I jogged and bantered, and she completed two loops of the reservoir (about 3 miles). After this test, she was ready for the hilly roads of Central Park. We ran 4 miles with a group of twenty men and women who had followed a similar program. Chatting all the way, they hardly noticed the hills, and all finished enthusiastically. The next Saturday, Mary Rodriguez ran 5 miles. The week before the Mini, she and several others like her ran the entire 6-mile course comfortably. On June 4, just seventy days after her first run, Mary started the 6.2 mile race, and finished in 1 hour, 13 minutes. She had progressed from a fifty-five-year-old woman who hadn't exercised in thirty-five years to a smiling, energetic "fun racer" in ten weeks! In 1983, a sixty-two-year-old member of Atalanta, Mary ran the eighth-fastest marathon time for an American female over sixty (4:16:05) to win her age division of the New York Marathon. As she says, "Stick with it. It's worth it."

GO! THE FIRST RACE

Your goal is simple: Finish.

Experience your first race, don't race it. Run it with a friend who is willing to chat with you all the way, holding you back at the start, and supporting you at the end when you feel like quitting. Your first race should be slightly longer or slightly faster than your usual jog. *Run* your first race. Later you can *race*.

Remember: You can walk during a race if you wish. You may need a slight breather, or the hills may be too much for you. Your goal is to finish the race in comfort.

Food and Drink

Beginners should not worry about, nor consume, special prerace diets. On race day, don't eat anything unusual, and nothing at all within a few hours of the race.

Do drink liquids, and drink them while you are running, even during a two-mile run on hot days. You should be used to drinking from doing so on your training runs. Also, pour water over your body on hot days.

Equipment

Beginner racers sometimes wear too much clothing. Start your runs, whether racing or training, feeling slightly under-dressed. Your body will heat up as you go. Try different clothing during your training runs; learn what feels best under which conditions. If the weather is cool, dress in layers you can remove: hat, gloves, even a sweatsuit. Tuck them in your shorts or hand them to a friend along the road. Don't discard clothing during your run; a drop in temperature, a sudden wind, rain, or snow, and you'll want those layers back. Take layers off progressively, until you find the right combination. In heat, cover yourself with loose, light, reflective clothing.

Don't race in new running shoes or fancy racing shoes. Wear your old, faithful, well-cushioned, broken-in training shoes. You don't need a brand-new pair for the race. They'll just cause brand-new blisters. If you want, run your first race in your old training shoes, and treat yourself to a new pair as a reward for finishing. Break those in slowly, however.

Fear Not

Afraid of finishing last? That's unlikely if you are well-prepared and follow these guidelines. Some runners will start too fast and struggle in last, or attempt to run the distance without proper mileage "in the bank" beforehand.

Gain confidence by planning your race strategy in advance. Break the course into small sections, and know where key landmarks and hills are located. Run from mile marker to mile marker. Be confident by being well prepared. Everyone is nervous before a race, even elite runners.

Race Day

Here you are. The morning of your first race may find your heart pounding. Prerace nerves strike the fast and the slow. You may take your leisure in the bathroom, eat toast, and drink orange juice (if that's your style) and read the paper. Carefully pack your bag: Vaseline, an extra pair of shoelaces, shoes, shorts, shirt, jock or bra, an extra shirt to wear after the race, tape, liniment, warm-ups, postrace first-aid equipment, toilet paper, a hat in case it's cold, a hat in case it's sunny, gloves in case it's cold, lock, and towel.

Arrive at least an hour before race time so you can check in, warm up, and of course chat with other runners. You should always preregister by mail so you can get right into line and pick up your number and perhaps a free T-shirt. If you don't preregister, you often must stand in line longer, fill out forms at the last minute, pay a higher entry fee, and get yelled at by tired officials. Warning: Not all races accept entries on race day. Better check in advance.

Proceed to the dressing area. Since you arrived early, you get a locker and have ample time to dress and apply your Vaseline, liniment, etc. Pin your number to the lower third of the *front* of your shirt, so the officials can see it as you finish. Fold or cut it so that the extra space at the edges is not in your way. Pin the number on each edge to make sure it is secure. I always bring extra pins in case they don't have enough. Also, memorize your number in case it gets destroyed by rain or splashing water.

Spend the next half-hour or more stretching, walking, and talking, and preparing your mind and body for the race. Tense runners arrive at the last minute to find you stretched and relaxed. Periodically jog for a few yards, and then stretch and relax. Half an hour before race time, take one last trip to the john, and be thankful you brought toilet paper. They've probably already run out. Proceed to the drinking fountain, and jog to the starting line.

Ten minutes before the start, peel off your sweats and place them in your easily recognized tagged bag. Carefully place the bag with the others. Very subtly jog behind the bushes for one last visit. Tie your shoes in a double knot. Line up toward the back of the pack to insure against getting trampled by the speedsters, or getting "pushed" into a fast early pace. Standing there among the crowd of runners, you may suddenly feel all alone, insecure, intimidated.

You're Off!

The crack of the gun propels you along with the flowing mass of runners down the road. "Why did I let Bob Glover start me on this madness?" you scream. But you're off. You fight adrenaline and hold back. Begin slowly, and if you feel good after a while, pick up your pace toward the end. Another approach is to start slowly and let as many runners get ahead of you as possible. (If you start too fast, they'll pass you later anyway.) Then, as you feel good toward the end of the race, pick up your pace and pass some of them; you're the tortoise passing the hares who went out too fast. This gives you confidence and the excitement of passing runner after runner over the last mile or two of the race.

Maintain a comfortable, slightly slow pace. Find a group of runners going at your pace, and join them. All will pull each other very easily for the first mile. You aren't out there to beat people. Your goal is to finish. Don't race against anyone who passes you or whom you pass—you'll lose your sense of an even pace. Chat with the runners around you, wave to your fans, laugh, have fun. This is a fun race for you, not a serious race as it is for those up ahead. Try to run the race as slowly as you can—that way you'll be sure to set a personal record (PR) in your next race. Then you hit a tough hill, or just run out of gas and feel the urge to quit. If you're running with a friend, encourage each other. Nina Kuscsik says, "You have a choice. You can quit or keep going. Just the knowledge that you can always quit sometime is often enough to keep you going to the finish line."

If you want to, take walk breaks, especially on tough hills. But keep moving. Don't stop unless you are hurt. Try to run the entire distance. But if your pulse soars, or you can't "catch" your breath and run at a conversation pace, or your legs tire, take brisk walk breaks. At water stations, stop, get some water, and walk as you drink. We know a runner who completed her first marathon by running from water station to water station, and walking at each station. Do not walk across the finish line, however. Jog across with a smile.

Don't be a hot dog, finishing the race with a face-twisting, arm-whirling, mad-hatter sprint. Finish in good form. Be in control.

Now comes the fun: You can brag to everyone in sight about how great you felt in your first race. Secretly, you may start plotting strategy for improving your time in the next race. After you cool down by walking and stretching, you can cheer the top runners as they receive their trophies, and know that you, too, are a winner. *

Most competitors remember that first race vividly, and each of their tales is instructive and often inspiring. Ellie McGrath is a *Time* magazine writer and a runner (who has now completed several marathons); her story sounds best in her own words:

I had started jogging to lose a little flab. Gradually I worked up to a 6-mile loop around Central Park, and was relieved just to finish. Then I joined a YMCA where I saw flyers for a 4-mile race for women only. I thought it would be fun to see how fast I could run.

So, two weeks before the race I traded in my white canvas sneakers for a pair of Onitsuka Tigers. I'll never forget how good it felt the first time I ran in them. After canvas sneakers, it was like running on air. Relaxed by this newfound comfort and egged on by the idea that I had "tigers" on my feet, I started getting psyched about running in a race. I had never engaged in any kind of physical contest; my closest experience to competition had been trying to ride a bicycle faster than my best friend.

The morning of the race was sunny, but cold. Should I wear warm-ups? A sweatshirt? I took a chance and wore just shorts and a jersey. My intuition was good because most of the other women were running in lightweight clothes. I was intimidated by the other starters, some wearing team colors and T-shirts, their jackets emblazoned with team names such as Golden Spikes.

But with the eagerness of a rank amateur, I elbowed my way to the front of the crowd. When the starting gun went off right over my head, I froze. The bang frightened me almost as much as the thundering hoofs around me. Then I bolted.

During the 28 minutes and 45 seconds it took me to finish the course, I learned several things. If you start too fast, you get really tired. If you underestimate the hills on the west side of the park, you'll be sorry. If you stop worrying about all the runners in front of you and think instead of all of them behind you, you'll enjoy the race a lot more. Having committed the first two mistakes, the last tactic was the one that got me around the course.

Crossing the finish line was a tremendous thrill. There was my boss, really amused by the whole thing, holding a congratulatory can of Diet Pepsi for me. Beside her was my boyfriend, bewildered, holding my parka. I picked up my medal for finishing, and went home to indulge myself with a hot bath, a chicken salad sandwich, and a magnum of champagne.

Recover

After the race, do less running and take it easy for the next few days. Recover carefully. Don't be in a hurry to make the transition from a beginner racer to a more serious competitor. The "too much too soon" syndrome will leave you injured or frustrated, or both. Remember, consistency and patience win in the long run. You need months, even years of "miles in the bank" to reach a serious competitive level.

GOALS: BEYOND THE BEGINNER RACER

After a few races, however, you may want to increase your goals. Gradually add to your training mileage and the intensity of your workouts. Set reasonable but challenging objectives. Don't neglect the fundamentals discussed in earlier chapters.

Try for three goals:

1. The safest, least competitive goal is to extend the distance of your longest race. If you have run 6 miles, enter a race for 10, then 15, then perhaps a marathon. Finishing will continue to be a reward; only now the distance will be tougher.

2. Another goal is to improve your time over the same distance, then improve your time over a variety of distances. You'll soon hear other runners talk about setting PRs (personal records). Keep a training diary: Record all your runs; what you wear, eat, drink; the weather; the time and place for all your races; your best time for each distance.

3. Aim for a certain place in the race, like the top 100 or even the top 1,000. Or, aim for finishing within a certain percentage of the field. Percentages sometimes sound better to you and your friends. I remember being thrilled by placing in the top half of the field in my first Boston Marathon. When people asked me how I had done at Boston, and I said, "I finished 1,012," they'd reply, "Oh, what happened to you?" Instead, by telling them I finished in the top half of a quality field they gave me the reply I sought: "Fantastic!"

Your individual goals should meet your individual needs at the time. For most of us, that means goals based on individual improvement. Let the elite run against each other.

THE RACER'S EDGE: BE PREPARED

To meet goals, be prepared for your race. Physical preparation comes first. You must have a base of endurance. Build up for the race, but also keep fit year round by properly spacing less important races. Enter race day with a well-conditioned and well-rested body. "Heat train" before summer races, "hill train" before attacking uphill struggles. Run cross-country workouts before attacking a rugged and hilly course through the woods. Before a marathon, run long distances to condition you physically and mentally for those last long miles.

Prior to a race, you may want to do some fast intervals to condition yourself to running in oxygen debt, and to practice the mechanics of running fast. Your weight should be down when coming into a race. Proper diet and exercise will gradually get you into "fighting weight" in time for the big effort. An extra five to ten pounds is a lot of extra weight, and will make a major difference in your time.

TRAINING: BEYOND THE BEGINNER COMPETITOR

How often should you train? How hard? What methods should you use?

Dr. George Sheehan finds that his aging body performs better on race day if he trains every other day. Most world class runners work out twice a day, and take a long run one day a week. I know runners who haven't missed a day in ten years, and others who take off a full two weeks twice a year. I've been beaten by both. Generally, I run six days a week, and rest a day.

Kenny Moore, fourth place finisher in the 1972 Olympic Marathon, wrote in *Road Racers and Their Training*:

"The basis for all training is that an organism exposed to stress will adjust if allowed to recover. But if it never rests, it just stays tired. I'm not in this to do work. I'm trying to improve. So I'm after the optimum formula of work, rest and racing, not the most difficult I can stand. I've found a dosage of one hard day and two easy brings improvement as quickly as any. It's something every runner must work out for himself."

The idea is to place enough stress on your body for training, but not enough to risk injury. Guidelines for doing speedwork and improving your race times from one mile to the marathon are detailed in *The Competitive Runner's Handbook*.

6 THE BEGINNER MARATHONER

→

"Marathon Mania" is sweeping the United States and most of the world. Every month, men and women run this classic event of 26 miles, 385 yards (42.195 kilometers) in a major city somewhere in the world. Travel agents will coordinate your holiday plans with marathon races in such exciting places as San Francisco, Honolulu, Boston, New York, Miami, New Orleans, London, Rome, Berlin, Paris, Montreal, Ottawa, Madrid, Stockholm, Rio de Janeiro, Athens, and even Peking and Moscow. What a way to see a city—by running through its streets!

The marathon is the longest and most difficult race most runners ever attempt. It is also the most popular. It symbolizes fitness and performance. Mention marathon, and most runners reply "Boston." The first Boston Marathon was run in 1897; 15 men competed. Until 1965, Boston usually had 250 to 400 starters. But by 1969 there were 1,152, and in 1970 the field had to be limited by imposing a qualifying time. The New York Marathon *turns down* more than 50,000 applicants each year. In 1964, there were six marathons held in the United States. By 1977, there were 166, and in 1984, there were more than 400. The National Running Data Center, which reports running's growth and records, listed nearly 140,000 marathon performances in 1984, up from less than 1,000 in 1970.

A marathon, says the dictionary, is any test of endurance. But almost every marathon runner knows the legend of a fierce battle on the plains near the small Greek town of Marathon in 490 B.C. The invading Persian army was caught by surprise by the out-manned Athenians, who charged into their ranks and saved the Greek empire. Pheidippides, a Greek soldier, was ordered to run to Athens with the news of victory. His run of about 22 miles from the battlefield is considered the first "marathon," but poor Pheidippides wasn't as fit as the modern marathoner. He entered Athens, exclaimed "Rejoice, we conquer!" and collapsed and died.

The marathon was added to the first modern Olympic Games held in Athens in 1896, and was won by a Greek, Spiridon Loues. Spiridon Clubs (Road Runner Clubs) have been established throughout Europe, and annual marathon runs are held over Pheidippides' route. In the United States, the first marathon was run 35 miles, from Stamford, Connecticut, to New York City. But the event was discontinued until 1970. Boston, with a marathon every year since 1896, remains the oldest continuous marathon in the world.

The distance of the marathon has varied until recent history. Pheidippides ran 38 kilometers as compared to the present standardized 42.195 kilometers (think metric!). From 1896 to 1908, the Olympic marathon distance was unset, but in 1908 the Olympics were held in London, and the races began at Windsor Castle and ended at the new White City Stadium. An English princess, so the story goes, wanted to watch the start of the race from her castle window and then view the finish from her seat at the stadium. The distance, set to please her highness, was 26 miles, 385 yards. That was about 2 miles longer than previous marathons, but it became the standardized distance. As you puff along those last few miles, all obscenities should be uttered to "Her Royal Highness" whose vanity created the distance.

In the Munich Olympics of 1972, Frank Shorter, Kenny Moore, and Jack Bachelor finished 1–4–9 for the greatest American Olympic marathon performance to date. Millions of excited Americans watched on television. This American triumph in an event previously dominated by other nations signaled the start of the marathon boom in this country. Within an hour of Shorter's greatest moment, I was on the roads training seriously for the first time in eight years. And so were a lot of other American runners.

Why would anyone want to run a marathon? The glamour and tradition of "the classic distance" captures the imagination. It's also "there," like the highest mountain or the tallest building. As the longest, most grueling, and most unpredictable running event, it is a symbol of superiority in physical and mental performance.

Most beginner marathon runners enter the first race to prove that their minds and bodies can meet the challenge, and their only goal is to finish. Then, they may set time goals of breaking three or three-and-a-half hours, and training toward those goals. They search to find their limits and then reach beyond them. They also begin comparing themselves to other runners; my original goal, for example, was to finish in the top 50 percent of the field, and now it has become the top 1 percent.

As a veteran of more than thirty marathons, I've learned many "secrets" of survival, although I never guarantee that any one of us will ever experience that beautiful, pain-free, fast marathon of runners' dreams. The marathon event is a true test of the runner. Proper training, diet, race experience, pacing, and so forth are important, but among the elusive elements that make the marathon special are the combination of Mother Nature and Lady Luck, and your mental ability to overcome physical torture for 26 miles, 385 yards. The marathoner learns to discover the peace inside of pain.

Sometimes you first discover that strength from the words

of others. When Carl Eilenberg was halfway up Heartbreak Hill during the 1975 Boston Marathon, he was about to stop. But Tom Coulter, a former Syracuse University All-America cross-country runner, came by and told Carl, in words that should be chiseled on those terrible hills, "Once you cross the finish line at Boston, there isn't anything you can't do." Eilenberg finished.

Another runner who finished a marathon against great odds is Dick Traum. He believes: "Anyone who honestly takes the time to train can finish a marathon. You don't have to be much of an athlete, just patient and disciplined. You have to put in the time." Traum has completed five marathons on an artificial right leg. His Achilles Track Club teammate Linda Down, who has cerebral palsy, finished the 1982 New York Marathon in eleven hours on crutches. In 1983, she ran two-and-a-half hours faster. Eighty-year-old Ruth Rothfarb completed her first marathon, the Avon International in Ottawa, Canada, in 1981, and thus became the oldest woman (so far) to go the distance. Mrs. Rothfarb then danced into the wee hours of the morning to celebrate.

SELECTING YOUR FIRST MARATHON

Most beginner marathoners enter their first race to prove that their minds and bodies can meet the challenge. Their goal—their *only* goal—is to finish. Later, they may set time goals; then training becomes more specific. For now, the object is to select your marathon, train for it, and finish.

Don't pick a hot race, a hilly one, or one that doesn't include a lot of first marathon runners like yourself. Choose a marathon near your home, when possible, to avoid the excitement of both travel and a race in a strange and interesting place.

TRAINING GUIDELINES FOR YOUR FIRST MARATHON

Here are some key tips for all marathoners:

1. *Mileage* Work from a consistent base of endurance training. As you get stronger, you should increase your weekly mileage at a rate of not more than 10 percent. Move gradually from a base of 20 to 30 miles a week to 40 to 50 miles a week. Hold at that level for *at least* eight weeks before tapering for the marathon. I prefer 50 to 55 miles a week, but no more than 60. Whatever your mileage, taper off during the last two weeks before your marathon. Don't even consider speed work until you've built a proper foundation of stamina. *Marathon running is a race where you avoid slowing down,* rather than trying to gain speed. Consistency in training—"putting miles in the bank"—is the key.

2. *Hard/Easy* The concept of "train, don't strain" that applies to the beginner runner also applies to all levels of marathon running. I feel that *all* workouts should be at a conversational pace for marathon training until the runner has built up a sufficient level of endurance to allow him or her to complete the race comfortably at a pace equivalent to or better than his or her normal workout pace for 5 to 10 miles. Then, to improve performance, he or she can practice going faster in intervals in order to develop the ability to push a marathon pace that is faster than the training pace. But beware of long, fast runs! Save them for the races.

A common-sense marathon schedule includes alternating hard or long training with easy or short days. The rest days are necessary so that the body can recover and strengthen itself for more progressive work. Tom Osler's plan for balancing long runs, average runs, and recovery runs is listed in *The Conditioning of Long Distance Runners* (see chart on p. 62).

		40-mile week	*60-mile week*
Day One	5% of week's total	2 miles	3 miles
Day Two	15% of week's total	6 miles	9 miles
Day Three	30% of week's total	12 miles (add a few runs of 15–20 miles)	18 miles
Day Four	5% of week's total	2 miles	3 miles
Day Five	15% of week's total	6 miles	9 miles
Days Six and Seven	Remaining 30% of week's total (use for race or just having fun)	12 miles	18 miles

3. *The Long Run* The "long run" is the key ingredient if balanced by a consistent base of endurance training. This run simulates the physical and mental stress you must endure in a marathon, and allows your mind to accept the fact that you can run long distances with some reasonable effort. Additionally, the body learns to adjust to different energy sources utilized in the late stages of a marathon.

The long run should be part of all marathon runners' monthly schedules and should cover a distance of 15 to 20 miles. Anything longer than that is unnecessary. Several top marathon runners like to put in regular runs of 20 to 30 miles to build up confidence and strength for the late stages of a race. But for the average runner, this is not necessary and runs beyond 20 miles could result in prolonged fatigue or injury.

Build gradually from a base of long runs of six to 10 miles run *each* week, to *at least* two or three runs of 16 to 18 miles within the eight weeks before your marathon. This is a minimum. I prefer three or four runs of 18 to 20 miles each during those eight weeks, but no longer than 20 miles or three-and-a-half hours, whichever comes first. If possible, don't run more than 15 miles on consecutive weekends. Then, no long runs beyond 15 miles during the two weeks before the marathon, or beyond eight miles one week before the race.

4. **Training**   Before beginning the stressful training for your first marathon, check with your physician. If possible, find a partner or two training for the same marathon, and work out together and run the marathon together.

• Shoes: Train in the shoes you'll run the marathon in. Do not run in racing flats. If you travel to the race, do not check your running shoes, but always carry them with you. Well-broken-in (but not worn down) shoes are the runner's most cherished possession.

• Schedule: Plan each day to the marathon date. Progress gradually according to the charts in this chapter. Build up mileage and long runs, which increase your confidence. Run only once a day; no two-a-days yet. Take one day a week off, sometimes even two. When you feel tired, or get injured, take more time off. Return gradually from injury. "Listen to your body" and avoid further injury. Gradually take shortcuts and work back into your schedule; you might repeat the week you were out, or take several weeks to catch up. Don't panic. A long-term schedule allows you to miss even a few weeks and still make it to the starting line. If you miss a month or more, however, seriously consider skipping this marathon.

• Stretch: Be sure to do all your warm-up and cool-down stretching carefully and slowly.

• Respect the heat and cold: Slow down in hot weather, drink lots of fluids, try to run during the cooler parts of the day. For cold, wear layers and vent excess heat. Don't discard any clothing, especially your hat or gloves; a change in wind direction will make you regret that move. Tuck your hat into your shorts, tie your windbreaker around your waist.

• Respect the changes in your life, such as family, work, diet, a new companion or baby, falling in or out of love. Be flexible with your training to adjust for life's stresses.

• Respect the long run: These runs build your confidence; don't neglect them. Practice drinking fluids on your long runs. Find the fluid your stomach likes best (we recommend cold water), and stay with it. Practice walking during your long runs, to get the feel of starting again, if you think you may need to take walk breaks on marathon day.

• Diary: Keep a detailed record of your training. Record the weather, what you wear, where and how long you run, how you feel, your weight, what you ate before and after, what you drank, any unusual occurrences, and so forth. Refer to this record in planning your race meal, fluids, and clothing.

• Race occasionally: This will teach you to start slowly on marathon day, and not blow all your training. Races between the 10K and half-marathon will build experience, mileage, and confidence. Race at least once a month during the last three months before your marathon, but not more than twice a month.

• Sleep: Increase your sleep as you increase your mileage. Eat well, but moderately. Avoid any unusual diets.

• Taper: This is important. Last-minute mileage will do you no good and perhaps a lot of harm. One runner we know decided three days before his marathon to run the 26.2 miles on an indoor track to see if he could cover the distance. He could—three days early, but not again on race day. Plan your workouts so you build to a peak work load about two weeks before the marathon, and then taper off.

• Be consistent: Train regularly and increase mileage gradually. Force yourself out the door when you feel lazy. Enter the marathon well prepared and confident that you will meet your goals. Treat the distance with respect; I've run too many marathons to take the race for granted. E. C. Frederick, author of *The Running Body*, writes: "It's a rare person who has the fortitude and mind control to force himself to finish a marathon when not properly trained for it. Even highly trained persons undergo much soul-searching and must dig deeply into their bag of tricks to endure those last six miles. Because they are prepared, most trained marathoners finish. Rarely does an unprepared person make it past 20 miles."

PREPARING FOR YOUR FIRST MARATHON: A TRAINING SCHEDULE

Anyone can start a marathon. But only the well prepared and carefully trained finish. Before starting forth on this quest, you should have one or preferably two years of running logged in your diary. You should also have run several races of varying lengths. You should have been running at least 20 miles a week for the last several months. (If you are not at these levels, I do not recommend training for a marathon yet. Be patient. Put the miles, and the shorter races, in your bank.)

To finish a marathon in comfort, you need the minimum mileage and long runs. You need to build your endurance base so you can finish the race. You need to balance the right amount of weekly mileage and the right amount and frequency of long runs. You also need to avoid overtraining: too little training, and you won't make it to the finish line; too much training, and you won't make it to the starting line. The percentage of marathon starters who cross the finish line is much higher than the percentage of runners who start marathon training and make it to the starting line.

Here are three training schedules for beginner marathon runners. They are based on your weekly mileage and the time until your first marathon, and are designed to prepare you gradually for the race.

1. *Six-Month Training Schedule/20-Mile-a-Week Base*   It would be best to plan six months ahead for your first marathon. This allows you more time to train for the race, and gives you a greater endurance base. If you lose time to injury, travel, or illness, this schedule allows greater flexibility.

The program takes exactly half a year: 26 weeks of preparation, or one week for every mile of the marathon. It is basically the same as the four-month plan, but is my preferred schedule and builds to a base of 50 miles a week.

THE FIRST-TIME MARATHON
SIX-MONTH TRAINING SCHEDULE
(from a 20-mile-a-week base)

Week	Mon.	Tues.	Wed.	Thurs.	Fri.	Sat.	Sun.	Total Mileage
1	Off	3	4	3	4	2	4	20
2	Off	3	4	3	4	3	5	22
3	Off	4	4	3	4	3	6	24
4	Off	4	5	3	4	3	7	26
5	Off	4	5	3	5	3	8	28
6	Off	4	6	3	5	4	8	30
7	Off	4	6	3	5	4	10	32
8	Off	4	6	4	6	4	10	34
9	Off	4	6	4	6	4	12	36
10	Off	4	8	4	6	4	12	38
11	Off	5	8	5	6	4	12	40
12	Off	5	8	5	6	4	12	40
13	Off	5	7	5	5	3	15	40
14	Off	5	8	5	6	4	12	40
15	Off	5	8	5	5	4	15	42
16	Off	5	5	10	5	5	12	42
17	Off	6	8	6	6	4	15	45
18	Off	6	6	10	6	5	12	45
19	Off	6	8	6	6	4	18	48
20	Off	6	6	12	6	6	12	48
21	Off	6	8	6	6	4	20	50
22	Off	6	6	12	8	6	12	50
23	Off	6	8	6	5	Off	20	45
24	Off	4	4	8	4	5	15	40
25	Off	5	5	12	Off	5	8	35
26	Off	4	6	4	Off	2	Race Day Marathon	16 + Race

Note: When you race you may need to adjust your daily and weekly mileage downward. Do not attempt to combine long runs and races on the same day or weekend.

2. *Four-Month Training Schedule/25-Mile-a-Week Base*

Thousands of runners have completed their first marathon comfortably following this basic schedule. This four-month program is

THE FIRST-TIME MARATHON
FOUR-MONTH TRAINING SCHEDULE
(from a 25-mile-a-week base)

Week	Mon.	Tues.	Wed.	Thurs.	Fri.	Sat.	Sun.	Total Mileage
1	Off	4	4	4	4	3	6	25
2	Off	4	5	4	4	3	8	28
3	Off	4	5	4	5	2	10	30
4	Off	4	6	4	5	4	10	33
5	Off	4	6	5	6	4	12	37
6	Off	4	6	4	5	4	14	37
7	Off	4	6	4	6	4	16	40
8	Off	4	10	4	6	4	12	40
9	Off	4	8	4	4	2	18	40
10	Off	6	8	4	6	4	14	42
11	Off	4	8	4	6	3	20	45
12	Off	4	10	4	8	5	14	45
13	Off	4	10	4	6	3	18	45
14	Off	4	6	6	6	4	14	40
15	Off	4	8	5	4	10	4	35
16 (Race Week)	Off	4	6	4	Off	2	Race Day Marathon	16 + Race

Note: When you race you may need to adjust your daily and weekly mileage downward. Do not attempt to combine long runs and races on the same day or weekend.

my minimum schedule for runners training for their first marathon.

3. *Three-Month Training Schedule/40-Mile-a-Week Base* This will work—and not be a disaster—only if you already have an endurance base of *at least* one or two months at 35 to 40 miles a week. From this foundation, you build to the marathon in three months. *This is not a shortcut for the beginner marathoner.* It is often a good schedule for your second marathon because it follows the longer training schedule and base for your first marathon.

From a base of 40 miles a week, start with Week 15 of the 26-week, six-month schedule, and count down toward the marathon.

For guidelines to improve your marathon training and times beyond this point, consult *The Competitive Runner's Handbook*.

PRERACE TIPS

- During the three or four days before your first marathon, eat plenty of carbohydrates. Don't deplete yourself (see Chapter 19). Don't stuff yourself with unfamiliar foods before long runs and races.
- Avoid the premarathon excitement and hoopla. Don't spend hours on your feet walking around to the prerace clinics or free meals. Stay off your feet.
- Do not stay up late. Don't avoid sex the day or night before the marathon. You'll be more relaxed, and sleep better.
- Two days before the race, go for a short, easy run (2–4 miles). Take the next day off. Many runners take a run the day before the race, resting on the previous day.
- Pick up your number early, if you can. Get to the race early with your number and equipment.

RACE-DAY TIPS

- If the marathon starts in the morning, get up at least three hours before race time. If your training included eating before long runs, eat three hours prior to the marathon.
- Wear the clothing you've already determined is best for you given the weather conditions on race day. Don't overdress or underdress. Peel during the race. Hint: It's better to start out a little cool than just right or too hot.
- Prevent blisters by applying Vaseline or foot powder to your feet. (Try this out during your long training runs to see which is best for you.) Apply Vaseline around your crotch and inner thighs to minimize chafing. Cover your nipples with Vaseline or Band-Aids to prevent rubbing. In a cold wind, Vaseline on your bare skin will protect it.
- At the starting line, pin on your number (right side up). Warm up, stretch, walk, jog across the starting line and out a few hundred yards to get the "feel" of the race. Use the toilet one last time.

- Drink fluids 10 to 15 minutes before the race starts, and also drink plenty of fluids during the race. On a hot day, pour water over you as well as in you throughout the race.
- Start at the back of the pack, and run slowly (30 seconds to a minute per mile slower than your usual 10-mile training pace).
- On a hot day, hold yourself back. Start slower than you otherwise would.
- Concentrate on maintaining good form. If you are injured (limping, in pain) or feeling ill—walk. If the symptoms remain, or increase, go to an aid station. Leave the race. Only fools continue. Men and women have pulled muscles, broken bones, collapsed, and even died during marathons. A lot of them also drop out and stay healthy—to return another day. Be sensible.
- Walk during the race if you feel tired or you have cramps. But try to keep moving. Sometimes a brisk walk will be faster than the slow jog of the other runners. Sit down only if you feel sick or are injured and plan to leave the race.
- Your principal goal is to finish in comfort. A 12-minute-a-mile run is a five-hour marathon. The first-time marathoner often takes between four and five hours; many finish slower than that. And remember—the slower you finish, the easier it will be to improve your time. Fear not. You won't finish last, and someone will be at the finish line when you get there.
- No one ever said it was going to be easy. You will need *fortitude*. If you have trained properly and do not feel ill or are not hampered by an injury, then you should finish. Dig down deep for extra strength and keep going. Friends and spectators offer encouragement. This is why you can go those extra six miles beyond your 20-mile training run—you have the support of all the runners around you and all the spectators along the course. If you can, find a group to run

with during the race to help each other along through periods of weakness. Everyone feels like quitting many times. You are not alone. Keep moving, take it one step at a time, one mile marker at a time, and *smile* when you cross the finish line. You're a marathoner!

POSTRACE TIPS

- After you finish, stretch and walk. Do not sit down. Drink fluids continuously. See Chapters 19 and 20 for guidelines to eating and drinking.
- Take a hot bath as soon as you can. Walk. Stretch gently. Repeat this the next morning.
- Treat all blisters and any aches or pains promptly.
- Return gradually to running. Don't train or race hard for at least four to eight weeks. Recover and rebuild.
- Analyze your race and the results. Create a new marathon training schedule. Plan well and race wisely. Your first comment after crossing the finish line may be "Never again!" But as you stretch, walk, stretch again, and emerge from a hot tub, you may find yourself telling your admiring nonmarathon friends, "If I had only . . ."—another month of training, a few more long runs, some speed work here and there, hill training, heat preparation, an extra helping of spaghetti the night before—". . . I might have lowered my time by 15 minutes." Now is the moment to get on with your new marathon schedule.

A CONCLUDING THOUGHT

Remember: You don't have to run a marathon. Don't let anyone push you into doing something you don't want to do. Your own desire is the only motivation that will carry you through the agony and across the finish line. You can't run it for someone else. Some runners never race. Others love the 10K and the half-marathon. Find your desire and follow it.

Also, if you have entered a marathon, but your training falls short of the miminum, don't go. The officials of the New York Marathon instituted a policy in 1982 that allows runners to cancel because of injury or undertraining and be guaranteed entry into the race the following year. In 1984 over 2,500 of 18,000 original accepted applicants took advantage of this offer. Start training for the next one. Treat the distance with respect.

Finally, don't take racing, or marathon running, too seriously. Rumor has it there is life after running. There is even life without marathon running. But there is nothing like the feeling of planning, training, and then running this great and classical race, and finishing with your head up, tired legs churning, arms pumping, waving to your envious sedentary friends.

7 RUNNING FORM AND STYLE

Every runner has his or her own form. I can spot a running friend at a distance. Some have faults in form such as a pronounced forward lean, high arm carry, bouncing motion, body sway, or flailing elbows. Others stand out because of structural faults such as bowlegs, or feet that point outward, or inward. Others run with good form but are quickly recognized by such quirks of habit as a rolling head, or long-legged or short, choppy strides.

Running should come naturally. Many of our faults of style come from the way we grew up and what impressed us. When I worked at the Y in Rome, New York, I coached a youth track team. One regular event for our kids was a mile run. It was the first exposure to distance running for most of them. Rather than teach them how to run, I decided just to let them run naturally and then work on apparent faults in form. The top runners of the future aren't necessarily the fastest, but those with an economical stride, patience, and will power. Form counts more than time when you're young.

I was amazed by the difference between the boys and the girls. The majority of the girls ran very smoothly and gracefully, with near perfect form. In fact, many of them ran faster over the mile than the boys. The boys, however, tended to run like football or basketball players. Physical education in the "ball sports" emphasizes this style which promotes power and speed. Therefore, many boys learn to run high on their toes and have a pronounced upper-body movement. Competitiveness, learned from a very early age and reinforced with Little League Baseball and Pop Warner Football, is reflected in their tense bodies. The girls, however, aren't exposed as much to highly competitive "ball sport" activities, and instead participate in sports that emphasize form, agility, and patience, like gymnastics and dance. A ten-year-old girl is probably the most natural runner in our running world.

Unfortunately, young girls often develop a less efficient running motion as they become teenagers. A girl at that age is sometimes told to run in a "ladylike" manner. She bounces on her toes, with her arms carried too high in front of her, elbows swinging in the air. The adult woman who begins to jog usually possesses these traits; she not only runs inefficiently but also bounces along with extra weight. She is susceptible to injury. Many women joggers complain of soreness in their upper back. This is usually because they carry their arms too high and force their shoulders back. Adult women also tend to lean forward too far, and have a lower knee-lift than men. The foot is often brought forward by swinging it out to the side rather than by raising the knee. All of this is correctable; women haven't had the "ball-sport" training, and learn new running methods quickly.

The teen-age boy often likes the power and speed of competitive sports. His coaches tell him to run on his toes with fists clenched and arms pumping. Later, men may be trained to concentrate on power and speed rather than relaxation and efficiency of motion. Sitting before the television set, watching football and basketball heroes, reinforces the running form of power-speed athletics.

We face a relearning process when we wish to "run for fitness." How can you teach running form? It can be detailed on paper, but must be practiced and refined in motion with a natural style that can be modified by a trained instructor. I don't tell my beginner runners how to run. I just allow them to start running naturally. Or, I'll observe them individually on the track. Either way, I can pick up obvious faults in their form, and correct them. I highly recommend that beginner runners start by running naturally, but under the watchful eye of someone who can correct obvious faults in running style before they become bad, hard-to-break habits.

Some runners have strange running forms that offset *any* musculoskeletal asymmetries naturally, and shouldn't be changed. Bill Rodgers, for example, flails his right arm to compensate for a short left leg. No one would change his form. Then there's Dr. Charles Ogilvie's Theory: Ogilvie, the winner of the 65–69 age division in the Chicago Marathon with a time of 3:16:52, believes that we have developed a right/left imbalance in our bodies and should compensate by adding some weight to the right side. When he races, Ogilvie carries in his right hand the bone of a pre-historic animal adorned with a feather—he recommends others do the same. You should run the way that feels best to you, as long as that form is biomechanically sound. Former University of Oregon and U.S. Olympic coach Bill Bowerman wrote in *Runner's World*: "Every human being is built on the same basic set of biomechanical functions: muscles working in concert with each other, muscles moving and augmenting bone structures, joints connecting rigid bones to allow them to support the body in differing planes. Every runner, therefore, starts with the same machine. No two bodies, however, have the same interaction of parts. Some are more efficient than others. Working with a runner's basic running form as dictated by the biomechanical structure, certain modifications can be made that merely make what nature gave the runner function more efficiently."

The four basic biomechanical principles of running are:
1. Footstrike
2. Forward stride
3. Body angle
4. Arm drive

These general principles apply to every runner, but no single running form works for everyone. The thing to remember is: Run with a relaxed, flowing, rhythmic style in the best biomechanical way possible. Running, when done properly, should be a complete, flowing action that occurs unconsciously. After you have been running for a while, you will find that you simply fall into your running style. It's an action that comes naturally, easily, to you.

The following sections analyze the basic elements of this movement. This should help you check your own form, or that of a running friend. Remember that a relaxed running form is essential to using your muscle energy efficiently. Your form should be the result of the best use of your body frame and size. The secret is to run naturally. Use the following sections to help you run well, but don't let them spoil your running. With time, you will improve your running form, and your running. But don't become obsessed with running perfectly. Your form will improve as you improve your fitness. If you want more advanced guidelines than those included here, consult *The Competitive Runner's Handbook* and its advice on running form for uphill, downhill, finishing sprints, improving your time, and so forth.

FOOTSTRIKE

For the beginner, running is like walking. The heel of your foot makes the initial contact with the ground, followed by the mid-stance or support phase, the toe-off or propulsive phase, and finally the leg swing. In walking, we always have one foot on the ground, but in running, there is a "floating" moment between the toe-off and the foot contact when neither foot is on the ground. We are, momentarily, airborne.

All runners land first on the outside edge of their feet, and then roll inward; the inward roll cushions the blow. Sprinters hit the ground high on the ball of the foot. Milers tend to strike on the ball of the foot also, but not as high as the sprinter. Running ball-heel produces speed and power for short distances. In longer runs, however, a ball-heel footstrike may cause leg fatigue, calf tightness, soreness in the Achilles tendon, or more serious injury.

Most long-distance runners and beginner runners strike the ground heel first. Many advanced long-distance runners hit somewhere between heel first and ball first. This is the method I use when I'm in good shape and running at a brisk or race pace. Otherwise, I run heel-ball.

I recommend heel-ball footstrike for beginner and intermediate runners; you don't benefit from the more advanced ball-heel footstrike until you can race at a seven-minute-per-mile pace or better.

The two most common errors in footstrike for beginner and intermediate runners are:

1. *Excessive Toe Strike*   Do not land high on your toes. You may quickly develop injuries to your shins, ankles, calf muscles, or forefoot. Some elite runners may appear to run on their toes, but they are actually landing ball-heel-ball: They are striking the ground just behind the ball of their foot, touching down gently on the heel, and pushing off the ball.

Do not copy anyone's style. Use the heel-ball footstrike, and run in your own easy motion.

2. *Excessive Heel Strike*   Do not hit the ground by jamming your heel into it and then slapping your forefoot down hard. This causes a shock to the body and may lead to injury. Often you can hear runners who hit like this, especially on a track: Their footstrike sounds like "*boom-slap, boom-slap.*"

You should land gently on the heel, and then allow your forefoot to come down quietly as your body rolls over the foot and pushes off the ball. The difference is in the impact, which must be a gentle heel-ball.

HEEL-BALL FOOTSTRIKE

This technique is recommended for beginner runners, for heavy runners, and for a pace slower than seven-minute miles. The runner using heel-ball footstrike lands gently on the outside of his or her heel, rolls inward lightly to the ball of the foot with the knee slightly bent to absorb shock, and then lifts off from the big toe. Toes are pointing as straight forward as possible. Done properly, this is a shock-absorbing method. The slight rocking motion between heel contact and push-off insures proper cushioning and strong forward propulsion. The result is a hitting and springing motion, which is less jarring and increases acceleration.

Some beginners run with a slow "flat-foot" technique: Their entire foot strikes the ground at one time, but as lightly as possible. The wide surface area cushions this footstrike, and it's also easy on the rest of the body. You cannot run very long or very fast using this style, however, and eventually will shift to the heel-ball.

STRIDE

As a beginner runner, you shouldn't worry about your stride. Just put one foot in front of the other and run. As you get in better shape, you will want to run a little faster and with more efficiency. The faster you go, the more you increase the length and frequency of your stride and your knee lift. A beginner runner will run with a low knee lift. To run faster using the advanced ball-heel footstrike, you will concentrate on lifting your knees higher. At first, the only time you need to focus on lifting your knees higher will be to help you run uphill.

Stride length is the distance between successive ground contacts of the right and left feet, heel to toe, as measured on the ground. Stride frequency is the total number of right and left foot ground contacts per minute. Running speed is the product of the length and frequency of stride. Therefore, there are only three ways to increase your speed:

1. Increase the length of your stride. (Be careful that you do not overstride.)
2. Increase the frequency of your stride.

3. Increase the length and frequency of your stride.

Each runner usually finds a stride that works best for him or her at a given pace, and then "switches gears" to adjust speed. The advanced runner runs with a ball-heel footstrike and drives the knees up, increasing the length and frequency of stride, to run faster. The beginner and intermediate runner uses a low knee lift, "shuffle" stride. The point of foot contact is directly in line with the knee, with the knee slightly flexed.

The foot should strike the ground after it has stretched forward and already started to swing back. If you overstride so that the leg hits the ground ahead of the knee flex—the leg is straight—the result is a breaking action rather than forward propulsion. Overstriding is also hard on the knees, back, and hips. A short, choppy stride is also inefficient because you use more energy to travel a shorter distance. A short stride is often the result of inflexibility. The runner with a relaxed stride and flexible leg muscles will not have to work as hard as the runner with a short, choppy stride. Runners with greatly pronounced or distorted knee-lift or back-kick are wasting energy.

BODY ANGLE

Too many runners worry about how they should run. Should they stand erect, slightly bent over, elbows high or elbows low, or whatever? The best advice is to relax. Allow your body to move as freely and with as little rigidity as possible. Bill Bowerman, former track coach at the University of Oregon, feels that an erect posture is most essential for a smooth running style. "Run tall," he preaches to his disciples. Running tall means running with your back as straight as naturally comfortable, the head up, and eyes straight ahead. The buttocks should be "tucked in" so that an imaginary line drawn from the top of the head through the shoulders and hips to the ground would be perpendicular.

A forward lean places an extra burden on the leg muscles and often contributes to back pain and shin splints. It should only be used when sprinting or going uphill. Leaning backward has a braking effect; it places a severe burden on the legs and back. The important point is that the runner usually runs erect. If you run faster with more ball-heel footstrike, you should lean forward slightly, which will allow you a more fluid and powerful stride.

Remember, run relaxed. Your shoulders should "hang" in a relaxed way, level with the ground. If you stick out your chest and throw back your shoulders you'll develop tightness in the upper back or even the lower back. Concentrate on not allowing the shoulder blades to pinch together. Tension first collects in the head and shoulders. Be aware of tension beginning at the base of the neck, in the jaw muscles, around the eyes, in the muscles of the forehead, and in the shoulders. Occasionally, let the head roll from side to side, shrug the shoulders and let them drop, or drop your arms loosely at your side to promote relaxation. Allow the chin to drop and flap, as if talking. This keeps the jaw and neck muscles relaxed. The arms should swing from relaxed shoulders; the eyes should look straight ahead.

ARM DRIVE

The movement of your arms provides the rhythm that pulls you along. The faster your arm movement, the faster you will be able to move your legs. "Pumping" the arms in powerful strokes is as important to the sprinter as high knee-lift. But the jogger and long-distance runner don't worry about arm pumping unless competing in a race or running up a hill. These runners are interested in two important factors relating to arm drive: balance and energy conservation.

The arms balance the runner. The left arm should swing forward, balancing right leg action; the right arm should swing forward, balancing left leg action. If the arms are carried too high, the result is a shortened stride, shoulder twisting, muscle fatigue, and tension in the shoulders and upper back. Arms carried too low often contribute to a forward lean, and to a side-to-side and bouncing motion. Arms moving across the body result in side-to-side motion and a shortened stride. Too little forward or backward motion results in lack of proper drive and balance. Flopping of the arms or rigidly held arms also contribute to inefficiency of motion, and thus waste your energy.

How should the arms be carried? The general guidelines are as follows:

- The arms should be carried low, between the waistline and the chest.
- At the midpoint of your stride, the forearms, wrists, and hands should be parallel to the ground, as are the shoulders.
- In the forward swing, the forearm moves slightly up and inward; on the back swing, it moves slightly down and outward.
- The thumbs should rest on your index fingers, with your fingers lightly clenched, palm turned slightly up, wrist firm but not tight, hand in line with forearms. Some runners prefer to put their thumbs in their middle fingers, forming a meditative circle.
- The elbows should be relaxed, not locked, and should not dramatically point away from the body, but should be loose at your sides. They should bend and straighten a little with each arm swing.
- The shoulders should remain level and should not move appreciably, although there is a rise and fall as the arms swing forward and backward.

It is important to concentrate on relaxing the shoulders, elbows, wrists, and fists. Body tension is often the result of improper arm carry. Occasionally let your arms drop straight down at your sides and loosely "shake them out"; this reduces the tightness that results from holding them up for a long time. According to the famous coach Percy Cerutty, "All running starts with the thumbs." Tension begins in the hands and improper hand carry can set off a chain reaction of form problems.

BREATHING

Many runners ask, "How should I breathe while running?" or "Should I breathe with my mouth open?" There is a theory that runners should breathe in through the nose and out through the mouth. Supposedly this promotes relaxation and filters the air. But running calls for lots of air to satisfy the body's need for oxygen. You won't last long breathing in through the nose and out the mouth. Open up your mouth and suck in all the air you need.

Some runners enjoy breathing in tune to their footstrike. They may inhale, for example, on every other left step, and exhale on every other right. Such breathing techniques may be relaxing during yoga exercises, but they would drive me nuts during a run, and I'm sure I'd get confused. If I had to blow my nose during the run, would it count as exhaling? What if I sneezed when I was due to inhale? Life is too short, and running too beautiful, to spoil with rigid rules. My advice is to breathe when you feel like breathing. On the other hand, Jack Shepherd—who will try anything once—has done special breathing exercises while running. He loves them, and we describe some in Chapter 17. You decide what's best for you.

However, there are two basic rules. Breathing should be relaxed, and should follow "belly breathing" principles. Most of us breathe backwards. We tend to suck the stomach in, and breathe from the chest. With proper abdominal breathing the belly expands as you breathe in, and flattens as you breathe out. The expansion of the abdomen indicates that the diaphragm is fully lowered, inflating the lungs to their fullest and allowing a more efficient intake of oxygen. Improper breathing can also cause the dreaded side stitch (see page 264).

To understand how to belly breathe, lie on your back and place a light book on your stomach. (Try this one.) Take a deep breath. If you are "belly breathing" properly, the book will rise as you breathe in, and fall as you breathe out.

THE THREE "R'S" OF RUNNING FORM

1. Run tall.
2. Run relaxed.
3. Run naturally.

No one can teach you how to develop your running style. For the most part, you are born with a certain style that changes as you do. The best we can hope to do is clean up bad habits. The "natural" runners possess a beauty most of us who run can recognize, and partially imitate. They run, as Tom Sturak writes of the great Filbert Bayi in *The African Running Revolution*, "like water flows or the wind blows."

Some days I feel as though my whole body is in complete synchronization and towing my mind along for the ride. I cleanse myself in the pleasant breeze I create with my free-flowing body. On these days I don't need to emulate anyone's form. I've created my own.

Study the mechanics of a proper running form, but always be yourself.

8 SUPPLEMENTAL EXERCISES

Training should be an enjoyable habit. And to make that habit more enjoyable, we suggest alternating your regular warm-up and cool-down exercises with some of the exercises below. We also include some aerobic alternative workouts you might want to try when running too much has made you stale, or to prevent or recover from injuries.

WEIGHT TRAINING

Running does little to strengthen the upper body or key muscle groups such as the quadriceps muscles. Runners who compete in distance races need upper-body strength and endurance. Just to hold your arms up during a long race or to find extra leg power through those last few miles requires added muscular strength. A good weight-training program done two or three times a week will supplement your aerobic work and improve your strength and body tone. Weight training is especially valuable for women runners, who generally have less well-developed muscles than men.

For men and women, a proper weight-training program should strengthen all the muscle groups of your body. Proper weight training can also help prevent injury due to imbalanced muscle groups. Increased overall strength should also better performance and help you drive up hills and continue running strong during the late stages of a long-distance run. Strength training also helps you increase the drive in your arms that propels your body forward.

You should select and follow a specific weight-training program and routine similar to your running workouts. Remember that heavy weights with few repetitions build strength and a bulky body; light weights and many repetitions build stamina and a lean, firm body. The rule for developing a runner's body applies equally to both men and women: light weights, many repetitions. The goal is to firm the body, not to build bulky muscles.

The following program was developed by Pete Schuder and myself for *The Competitive Runner's Handbook*. I recommend a three-step approach to weight training: warm-up, workout, cooldown.

THE WARM-UP AND THE COOL-DOWN

The warm-up for weight training is basically the same as warming up for running. Spend about 15 minutes before lifting performing the four groups of stretching exercises outlined in Chapter 2. These exercises will loosen up the muscles connecting tissues and joints, and permit you to work out with little danger of injuring yourself from tightness.

One pattern might be to lift after an easy run: Perform your stretching exercises after the run, lift, and then do your regular cool-down stretching.

After your warm-up stretching, you should do some warm-up lifting. This would be 10 to 12 relaxed repetitions using very light weights. This will also allow your muscles to warm up and loosen.

The cool-down, as with running, is the warm-up in reverse. Walk or swim for about five minutes, and then do your stretching and relaxation exercises.

THE WORKOUT

Remember: light weights, many repetitions. Weights lifted about 10 to 15 times build both muscular strength and endurance while increasing bulk very little, if at all.

The easiest and safest weight-training equipment to use are the Universal and Nautilus machines. The weights are connected to a main housing, which prevents you from dropping the weights on the floor or on your toes. Weights are changed quickly and easily by moving small levers or rods. You may want to modify your program by staying with one weight for each set of exercises, and doing the 10 to 15 repetitions without changing the weights frequently.

A set of barbells is also good. They may be more handy than the machines since you can keep a set at home and not have to go to your local gym or Y. Be careful if you have not lifted weights before. If possible, get some advice and supervision from a professional instructor.

The following routine can be done with any equipment. It is simple to follow, and takes about 15 to 20 minutes twice a week. This is a medium-weight workout to build stamina. Each weight-training routine consists of the following steps:

1. Select the exercise and the weight to be lifted.
2. Do the specified number of repetitions, exhaling as you lift the weight, inhaling as you release the weight.
3. Rest one minute at the completion of the first set to recover, and do some flexibility exercises to keep your muscles and joints loose.
4. Do the second set the same way as the first set.
5. Rest one minute at the completion of the second set, doing flexibility exercises to maintain muscle flexibility.
6. Do the third set (if possible) the same way as the first two sets.
7. Rest one minute at the completion of the third set, do flexibility exercises, and set up your next exercise.
8. Continue with the next exercise following the above seven steps.

A difficult choice in weight training is knowing how much weight to use, and when to increase the weight for each particular exercise. Here are two general rules to follow:

Rule One: Start Light Always start every workout with a very light weight. Allow your body to adapt to the increased resistance. Do only a few repetitions. We recommend one set of 10 to 15 repetitions.

Rule Two: Increase the Weight Gradually Increase the amount of weight you lift for a particular exercise only after you can easily repeat three sets of the recommended repetitions. Then increase the weight, but only by five to ten pounds. Reduce the number of sets to two, and gradually work your way back up to three sets at the recommended number of repetitions.

THE EXERCISES

A good 15- to 20-minute program might include the following exercises. The quadriceps exercises are especially important, for these are the muscles that lift your legs and the muscles that often tire in long races.

The Bench Press

Lying flat on your back, face up, press the weight straight up from your body. This exercise strengthens your arms, chest, and upper torso.

Do three sets of 15 repetitions.

Sit-Ups with Weights

Lying on the floor, knees bent and feet hooked under an immovable object, put your hands behind your head and bring your upper body, bent at the waist, to your knees. Place a weight behind your head as you become stronger. This exercise strengthens your abdominal muscles.

Do three sets of 20 repetitions without weights.
Do three sets of 10 repetitions with weights.

Step-Ups

Standing, holding the weight with both hands behind your

neck, put one foot on a stationary box about 18 inches high, and step up with the other. A set is complete when the recommended number of repetitions is done with each leg. This exercise strengthens the Achilles tendons, calves, and quadriceps.

Do three sets of 10 repetitions with each leg.

Toe Raises

Standing, holding the weight behind your neck (as with step-ups), raise yourself up onto your toes. This exercise strengthens your calf muscles, Achilles tendons, and ankle joints.

Do three sets of 15 repetitions.

Reverse Curls

Standing, hold the bar with the weights palms down in front of you, resting the bar on your quadriceps. Keep your back straight, thus not allowing your body to swing, and bring the bar up to your chest. This exercise develops the forearm for better arm swing.

Do three sets of 15 repetitions.

GENERAL RULES FOR WEIGHT TRAINING

- Weight training is progressive, just like running. You begin with low weights and gradually increase the weights as you become stronger.
- You lift twice a week, allowing two to three days between each lifting session to let your muscles rebuild themselves. Weight workouts should be separate from your runs; or, lift first and run second, taking it easy.
- Limit the number of repetitions to 10 to 15 and the number of sets to two or three in order to build muscle strength without building bulk.
- Begin each weight-training session by exercising the large muscle groups first and then the smaller muscles. Alternate upper-body lifting with lower-body lifting.

- Do flexibility exercises before and after each repetition lift.
- All lifts should be done through a full range of motion to work the muscles completely.
- Lifting is done to a four-count pace: count to four as you lift the weight, and count to four as you release the weight.

For more complete guidelines, see *Weight Training for Runners* by Ardy Friedberg.

SUPPLEMENTARY EXERCISES WITHOUT WEIGHTS

Too often I hear runners complain because they can't keep up with their running programs. They've been injured, or are in pain. When I hear this, I ask: How long have you been running? How far do you run? Are you doing your warm-up and cool-down exercises? Too often, the slowed-down runner is beyond the beginner stage and has increased his or her mileage but given up the warm-ups and cool-downs because "they're boring." Here are some exercises that you might add to your running program to prevent injury and to make your running stronger. They are arranged by body area to be stretched, and then by special exercise.

Abdominals

Weak abdominals contribute to poor form and to back pain. Do bent-knee sit-ups (see page 19).

Upper Body

Weak arms and chest muscles can be strengthened to improve arm drive. Do push-ups (see page 18).

Quadriceps

Weak quads, especially in relation to strong hamstrings, can cause imbalance, which affects the pull on your kneecaps. These muscles also help pick up your legs and are important in the late stages of long runs and for running uphill. Some supplementary exercises:

- Sit in a chair, straighten the leg and tighten it, holding the kneecap parallel to the floor. Hold for 20 to 30 seconds in isometric contraction. Repeat 10 to 20 times.
- Sit on a table and lift any type of weight suspended from the legs, with legs straight. (One leg at a time.)
- Walk up several flights of stairs regularly.
- Walk in water, emphasizing knee lift.
- Hike or run on hills.
- Tuck your toes under a desk or couch and try to lift it with your toes. Your knees can be either bent or straight. Hold for ten seconds. Relax. Repeat 10 times.
- Stand with your back to the wall. Lift one leg as high as you can, keeping the knee straight. Hold for a five-count. Now bend the knee to relax for the count of five. Straighten the knee again. Do each leg five times, increasing to ten.

Adductor Muscles

These muscles contribute to inner leg pain and groin pull. For strengthening the adductors, try the following:

Lie on your right side with your right hand supporting your head. Your left hand is placed on the floor in front of you for support. Your left foot is flat on the floor in front of your right leg. Your right leg should be slightly ahead of your body. Now, flex your right foot so that the toe points up toward the knee. Keep the knee firm and straight throughout the exercise. Then lift the right leg as high as you can, and then lower it. Start with 5 to 10 repetitions and work up to 20. When you lower the leg each time, do not touch the floor with your foot and do not relax your leg. Keep it firm throughout this exercise. This can also be done with a one-pound weight on your ankle. Turn on your left side, and repeat with your left leg.

Hamstrings

Here is a strengthening exercise to prevent pulls.

Attach a one-pound weight to each ankle. Lie on your back on the floor, arms at your sides. Your knees are bent, feet flat on the floor. Stretch your right leg up as straight as you can. Then put your foot back on the floor. Repeat 10 times. Now repeat with the other leg. Your aim is to straighten the leg so that it is almost at a 90-degree angle to the floor. Start with three sets of 10 extensions for each leg. At first, do this without the weights.

Arch
The following exercises may relieve arch pain.
• Pick up marbles with your toes.
• Roll a bottle under your foot.
• Stand on a towel with your toes over its edge and pick up the towel with your toes.

Postural Muscles
These muscles are important for good running form. The following exercises should strengthen the abdominals, the gluteal muscles (fanny), and the erector spines (back muscles along your spine).
• Lying on your back, tilt your pelvis toward the floor, tighten your buttocks and stomach, and push the lower back into the floor. Hold. Count to 10. Relax. Repeat two more times.
• Stand with your back against a wall, push your lower back toward the wall as you tighten the buttocks and stomach. Count to 10. Relax. Repeat two more times.

Shins
These exercises will strengthen the anterior leg muscles to minimize shin splints.
• Lying down or sitting in a chair, put your right foot on top of your left foot. Now try to pull your lower foot toward your body as your upper foot pushes it away. Hold for 10 seconds. Switch feet and push-pull for 10 seconds. This is one set. Do five sets.

- Sit on a table with your legs hanging freely over the side. Flex one foot to lift a weight, perhaps a bucket of pebbles or a sandbag or other weight suspended over the foot. Do not try to lift too much. Do 10 lifts with each foot. Repeat once.
- Attach a rubber bicycle inner tube to a board. Standing, slip your toes under the tube and lift them against it. Hold for a ten-count and switch legs. Do two or three sets.
- Turn your feet inward while standing and make a rolling motion. Do for a few seconds with each leg. Repeat.
- Stand on the edge of a towel and curl your toes to pull the towel under your feet.

SUPPLEMENTAL AEROBIC EXERCISES

Swimming, biking, cross-country skiing, race-walking, and even brisk walking are aerobic exercises of benefit to the runner. They can be used to replace running when you are injured, or they can be done along with running to help prevent boredom or injury. These exercises, combined with weight training, will enhance an overall fitness program and help balance musculoskeletal development. Running primarily strengthens the antigravity muscles along the back and the back of the legs. This creates a muscle imbalance, and most runners should strengthen the opposing muscle groups: abdominals (stomach), quadriceps (thighs), and shins. Running does little for the upper body, and you should also strengthen your chest and arms. Here are the important muscle areas, with alternative exercises that will help develop them.

- Ankles: swimming
- Shins: biking (with toe clips)
- Quadriceps: biking, race-walking
- Upper body: swimming, cross-country skiing, race-walking
- Buttocks: cross-country skiing, race-walking
- Abdominals: cross-country skiing

Maintaining aerobic fitness is important to the runner. The activities listed above can both supplement your running and increase your fitness. For example, a novice marathoner who runs 40 miles a week can increase his or her aerobic level to the approximate equivalent of 50 miles a week or more by also swimming 30 to 60 minutes a day, three days a week.

Be warned that these are supplementary workouts. Hour for hour, running is still the best training for a runner. No other activity uses the same specific muscles groups; you still have to get out there and pack in the miles. Cross-country skiing, biking, rowing, swimming, and race-walking are excellent aerobic alternatives, but you must keep up your intensity and not cheat. Obviously, a good choice is to combine alternatives: biking and weight training, for example, provide good overall workouts for the upper body, legs, and cardiorespiratory systems. The beginner runner may wish to alternate days of running with days of swimming, for example, to extend fitness, minimize injury, and ease muscle tightness.

Walking, biking, and swimming after a workout or a race will help you relax and recover. The exercises may be used in the days following a long race, such as a marathon, to ease sore muscles back into shape, or to relax previously little-used muscles for the beginner marathoner. Swimming is particularly good for relaxation and postrace recovery, since it provides aerobic work without the trauma of weight-bearing exercise. The water also has a massaging effect on your tired muscles.

If you travel, remember that many hotels now have exercise equipment, and some also have pools. A few offer guests the opportunity to work out in a nearby health club. You can also check out the pools and indoor exercise equipment at a local YMCA.

Atalanta's national class masters runner Patty Lee Parmalee faced a dilemma. She was on a sailboat in the Virgin Islands for a vacation, missing the team training runs in the cold, icy month of January. What to do? I convinced her to jump overboard and train daily in the ocean, just as she would have on the roads of Central Park. She built up to swimming for half an hour a day and twice a week simulated her team speed workouts by "running in the water" using a life jacket or by flutter kicking holding on to the boat rope ladder. Since she isn't a skilled swimmer, she found that she felt more tired, especially in the upper body, than if she had run. But she proved she could stay in shape under very unusual conditions, and returned to the roads and racing in fine shape.

Every year her teammate Nancy Tighe, winner of the 1981 Long Island Marathon in the 50–59 age group, spends two to three weeks traveling by bike with her husband, John. Although they make it a "fitness vacation" away from career work, she gives up running entirely during this time. They tour the countryside in such places as Ireland, Austria, England, Vermont, and Kentucky at a rate of about 50 miles a day. Upon her return, she looks forward to running again. Besides maintaining aerobic conditioning, the bicycling has also strengthened her quads considerably.

GUIDELINES FOR SUPPLEMENTAL TRAINING

Plan your supplemental exercise as carefully as you plan your running program. Here are some guidelines for adding other exercises to your running program:

1. Whichever alternative exercise you select as a *change of pace*, continue to run a few times each week to keep your "running legs." This will ease the transition when you return to running full-time.

2. If you select an alternative exercise to *increase your aerobic fitness*, be careful. You should not exceed about 25 percent of your total running training doing alternative exercise. You are, after all, training to be a runner, not a swimmer, cyclist, or racewalker. The activity supplements your running, it doesn't replace it.

3. If you wish to cut back your running in order to rest or treat an injury and wish to *maintain approximately the same level*

of aerobic fitness, try to cut back no more than one-third of your running time. A runner doing 30 miles a week would cut back to 20.

4. Ease into the activity. Treat your new exercise just as you did running during your first few months: don't overdo it. Too much is worse than too little.

5. If new techniques are required, take lessons (for example, cross-country skiing). Start the new exercise slowly, and do it every other day, alternating with running if possible.

6. Training principles that apply to running (as explained previously) also apply to your alternate activity—especially the principle of alternating hard and easy days and training without overstraining.

7. Your alternative exercise should be performed at a training heart rate, or perceived exertion, equivalent to your rate during running.

8. If your exercise is less demanding than running, do it longer. The rule of thumb is: if you can't reach your training heart rate, exercise for twice as long.

9 THE YOUNG RUNNER →

If you're young enough to walk, you're young enough to run. And if you're old enough to walk, you're old enough to run. At age two, Christopher Glover, who sprinted into my world in 1981, swerved his way to the finish line of the "Pee Wee 100-Yard Run." And Larry Lewis ran every day until his death at age one hundred and six, ending a string of ninety-seven years of running life.

The running scene has become a family activity. Children are running, and now make up a significant percentage of entrants in races. Is this wise, or healthy? Should our children run so much? And how much is medically and emotionally correct?

Our children need four to six hours of vigorous and encouraging physical activity every day, but they aren't getting it. A recent national survey shows that American children have not improved their physical fitness at all during the last decade. In fact, the results of federally funded standardized fitness tests of American public-school students during the last 25 years are discouraging. There were significant gains in fitness between the first study in 1957–58 and the one in 1964–65, but little or no improvement was shown in tests in 1974–75. During 1979–80, an AAU test of more than four million children, six through seventeen years old, showed that 57 percent of these youngsters failed to achieve fitness standards thought attainable by the average healthy child. By 1984, the AAU test showed that 64 percent failed to meet these standards.

In 1979 Thomas B. Gilliam, then of the University of Michigan and now a health consultant, examined Michigan schoolchildren. He found evidence of one or more of the common risk factors for heart disease—high blood pressure, obesity, high cholesterol levels, low cardiovascular fitness—already characteristic in half of these schoolchildren. Their lack of fitness and exercise, and their high-salt and high-fat diets, seem to assure that they will develop the American health standard of coronary disease and heart attacks. Despite the nation's current heart-attack rate, rising medical health costs, and sagging academic achievement in the public schools, physical education is being cut back for our youngsters. Physical fitness, as part of mental fitness in the schools, is also losing. As one New York State educator lamented: "If you don't have a healthy child, you can't instruct a healthy child."

We know today how beneficial regular aerobic exercise is for adults. The studies and evidence are presented throughout this book. But what about children? If they can't get any exercise during school, what can be done for them afterward? As Dr. Wynn F. Updike, associate dean at Indiana University's School of Health, Physical Education and Recreation, says, "Exercising tends to be an ongoing phenomenon once youngsters experience fitness and its positive characteristics."

Running is a comparatively inexpensive form of sport and exercise. There is little dependence on equipment, other than shoes, and class sizes don't have to be restricted. It's social, healthy—and it always should be fun. This does not mean that instruction should be eliminated. Getting any boy or girl started down the road to fitness should include patient, noncompetitive instruction and honest enthusiasm. Moreover, running doesn't have to replace other sports for kids; it is a much-needed aerobic activity that complements other sports.

Running is a natural extension of play. Dr. Ernst van Aaken of West Germany, who spent much of his life in sports medicine and working with children, spoke in 1976 at a Road Runners Club clinic in New York City. He said that "a child is born a long-distance runner, his play is running, and innumerable X-ray exams have demonstrated that the heart of a child has a more favorable volume relative to body weight than adults." Studies show that the typical nine-year-old has the biggest heart volume for his weight that he will ever have, unless he trains hard to be a world class endurance athlete.

Dr. van Aaken added that the play of children is really a long-distance run interrupted by several breaks. He once measured the total distance covered by a seven-year-old boy at play. The lad covered five miles in 90 minutes, taking 400 breaks. A healthy child, according to Dr. van Aaken, can run and play all day long and thus should be encouraged to participate in endurance sports rather than "ball sports" that only promote speed and power.

Other recent medical research shows that even "untrained" children have high rates of oxygen intake, which is considered a good measure of endurance fitness. In fact, many nine- and ten-year-old children score higher than all the highly trained distance runners. Most interesting is the fact that the untrained children scored as high as the trained children, which may indicate that endurance is something we are blessed with as children, but squander as we age.

I like to see children introduced to running at an early age, but not pushed into it. Running should be self-motivated. Bennett Gershman is a New York attorney and a top marathon runner, representing the Central Park Track Club. In a 1976 six-mile race, I was surprised to see Bennett far back in the field. Then I noticed that he was running with a big smile on his face, accompanied by a similar one on the face of his eight-year-old son, Seth, who was running his first race. Was the father pushing the son into his sport? Bennett said absolutely not. "During the summer I often run along the beach at Fire Island. Seth would see me run and occasionally, as a five-year-old would, ask if he could come along.

It was his idea from the beginning. We now run together early in the morning a couple of times a week. We go an easy two or three miles in Central Park. It gives us a chance to be alone together and creates a stronger father-son bond. Seth used to watch me at races; he asked if he could run one, so we did. He was really excited about the whole thing, especially when he received a trophy for being the youngest finisher, as well as lots of applause from a big crowd. We ran another race and he didn't get a trophy. He was disappointed, but I think he understood. I definitely believe that my son enjoys his running, and I don't want to see his fun ruined due to either one of us taking it too seriously."

He was right. I think there are some specific guidelines, and warnings, for working with kids interested in running.

WHEN TO START

Let the child decide when the time is right to start a sports exercise like running. Eight or nine years may be the right age, but wait for the child to make the move. Don't push your child into the activity. Make the early experience positive, successful, and *fun*. Focus the running or exercise on your child, the way Bennett Gershman did.

1. *Ages Two and Under*   When my son, Christopher, was born, Virginia and I found that our exercise dropped almost to zero. We spent our time living for the baby. Within a few months, however, we discovered baby-carriage running. Every Saturday and Sunday we "ran" together as a family. We shared the joy of being together, although in truth Chrissy often slept for most of the four-mile loop of Central Park. Cameras clicked, and people would say: "Look at that family running together!"

This led to our sponsoring a "Baby-Carriage Running Clinic and Fun Run" for the New York Road Runners Club. We wanted to encourage families with babies to run together. We even had a diaper drawing to award a pair of baby running shoes donated by Nike. Best of all, we learned a lot. Here are some of our conclusions.

Safety: Use well-built carriages, with good shock absorption, such as the Baby Jogger (from Racing Strollers Inc., P.O. Box 9681, Yakima, WA 98909). Do not use the lightweight, collapsible strollers. The front wheels can catch in a crack and catapult both baby and running parent. Strap in baby with a full harness.

Run at a slow, comfortable speed. Running at high speeds will decrease your ability to control the carriage. Walk down steep hills, and stop if any danger, like bikers riding toward you, appears.

Run in parks where roads are closed to automobile traffic.

Training: Baby-carriage running is a great way for beginner runners, or mothers who stopped running to give birth, to ease into the sport. Start with brisk walking while pushing the carriage. The resistance of the carriage will push up your heart rate. Next, alternate slow jogging with walking until you can run 20 minutes without stopping.

Run at about the same heart rate you would maintain if you weren't pushing a carriage. For example, if you normally train at 140 beats per minute, find the pace-per-mile that is equivalent while pushing the carriage. That will probably be one-minute-per-mile slower.

Also, you can do some speed work while pushing the baby and the carriage uphill. You'll find that the increased weight will make you work a lot harder, and you'll still be able to control the carriage safely.

Remember:

- Increase your comfort by adjusting the carriage handles to fit your height. Increase the baby's comfort by shifting the child to different positions during the run.
- Be sure to bring extra clothes to keep you and the baby comfortable, and include a good supply of diapers.
- The best time to run is before a baby's nap. Often he or she will doze off to the rhythmic sound of your running. When the baby wakes, talk to him or her and point out things of interest along the way. You may want to stop sometimes

and let your baby out for a crawl-run. When Christopher shouted that he wanted out—and he began "running" on his own at ten months—we'd stop our run and let him out for his.

2. Ages Two to Six   Exercise of any type at this age level should always be fun and play. The New York Road Runners Club sometimes holds "Pee Wee Runs" of 440 yards, and every kid gets a balloon and animal crackers. But parents can become awfully involved in their children's sports, even at this age. Keep communications open between you and your child, and be sure that he or she really wants to run in a group or exercise formally. Remember what Dr. van Aaken said: that the play of children is really long-distance running. We don't need to encourage them much, but we do need to keep their competitions and running in perspective. Never force a child to run.

3. Ages Six to Twelve   This is the age when a lot of kids, especially boys, start becoming very competitive. Hold them back, and give them perspective. I never encourage children under twelve to compete in long-distance running. I prefer that they experience the joy of running for fitness and racing for fun. I feel strongly that any youth running program be low-key, and begin with the objective of teaching kids to have fun. Here are some guidelines:

- Always emphasize sportsmanship. There should be no winners or losers.
- Stress teaching skills that include proper running form and technique in all aspects of track and field. Kids should participate in any events they want, and avoid specialization.
- Praise each runner, and give each special attention, regardless of ability. If records are kept, they should be used only to give incentive for personal improvement.
- Limit mileage to runs of one to four miles, and races to two miles.

- Limit "speed workouts" to one a week.
- Let the children choose to run, and encourage them to let their bodies fly, their legs run.

Low-key—that's important.

Noncompetitive. But why bother? One day, after handling a group of a hundred screaming and yelling nine- to twelve-year-olds on a hot summer afternoon, I also wondered why. As I packed away our equipment, a shy eight-year-old came up, eyes sparkling with excitement and pride, and asked, "Coach, could I please run another mile?" My outer smile didn't match the one inside.

4. Ages Thirteen to Nineteen Teenagers vary in size and growth so radically that accurate advice needs to be given to each one individually. A boy at thirteen or fourteen who cannot descend a flight of stairs gracefully can become, at age sixteen or seventeen, an athlete of formidable skill. A girl of fifteen who is an outstanding team player may at seventeen be a plump, nonathletic person. The simple point is: Kids in this age group change physically and emotionally almost week to week.

Exercise, therefore, must first of all be fun for these youngsters. They should also be praised and coached individually. They should never be evaluated only negatively: that gawky freshman soccer player, or runner, may become an all-state athlete in two years.

Here are some guidelines for teenage runners:

- These runners should learn how to run fast over short distances. They should concentrate on distances run by their school's track team, up to 5K. They may want to run road races up to 10K.
- Older teenage runners will have increased stamina over longer distances. I do not recommend marathon training until an adolescent is able to handle both the training and the racing physically and emotionally. This is one of the reasons why the New York City Marathon has a minimum age limit of sixteen.

GUIDELINES FOR YOUTH

There are some specific guidelines for parents of all runners and their coaches:

• Don't let the sport shift from being playful to being too goal-oriented. An adolescent especially can be helped or crushed by running competition. As a shy, skinny teenager, I felt that no one recognized me until I was a track star. Suddenly my confidence rose and I became more outgoing. The discipline of running can also give a kid a steadying influence—as it can an adult—at a time when life may seem to be "a real bummer." One of the teenage girls on our team asked me to write a letter of reference for her college résumé. I did, emphasizing the fact that anyone who could make the sacrifices to train for and successfully complete long-distance races—in her case a marathon—would indeed have the self-discipline to make a good college student.

• Beware of the pressures involved with the sport. Dr. George Sheehan warns that "competition and parental ego are the main stumbling blocks to young runners." I've seen parents scream and yell at children after races because they didn't perform as well as the adult thought they should. Parents and coaches should step back from the kids and leave them alone. Adult training methods are for adults, not kids. (Incredible as it may seem, I once discovered that a parent was introducing a young runner to carbohydrate loading before a marathon, a process that includes the possibly dangerous depletion cycle.)

• Let kids learn to lose. You can only appreciate winning by losing a few. I also think we are too award conscious. The New York Road Runners Club used to give out awards to the youngest finishers at races. It was a cute idea—until the parents began arguing over the trophies and withdrawing kids from races.

• Praise the child, win or lose.

• Practices should be fun. There's enough competition in the races. Parents should encourage their children to run with them, but only at the child's suggestion and his or her pace.

• Remember, children, like adults, have their ups and downs. Barry Geisler, National Road Runners Club age-group running chairman, emphasizes that "the body has just so much energy. When more is needed during growth stages, less will be available for running, and performance is affected. Coaches need to be aware of this concept."

• If the child wants to join a team, be sure that the coach is responsible and that he or she puts the emotional and physical health of team members before winning.

• The ultimate goal should be long range: It should be the fun of running and the need for fitness, not the compulsion to win. There's a whole, big, overcompetitive world waiting for the child when he becomes an adult. A balance should be maintained between preparing the child for competition and depriving him of his right to grow up at his or her own speed through play and sports.

Training

Be sure that your child learns to stretch before each run. He or she should follow the instructions in this book for warming up and cooling down. Your child should also start with the walk-run system, and train only at a conversational pace. This must be fun, and gradual. Add distance in a very slow progression; balance energy and enthusiasm with patience and moderation. If your child expresses interest in joining a group, help him or her select a YMCA program for kids or some other program that is not overly competitive and is for children only.

The important thing is to establish a reasonable and fun training routine based on your child's age and conditioning. Equip your child with running shoes especially designed for shock protection and support in running, and try to have the child run on soft surfaces.

Competition

More and more children are running long-distance races. The

American Academy of Pediatrics recommends that preadolescent children not run long-distance races held primarily for adults. Especially, children should not run marathons. Dr. Lyle Micheli at Children's Hospital in Boston suggests that children under 14 not run distances greater than 10K.

Also, too much emphasis placed on winning, or even on competing, may spoil a young child's enthusiasm for running. After all, the exercise is more important than the race. "Running is an adult sport," said Dr. George Sheehan. "One derives the pleasures of contemplation, conversation, and competition from running, which is fine for someone who is searching for his place in the universe." Kids like the excitement surrounding the race, not the race itself.

Injuries

Children can get the same overuse injuries from running that their parents get. Moreover, children do not tolerate extremes in temperatures as well as adults do. A young body has not fully developed, and its thermoregulatory system, which maintains proper body temperature, does not adjust to severe heat or cold. The young runner, therefore, should dress lightly in warm weather, and in layers for cold. As with adult runners, they should learn to train in clothes that keep them comfortable.

Because they are still growing, children also suffer injuries that may complicate the natural growing process. There is some medical evidence that young runners may damage their epiphyseal growth centers, which generate growth at the ends of long bones. Studies from Children's Hospital in Boston indicate injuries to young runners' joint surface of the talus, similar to Little League elbow, and some apparent avulsion of the ankle bone in children. Excessive training, in the 50- to 80-miles-per-week range, may cause a painful knobbed-out bone condition called Osgood-Schlatter disease.

Studies in 1980 by Dr. Bernard Gutin at Columbia University

showed that children's bodies change with training much as adults' bodies do. Their hearts become larger and stronger, they use oxygen more efficiently, and their muscles burn increased amounts of fat.

The longest-lasting injury is psychological. A California study in 1980 by Dr. Harmon Brown found that after two years, half the children who started a running program had quit. After three years, 75 percent had stopped, and after four years 85 percent weren't running at all. Why? Most of them had taken up long-distance running because their parents made them. The impetus, of course, must come from the child, and support and direction from the parent. Never force kids to run or race. *Never.*

What is best? Perhaps something between the East German approach of training kids seriously at a young age for possible future stardom, and the run-for-fun approach. I think the emphasis must be on fun. And the idea for having fun must come from your child. Perhaps the nicest dream of the addicted adult runner is to be awakened from a Sunday afternoon snooze by a young son or daughter who pleads: "Daddy, would you like to go for a run with me?"

10 THE OLDER RUNNER

America is aging. By 1990, more than 28 percent of all Americans will be over age sixty. Thirty years from that date, approximately one out of every three Americans will be a senior citizen—including all the top men and women runners of today.

But with health costs rising, and government monies for medical and health care falling, keeping yourself healthy as you age makes sense both physically and financially. All of us, whatever our ages, should protect and care for our health.

More men and women are running and exercising now than ever before, and many of them are middle-aged and older. The Masters group of runners is getting larger every year. In some major races, more than half the field consists of men and women over forty years old. Running, and especially racing, is one of the few sports where the participant is rewarded for aging.

In most parts of the country, men and women in the Masters category (over forty) race against each other and are scored separately in five- or ten-year age breakdowns. The Road Runners Club of New York, for example, categorizes runners this way: Sub-vet (ages thirty to thirty-nine); Veteran A (forty to forty-four); Veteran B (forty-five to forty-nine); Masters (fifty to fifty-nine); and Seniors (sixty and older). Some races now even have a seventy-plus division.

As a result, this breakdown by age gives each older runner "a new life." How many sports allow a fifty-year-old to compete against his or her peers for a trophy? Runners secretly watch the calendar as they await their chance to move into a new age group, and be called "the new blood" or "kids." Team competition further enforces this breakdown, and the pride in being fit. The spirit of the Masters runner is very high. Dr. George Sheehan, himself a Senior category runner, wrote in *Dr. Sheehan on Running*, "We are continually capable of doing everything we did in our prime—a little slower, perhaps, somewhat weaker, surely, but if they wait around long enough we'll finish." One of the Masters groups that has a lot of fun is the Scarsdale Antiques. This club was formed in 1971 by men and women in their fifties, sixties, and even seventies to promote running for young and old alike. The Antiques often place several members in races around the metropolitan New York area, and annually send a full bus of older—and younger—runners to the New York Marathon.

So what are you waiting for? Maximum life span now averages 85 years. Yet too many Americans reach their 50th birthday and start shopping for rocking chairs. They should shop instead for running shoes.

As we age, our bodies betray us. Science tells us what to expect: We will lose about two centimeters in height after age fifty; our ears, nose, and head will actually grow; we'll gain weight until age fifty-five, and then slowly lose it; we will lose both matrix and minerals from our bodies; we'll also lose lung function, muscle strength, joint mobility, and elasticity, and our cardiac output will decrease by about one percent per year. When one middle-aged runner at a Road Runners Club sports medicine clinic complained of a series of nagging injuries, Dr. Richard Schuster summed up this problem by saying: "Look at the calendar, my friend."

Our running does indeed drop off. Studies by Dr. L. E. Bottinger, a professor of medicine at the Karolinska Hospital in Stockholm, showed that endurance runners peak in performance between the ages of twenty-six and thirty. His work indicates that racing times become slower from that point almost linearly with age, while decreases in performance drop about 6 to 7 percent with every decade.

But a long-term study being conducted at Washington University School of Medicine in St. Louis involving competitive runners aged fifty and older reports encouraging news: People who exercise don't slow down with age as fast as many have believed. That research shows only a five percent per decade decline in performance after the age of thirty if training continues steadily. Research study by a University of Minnesota graduate student, J. Hodgson, showed that in exercising individuals over age 50, the rate of decline is comparable to that of unexercising men and women forty years younger; that is, an exercise program may help you recapture forty years' worth of oxygen-transporting capacity. And, a recent study by Dr. Michael L. Pollock of the University of Wisconsin Medical School–Mount Sinai Medical Center, following runners aged fifty to eighty-two for ten years, shows that exercisers who continue to train at the same level hold their own in terms of conditioning well into their seventies.

Other studies have compared very fit older people with unconditioned sedentary men and women. Results show that heart function (notably stroke volume and cardiac output) and muscle enzyme activity in the older exercisers is equal to or superior to those of average, unfit twenty-year-olds. Continued, regular training appears to slow down, and all but stop, loss of aerobic capacity. Regular exercise also controls the accumulation of fat, and aids in maintaining mineral mass in bones, especially calcium, whose loss is a particularly insidious disease of older women. Further, the active older person also has a healthier supply of lipoproteins, those anti-cholesterol agents in our blood, and older male runners have shown blood-lipoprotein patterns similar to those of young women, who have the lowest coronary-disease rate known.

Running may not be the answer to aging, but clearly some form of exercise is beneficial. For one thing, older people lose the pleasure of movement simply for the sake of moving, which children enjoy. The sense of confidence in moving that a regular exercise program brings is itself a reward. And, as we've indicated above, regular exercise may also play an important role in the relief of the nemeses of old age: coronary artery disease and heart attack, osteoporosis, and osteoarthritis.

According to Dr. Hans Kraus, a skier and rock climber at age eighty, "Unfit persons age more quickly. They suffer from a deficiency of sufficient exercise and all the benefits exercise means to the body." When I return home and see the deteriorated condition of some of my classmates, I'm convinced that too many of us get old before our time. It may be that the elderly do not exercise because society doesn't expect it of them. An old man jogging along the road is still considered a nut. But fitness programming for the middle-aged and elderly is now becoming more popular as a greater percentage of our population consists of men and women over sixty. Dr. Kraus believes that we need to do more than mere "reclamation jobs" with the elderly. Since many of the disabilities we associate with old age result from years of inactivity, he recommends regular exercise (preferably begun in childhood) including a program of flexibility exercises, walking, or swimming to prevent aging.

Physical exercise will not solve the problems of aging, and for some it may even be dangerous. Alternative forms of exercise should be considered. Dr. Ken Cooper, for example, does not recommend jogging for men and women age sixty or older who have not been running most of their adult lives. He recommends instead walking, swimming, or stationary cycling. Here are some guidelines for older runners who want to start a vigorous exercise program like running:

• If you are over age forty, check with your physician before starting to exercise. An electrocardiogram will evaluate your heart's health, and many doctors now also suggest a treadmill stress test. The stress test takes about an hour, and monitors your heart rate while you walk at varying speeds on a moving treadmill. It is not painful, although some older men and women with knee or hip problems or arthritis in the lower extremities may wish to take a bicycle ergometer test instead. In either case, your doctor monitors your heart rate before, during, and following exercise, to determine how it responds to such physical stress and how it recovers.

• Older people who wish to exercise should start with an easy walking program. When they are able to walk a comfortable distance, perhaps two or three miles, without stopping, they might try a gentle jog. They should do this only after a proper physical examination reveals no physical reasons not to jog. Dr. Ronald M. Lawrence, M.D., president of the American Medical Joggers Association and member of the National Council on Aging, also says: "Plain old walking is one of the best, if not the best, forms of exercise for older people."

• As with any exercise program, walk and then jog at a conversational pace; do not exercise at a pace that leaves you gasping for breath. Slow down if you have trouble talking, and follow your body's signals.

After exercising and stretching, if you feel unwell or have lingering aches and pains, you probably overdid it. The absence of body aches is a good measure of the progress of your exercise. Do not exercise until you are in pain! This should be fun—and beneficial, not painful.

Bring your body back into condition slowly. If you ache, try hot and then cold packs on the aching muscles. Moist heat is best. Apply heat for 20 minutes, then ice for five.

• During the first week, walk as far as you feel comfortable. Be careful: Don't walk in one direction until you feel tired. Cut the distance in half: walk out half your "comfort range" and walk back the other half. This might mean walking around a city block, walking along a road for a quarter mile, or walking a small number of laps around a track. Hold this level for several weeks, or until you can do it without any trouble at all. Gradually increase your distance by a quarter mile per week. Remember the runner's rule: Increase distance, and hold; then increase again, and hold.

• Once your initial physical response to this new exercise routine levels off, try to get your heart rate into your aerobic target area. Try to keep it there for 15 to 20 minutes, three times a week. (See the aerobic chart on page 7 to find your range; or subtract your age from 220, and find 75 percent of that number; that's your target rate.) If you don't want to check your pulse, at this level of exercise simply work out at a comfortable, easy-breathing level for 30 minutes.

Runners and other exercisers of all ages face similar hazards. But one of the most serious is exceeding the body's ability to regulate body temperature. Older exercisers must be very careful on hot and cold days, because of their increased vulnerability to heat and heat stroke, and to frostbite.

Older runners may also have poorer vision and hearing, and slower reflexes. They are less likely to see or hear a dangerous situation, and are slower to respond to it, than other runners. They should exercise and run with others, and be extremely cautious if their workouts take them along roads or even pedestrian and bicycle paths.

All the precautions aside, the older runner is an inspiration to us all—and to other, nonexercising older Americans. Miki Gorman, for example, started running at age thirty-three. Five years later, in 1973, she held the world's record for the women's marathon: 2:46:36. In 1976, then age forty-one, Miki ran 2:39:11 in the New York Marathon, at that time the third-fastest women's marathon time in American history. Dominican nun Sister Marion Irvine of California ran a record for runners age 50 and older of 2:51:01; she was 54 years old, and qualified for the 1984 Women's Olympic Marathon trials.

Toshiko d'Elia is another inspiring older runner. She teaches deaf children, and was a mother in her late thirties when she started jogging. Her first race was a two-mile cross-country run; her twenty-year-old daughter Erica had pushed Tosh into it so that none of the high school girls would come in last. But Tosh finished third and won a trophy, and has been hooked on running ever since. She is now a member of our Atalanta women's team.

Within two years of her two-mile run, Tosh was a nationally known runner. In 1975, at the age of forty-seven, she competed in the United States Masters National Track Championship and ran third in the 5,000 meters. She then went on to Toronto for the First World Masters Track Championship and won second place in the same event with a time of 19:26.5—only a tenth of a second off a world record! In 1977, she finished second in the forty-five to forty-nine age group at the World Masters Marathon Championship in Sweden. Her time was 3:05:20.

Her first marathon was the Jersey Shore Marathon, run in 1976 in icy, snowy conditions with a windchill factor of −19°F. She intended to run only halfway, but the friends who had arranged to pick her up in a car never appeared and she was forced to finish—running a 3:25 marathon that qualified her for Boston. In 1980, at the World Masters Championship marathon in Glasgow, Tosh became the first women aged fifty or older to break three hours—2:57:21. Her autobiography, *Running On*, became a hit in her native Japan, and a television movie has been made of her life.

Ruth Baker, an over-sixty soap-opera actress, enrolled in our beginner's fitness program in 1976, lost twelve pounds and found running "a natural high." Says Ruth, "I find that the more I run, the more confidence I get. It's really increased my belief in myself. Now I have proof that I don't have to be limited because of my age." Ruth ran in the 1976 Mini-Marathon, and finished with a huge smile. Later that evening on her way to dinner with her husband, she was wearing her medal proudly around her neck for all to see. With a bit of encouragement, more older women could know the joys of running. It's too easy to say, "Hey, I'm too old to do it." That's just not true. Nobody should give up because of age.

Ruth Rothfarb is a grandmother in her eighties. But she can run the socks off a lot of nonexercisers half her age. Ruth winters in Miami and summers in Cambridge, Massachusetts. Every day she laces up her running shoes and covers about ten miles. Here's how she does it: In the morning, Mrs. Rothfarb stretches and works out to the television programs starting at six, then she jogs (at a 10-minute-per-mile pace) six miles. Next, she swims for half an hour. Later that day, before dark, she jogs another four miles; when she has errands, she substitutes brisk walking for her jogging.

Although she is now a well-known Senior runner, Ruth Rothfarb had to overcome the shock and dismay of her elderly neighbors. "They thought I was going to kill myself," she told Carol Morton of *Running* magazine. "At first they thought I was a crazy woman. They said, 'You're going to have a heart attack.' " Mrs. Rothfarb, a widow since 1962, started running partly to stay active; she refuses to be dependent on anyone. Her family is grown and occupied with their own lives. "I can do whatever I feel like doing," she says. "Being dependent is a bad thing."

In 1980, Ruth completed the Avon International Women's Marathon, her first, in 5:37. She's still running. "Every race, I get so much applause, but I'm not impressed with myself." We are. Ruth Rothfarb has lowered her marathon time by ten minutes, and completed the Boston Bonne Bell 10K Championship run in 1:08:27. Her marathon training may cover nearly 100 miles in a week. But she follows a very sensible rule: "On days when I don't want to run anymore, I just walk."

Ruth Rothfarb's workouts are almost identical to those of Dr. Paul Spangler, also in his eighties. Dr. Spangler gets up at five a.m., runs six to 10 miles, then swims for half an hour to stretch and work those muscles not used in running. Like Mrs. Rothfarb,

Dr. Spangler increases his mileage up to 70 miles a week when training for a marathon. It's paid off: in 1979 he ran a 3:59:47 Avenue of the Giants marathon. At the 1982 World Veterans Road Racing Championships, Dr. Spangler won gold medals in the 10K (56:24) and 25K (3:06).

Another runner to keep your eye on as he passes you is John A. Kelley, now in his late seventies. Johnny Kelley is still the legend of the Boston Marathon, which he first ran in 1928, at age 21. Kelley has run Boston almost every year since 1932, winning it twice (best time: 2:30:40 in 1945) and finishing second seven times and in the top ten 19 times. Kelley also made the U.S. Olympic marathon team three times, and finished 18th in 1936 and 21st in 1948, when he was forty-two years old.

Catching Kelley will be tough. He runs Boston every year wearing the number one, and his fans cheer him every step of the route. In 1976, at age sixty-eight, Johnny Kelley ran the Boston Marathon in 3:20 despite 100-degree heat.

There are some young upstarts moving in. One, Don Dixon, threatens Kelley's records. In 1977, when he was 50 years old, Dixon, completed the New York Marathon in 2:39:57. He had started running at age forty just to get in shape, and became a typical YMCA two-mile-a-day jogger. By age forty-four, however, Don had entered his first race, the tough Yonkers Marathon, which he finished in 3:35. He later found that he could maintain a fast pace throughout a race, and he discovered something about himself: "I think the secret to my success is consistency. I run year around and thus have accumulated lots of miles in the bank." Don admits that it takes him longer now to recover, but he picks his races and runs with the best. He adds, "I plan my running schedule better now. Also, when I lose the desire to run and my body tells me I need rest, I don't hesitate to take a day off. I feel it's important for older runners to ease off in training at least twice a year and come back strong, keying for a big race. As we get older, we need more rest. Many of the Masters runners run too much, or run too little and then try to race too hard." Don trains 40 to 60 miles a week, and leaves many younger competitors far behind. Most important, he says, "I feel as good as I ever have in my life. The more I run, the younger I feel."

Ted Corbitt is so famous as a runner that a book was written about him (*Corbitt* by John Chodes). He ran his first marathon at age thirty-one. In 1968, at forty-eight, Ted won the National 50-Mile Championship in 5:39:45, and became the oldest runner ever to win the national distance racing title. The next year, he ran 100 miles on a track in 13:33:06, and cut three and a half hours off the American record. At the age of fifty-three, in 1973, he ran twenty-four hours on a track and completed 136.4 miles. Corbitt, who was the first New York Road Runners Club president in 1958, says that as runners age they must learn to adapt to the changing condition of their bodies. "Fitness can't be stored," he says. "It must be earned over and over, indefinitely. If a man runs for twenty years and stops completely, it is just a matter of time until he is in the same condition as the fellow who has never done any running."

Larry Lewis may be the most celebrated runner in history. He was 106 years old when he died, in 1974, of cancer. Up until his death, he ran 6.7 miles every morning at 4:30 a.m. around San Francisco's Golden Gate Park; he then reported to work as a full-time waiter at the St. Francis Hotel. Sometimes he walked the 5 miles to work as well. In the March 1974 issue of *Runner's World*, Larry Lewis said it all, "Never say a person is so many years *old*. Old means something dilapidated and something you eventually get rid of, like an old automobile or a refrigerator. I'm not in that category. You may become mellow, but never old."

Still unsure about exercising after fifty? Mike Tymm, columnist for *National Masters News*, puts it all in perspective: "Aging is more like easing yourself down the face of a cliff. It can be a pleasant descent. The key is not to look up or down, but to focus straight ahead while keeping a firm grip."

Take the case of Zachariah Blackistone of Washington, D.C., who at age one hundred and seven commented on his excellent physical condition and mental awareness (he was an active millionaire): "I owe it all to exercise, especially jogging. When I wake up I think I'm dead. Jogging brings my blood pressure up and I feel like a man. I'm ready for the whole day."

11 WOMEN ON THE RUN

Before the mid-1970s, a pregnant woman jogging in a city park was a major focus of attention and concern. Before 1972, a woman running in the Boston Marathon was *illegal.* By 1984, women were racing the marathon distance in the Olympics, and, more important, thousands of women were crossing the finish lines of races and fun-runs, while tens of thousands more were lacing up their running shoes and putting in mileage on their own. A 1983 survey on American attitudes toward sports asked: "Does participation in sports diminish a woman's feminity?" Some 84 percent of the nationwide male/female sample responded no.

Gloria Averbuch, in her book *The Woman Runner*, describes this as a "new celebration of women's athleticism" that has not been seen before. "Testimony of women everywhere reveals that we are bound today by a new camaraderie. Together we are realizing our physical abilities and discovering the joy of doing for ourselves."

As the barriers fall, it is difficult to remember how ridiculous they were. In the early 1900s, women were allowed (by men) to whack a tennis ball in ladylike fashion, or swim—if properly covered up. British women who dared to run in any footraces were called "brazen doxies." Not until 1928 could women run in the Olympics, and when several untrained ladies collapsed at the finish of the 800-meter race, the race was labeled "frightful." The event was not held again until 1960, and not until 1984 was the longest race for Olympic women extended beyond 1,500 meters—less than a mile. By that year, women could compete in the Olympic 3,000-meter and marathon distances.

In days when names like Grete Waitz, Joan Benoit, and Mary Decker are immediately recognized, it is easy to forget those who ran the hazardous path first, and how recently that was. The feminist awakening of the 1960s gave women the tools to fight for their rights, and one is the right to run as far and as fast as they are able. One myth women faced was that long-distance running would make their breasts sag and their muscles bulge. Chris McKenzie, a former world-record holder at 800 meters and now a top age 50+ runner, decided to convince American male race officials that they were too protective of women runners. She arrived at a monthly meeting wearing only a bikini and a coat. When the subject of sagging breasts and bulging muscles came up, Ms. McKenzie peeled off her coat and asked for opinions. Only then was she given permission to run longer distances.

Still, men were slow to learn. In 1966, Roberta Gibb Bingay ran the Boston Marathon—unofficially because her entry was refused. The next year, Kathrine Switzer got an official entry number when she sent in her application as "K. Switzer." Race officials, thinking she was a he, let her run; she was several miles into the marathon before being discovered. When Jock Semple, the race director, caught up to her, he tried to rip her number off. Kathy Switzer's boyfriend deposited Jock on the curb, and because the action took place before the press bus, the media couldn't miss the message. Kathy's plight and photos were in newspapers coast-to-coast.

A few days afterward, Kathy was thrown out of the AAU. They gave her four reasons: She had fraudulently entered the race; she had run with men; she had run longer than the allowable distance; and she had run without a chaperone.

Yet, she had completed the race in 4:20. In 1973, in her home town of Syracuse, she paced me to my first sub-3:30 marathon, which qualified *me* for the Boston run. In 1975, she was the first American woman across the Boston finish line, running a 2:51:37 marathon. The boys behind her ate their hearts out.

Before the 1972 New York City Marathon, the AAU suddenly decided that women would not be allowed to run with men. The women would run separately, beginning their race 10 minutes ahead of the men. (Ladies first!) But when the starting gun fired, the women, in protest, sat down behind the starting line and waited for the men's race to begin 10 minutes later. When the men started, off went the women, too—all of whom voluntarily had 10 minutes added to their running times. This discrimination prompted a civil rights lawsuit against the AAU, which finally gave in and ruled that men and women may start "from a common line at a common gunshot," but must be scored separately and compete for separate prizes.

This took place a year after an important New York Marathon—as important to women's running as Englishman Roger Bannister's classic race in May 1954 in which he broke the four-minute mile barrier was to running in general. The goal was for a woman to break the 3-hour mark. On a hilly Central Park course, Beth Bonner made history by holding off the challenge of Nina Kuscsik, 2:55:22 to 2:56:04.

In 1976 Nina Kuscsik, the first woman to officially win the Boston Marathon, spoke at a Marathon Conference held by the New York Academy of Sciences. "Girls and women, ages ten to seventy, have become marathon runners," she told the conference. "It is an exciting time to be a female long-distance runner. National and international competition exists for us.

"Since the marathon is an event that comes to the people, we and the public share a unique spontaneity; that of our reactions toward one another. And in only a few years the reaction has changed considerably. Spectators appreciate our athletic abilities more and have become less concerned that we are women.

"Like our male counterparts, we sometimes wonder what cravings keep us on the road. Prerace nerves and the fatigue that inevitably envelops us en route have no sexual preference. Women, too, feel a tiredness that affects our whole psyche. . . . Indeed, we love to run and we welcome the intensities of a lifetime that can be captured in the span of our races. There we find an admirable interdependence of our mental, emotional, and physical energies. We've concluded that marathon running is a truly human and healthy endeavor. This, however, is a very contemporary conclusion."

Nina is right. Only since 1975 or so have all of us become accustomed to seeing women run with men in Boston, New York, or other marathons. In fact, women are not only welcomed but expected competitors in races of all distances, including those beyond the marathon.

Moreover, women have lowered their world-record marathon time from 3:21:54 in 1969 to 2:22:43, set by Joan Benoit at the 1983 Boston Marathon. This is an improvement of nearly an hour compared to an improvement of only a few seconds for the men over the same period. I believe that we will continue to see women's marathon times drop.

In 1984, 267 American women—including six Atalantans—officially qualified for the first women's Olympic Marathon trials. Every one of these women had run the 26.2 miles in 2:51:16 or better, a cutoff time selected because it was the 100th fastest by an American woman in 1983.

There were some surprises among the qualifiers. The youngest was Cathy Schiro, sixteen, who placed ninth at 2:34:09, a world record for junior runners. The oldest was "the flying nun," Sister Marion Irvine, fifty-four, who crossed the finish line in 2:52:02. Fordie Madeira, thirty-nine, was nineteenth (2:36:35).

One of the best races for women, in my opinion, is the Mini-Marathon, organized by the New York Runners Club. The Mini was the first race in the world for women only, and it is now an accurate measure of just how popular running has become for American women. In 1972, only 72 women showed up in Central Park for the race, but by 1984, more than 5,000 women, ranging in age from nine to eighty-three, ran the Mini.

The race covers 6.2 miles, a little more than a complete loop in Central Park. The run offers any woman the chance to race. Kathy Switzer, writing in the Road Runners Club *Newsletter*, caught the true magic of the Mini, "Here was a race with publicity, planning, a strong competitive field and one other ingredient for spice. When you add that elusive element—the individual, noncompetitive, otherwise ordinary woman—the race fairly bulges with hundreds of hearts all pumping wildly with determination to succeed personally, to accomplish, and to mix dreams and fantasy with sweat, sisterhood and liniment. It seems only for that one day, but indeed!—the Mini is that one moment in time that pulls hundreds of women through the months of slogging rainy-day workouts, carping secretarial pools and screaming kids, and it is the one moment that they can savor and use for fuel the rest of the year."

And so the baton has been passed to a new generation of women runners. There are new studies and new information about women and running. The old myths are dying—slowly. According to Dr. Ernst van Aaken, "Psychologically, men are more explosive, inconsistent, not enduring, and in pain and exertion—especially among high-performance athletes—somewhat sniveling. A woman is the opposite: tough, constant, enduring, level and calm under the pain to which her body exposes her (during childbirth). On the average, she is more patient than a man. Armed with these advantages, women are in a position to do endurance feats previously considered by men to be impossible."

Women, like men, need to exercise, and run. Increasingly, their liberation is freeing them to suffer the same diseases of high-pressure occupations that men suffer: high blood pressure, stress, added fat, loss of body tone, heart attacks. In fact, the rate of heart disease among younger women is now increasing dramatically.

One woman runner, a good friend of mine, is Kathryn Lance, author of *Running for Health and Beauty: A Complete Guide for Women.* Kitty started as a beginner runner at age thirty. I helped her with her book, and she helped me with this chapter. She also gives a woman good reasons to run. "You have been cheated," Kitty writes in her book. "Throughout your entire life, your family, your schools, society itself—all have systematically cheated you of one of your most fundamental rights: the right to a healthy, active body.

"Studies show that girls tend to reach their peak of physical fitness at about age thirteen or fourteen—and from there on it's straight downhill. This is because from the time we are very young our culture simply doesn't encourage females to take care of their bodies. Worse, in subtle and not-so-subtle ways, we are actually discouraged from using our bodies in a truly athletic way. . . .

"Today, almost everyone agrees that women have a right to earn as much money as men for equal work. But where you stand on the question of woman's place in society is irrelevant. . . ."

One major outcome of this decade of liberation has been the discovery that men and women respond to vigorous exercise in very similar ways. The primary differences between the sexes come only in the levels of performance. That is, your level of physical fitness is more significant than your sex in determining the benefits of exercise. To be sure, there still remain physical differences: women are smaller than men; men usually develop longer arms and legs, broader shoulders, greater muscle mass, and less body fat. Women are 10 percent fatter and have less muscle mass. They have smaller lungs, and only 85 to 90 percent of the heart size of men. Women generally weigh less than men of the same height, and have less power to propel their body mass.

Women may be slower over short distances, but they have more endurance, and they suffer pain better. Dr. van Aaken believes that "women are born with greater natural stamina. Men, on the other hand, will always throw farther, jump higher, run faster for shorter stretches. Forty percent of man's body weight is muscle; in women, muscle amounts to only twenty-three percent. Instead of this, women have more hypodermal fatty tissue—and that is the source of energy for hours'-long exertion." Women runners, Dr. van Aaken suggested, may become very competitive with men at long distances.

So, in the long run, these differences may not be obstacles at all. Still, the woman who runs must be concerned with her menstrual cycles, and possibly birth control devices, pregnancy, and motherhood. All may be shared with the man in her life, but only two can be exchanged: You can let *him* watch the kids while you run, and you can let him practice birth control.

Women runners have helped prepare this chapter, and here are some topics they feel important to women who want to run.

TRAINING

Women are easy to coach, especially beginning runners who want to move up into competitive running. I have coached a women's running team since 1975 and my current group, Atalanta, has 30 elite women runners ages 20–65. My practice has always been to treat the women like the men: There is no reason to train women any differently than men.

I strongly suggest, however, that women who are just beginning to run join a group of other women (and men) who are starting out, and avoid being coached by a husband or boyfriend. Either one may be condescending as you make him run slower than usual. Later, he may get hostile when you are fit enough to run faster than he does. Don't run at all with your husbands or boyfriends unless they enjoy and encourage your running. Beware, as detailed in Chapter 22, of the dangers to your relationship if you run and he doesn't. Runners may make better lovers, but sometimes lousy spouses. The New York City Marathon has been named in at least one divorce proceeding for causing "incompatibility" between husband and wife runners. The best solution may be for the two of you to run—separately.

SAFETY

Too many women I have helped train get onto the running paths full of enthusiasm and spirit, and run smack up against the worst kind of male chauvinism from nonrunners. They become targets of verbal and sometimes physical abuse. They become afraid of running alone. They find that they have to learn not to be targets.

Various running clubs around the country have put together a list of precautions. Here is what they recommend:

- Run with other people whenever possible.
- Don't run alone in unpopulated areas, or after dark.
- Keep alert at all times. Observe the traffic, terrain, your fellow runners—every person you see.
- Assert yourself with confidence, using your voice and posture.
- Establish an imaginary safety area around yourself. Avoid confrontations with anyone who invades this area.
- Respond with anger when approached in a threatening manner. Practice angry responses.
- Carry some form of protection, such as Mace, a giant safety pin, or other device. Practice using them, and know what to do.
- Avoid running in alleys, bad neighborhoods, trails or sections of trails in heavy brush or dense trees, or along a secluded trail near a roadway.
- Vary your running pattern and don't run by the same spot at the same time every day.
- Dress conservatively.
- If you hear someone coming up behind you, pick up your pace slightly and look back.
- Be in shape. I know of several women who have broken away from attackers and outrun them.

- Don't be careless. If you run alone, look as though you mean business and know where you are going. Remember that a lonely country road can be as dangerous as an unsafe city park.
- Women and men should also wear identification either on a small plastic card or a bracelet. Also, we all should let a relative or friend know where we are going and when we will be back.

MENSTRUATION

Most women experience bothersome symptoms related to their menstrual cycle. These symptoms may include cramps, depression, irritability, backache, nausea, weakness, a feeling of "heavy legs" or of being bloated due to water retention. For some women, a heavy blood flow during the first two days of their menstrual period may make exercise impractical; severe cramping may make it uncomfortable.

Most doctors agree, however, that reasonable exercise during menstruation is not only acceptable, but also helpful. Exercise that improves blood circulation and muscular strength and flexibility in your abdominal area is desirable. Further, it frequently relieves the discomforts of cramps and backache. Exercise may also relieve irritability and other emotional symptoms. A conditioned body is simply better prepared to handle this monthly stress.

Women report that their menstrual periods do not affect their performance in races. One study of Olympic athletes found that they won gold medals during all phases of their monthly cycle. In fact, training may be more troublesome than racing. The reason is logical: The runner will overcome discomfort in the excitement of a race, but not in the drudgery of practice.

Most women runners we talked with find that running doesn't make menstrual cramps worse, but running may be slower during this time. Many find that cramping actually diminishes or disappears while running. Some women runners report that running regulates their periods, while others experience the cessation of menstruation, or secondary amenorrhea. The latter occurs in some 15 to 20 percent of women runners, usually those who are running high-mileage training routines. Dr. Joan Ullyot, M.D., author of *Women's Running* and *Running Free*, attributes amenorrhea to dramatic reductions in body fat, which can occur for a variety of reasons, including starvation and rigorous exercise. The theory is that such a loss of body fat leaves the body without sufficient reserves to support a pregnancy, and the system simply "shuts down." The condition is not considered harmful, and regular menstrual cycles reoccur when these women runners return to their original body fat levels, or the woman runner cuts her mileage. A 1978 survey of women runners indicates that the percentage of runners experiencing amenorrhea is directly proportional to their increase in mileage.

A second area of concern here, and about which less is known, involves the delay of onset of menarche by strenuous exercise. Dr. Jack Wilmore, of the University of Arizona, has reported a tendency in girls participating in heavy competition before menarche to have onset delayed until ages 17 or 18. Physicians are uncertain whether this is good or bad.

Running may help eliminate or lessen some of the physical problems accompanying menstruation by increasing blood flow and reducing body water retention through sweating. Moreover, as a runner experiences various pains associated with running, she may more easily adjust psychologically to the discomforts of her menstrual period.

Kathryn Lance has some good insights into the psychological factors of women and menstruation. "Many of us have been taught that we are in a weakened condition at this time, and so we are used to doing as little as possible while we are menstruating, if not actually taking to bed. Because of these years of conditioning, the thought of any really strenuous activity seems foreign and a little dangerous to most of us—almost against the laws of nature.

"Unfortunately, what most of us *didn't* know all these years was that something strenuous might have been just what we needed to help avoid menstrual problems in the first place. Running not only seems to relieve cramps in many women, but also helps to *prevent* them in some cases."

ANEMIA

Blood loss from menstruation results in a depletion of iron, which may lead to anemia. Mild anemia may not affect the average woman, but it will affect the performance of the average woman runner because anemia limits the oxygen-carrying capacity of the blood.

There are several reasons why women runners are probably deficient in iron. One is that the average American diet does not contain enough iron, and all of us lose small amounts of iron daily through normal body functions. Also, women can store only 250 mg. of iron (compared to a man's 850 mg.) and have about one million fewer red blood cells than men. Moreover, a woman loses iron through menstruation, and faces an increased need for iron during pregnancy.

Women runners may want to supplement their diets with iron; the recommended daily allowance for women between ages 11 and 50 is 18 mg. Women may wish to take iron capsules of at least 30 milligrams a day, or eat more iron-rich foods such as liver, leafy green vegetables, wheat germ, soyflour, edible seeds, and blackstrap molasses. There are some negative side effects that may occur with iron supplements, such as constipation, gastric distress, and even the possibility of "iron overload." Your doctor should be consulted, and he or she may want to give you a blood test to determine whether or not you are indeed anemic or iron-deficient.

CONTRACEPTION

Women who are taking birth control pills probably don't have any problems with their running. However, Nina Kuscsik, a registered nurse, believes that as women become more attuned to their bodies through running, they may not want to use a drug like the Pill. It does make some women runners feel bloated and unenergetic at times.

The intra-uterine device (IUD), however, has caused pain and discomfort in some women, which worsens when they run. Others have complained that the IUD makes them bleed so heavily during their periods that they can't run long distances. In that case, if you are wearing an IUD, you might want to have it removed for long-distance running, and switch to some other form of birth control. Or, have your husband or lover practice birth control so you can run free.

Running can work in other ways, too. We know of women with sterility problems who became pregnant after starting a regular exercise program. Of course, their inability to become pregnant may have been due to psychological reasons, but running does put women (and men) more in touch and tune with their bodies; it makes us aware of how we are caring for ourselves.

FERTILITY AND PREGNANCY

There is some debate about whether or not strenuous athletic participation, like consistent marathon training, causes a higher infertility rate among women runners. Changes in the menstrual cycle do occur, and Dr. Mona Shangold, co-author of *The Women's Sportsmedicine Book*, suggests that "there may be a relationship between reproduction problems and chronic exercise such as extensive training done by long-distance runners." As with the interruption of a woman's menstrual cycle, any of the reproductive problems encountered appear to be reversible with a decrease in exercise.

Should you continue running during pregnancy? Yes, if you have been running regularly for at least six months before becoming pregnant, and you are healthy, and you have no musculoskeletal problems. A 1984 study at the University of Illinois, of women who had been running an average of three years before becoming pregnant, shows that healthy women can safely exercise throughout their pregnancy. These women ran an average of 16.5 miles a week during their first trimester, and tapered to six miles a week during the last trimester. Some even ran up to the day they delivered, without any problems.

Other studies indicate that exercise during pregnancy brings more oxygen to the placenta, which in turn helps nourish the fetus. The exercise also continues your excellent muscle tone and cardiovascular conditioning. It may have additional side benefits in terms of relieving constipation during pregnancy, and reducing the possibility of hemorrhoids, varicose veins, and insomnia. Finally, running during your pregnancy will certainly give you increased strength and endurance during labor and delivery, and a rapid recovery afterwards.

There are wonderful stories about women who were runners, and then became pregnant. One ran throughout her pregnancy, and walked out of the delivery room with her newborn in her arms. Or, take the case of Mary Jones, of Dallas, Texas, who at age 32 and eight months pregnant ran a 2:05 half-marathon at the White Rock Marathon in 1976. Her preparation was jogging 40 miles a week. "My doctor told me to listen to my body, and as long as I felt good about running, continue to do it," she said. "My idea of a beautiful delivery would be to run 13 miles in the morning and have the baby later that day."

Deborah De Witt began exercising regularly when she reached thirty. Her husband, a member of the New York Road Runners Club, convinced her that running was fun and healthy. Little did she know just how healthy. "I would typically jog three times a week for a mile or a mile and a half. I am not a gung-ho runner by any stretch of the imagination, but I was getting to the point that I could run two miles with not much effort and some enjoyment. Then, we decided to have a baby. I had read Cooper's aerobics book, and I consulted with my obstetrician, who assured me that I could continue jogging as long as 'everything was going well.' "

Everything went well, and Deborah kept running. Six months came and went. She reported to her doctor monthly and told him she was still jogging. He encouraged her. "Since I felt good, I decided to continue. Of course, my pace was slowing because I was carrying a lot of extra weight, twenty pounds in all. And by the end, I was having swelling in my legs which frequently caused cramps during running, but I tried to push through. Since I was jogging three times a week regularly, I never had any sensation of a large belly swaying back and forth. But I was a sight at the YMCA track in my green man's extra-large T-shirt and my maternity shorts."

Deborah ran a 10-minute mile during her exercise class on a Monday, and on Wednesday began labor. She was in labor eighteen hours with no medication. "Because I was in good shape from the jogging and exercise and had been through childbirth classes, I was able to rotate the baby's head—it came out face up instead of face down—and did not have to have a forceps delivery." She gave birth to a 7-pound, 13-ounce boy. "I came home from the hospital with a flat stomach (I did sit-ups until about two weeks before Andrew arrived), weighing what I did before the pregnancy.

"If this sounds like a testimonial to running, it is. But it is a testimonial from an average, run-of-the-mill jogger, not a super athlete." Deborah continued her jogging after her six weeks' postpartum checkup.

Even well-trained athletes are not stopped by pregnancy; some have won Olympic gold medals while pregnant. Dr. Gyula Erdelyi of Hungary studied 172 women athletes through their pregnancies and found that two-thirds of them were able to continue training through the fourth month. The quality of their performances did not decrease during the first three months.

Dr. Erdelyi found that pregnant runners had fewer complications during pregnancy, and 50 percent fewer cesareans. He also found that duration of labor was shorter for athletes than for nonathletes.

Dr. Evelyn Gendel, director of the Kansas Division of Maternal and Child Health, sees no reason for women not to continue running during pregnancy if that is what they were doing before they got pregnant. But run first, get pregnant later. It is not a good idea to start a vigorous exercise program after pregnancy occurs.

There are some other rules to follow. Dr. Ullyot notes in her book *Women's Running*: "A general rule for any form of exercise during pregnancy is, 'Do what you're accustomed to, as long as it feels comfortable.' If you've been jogging five miles a day, keep it up. If you find yourself getting tired more easily, cut down the mileage. If your uterus contracts wildly whenever you jog late in pregnancy, walk or swim instead, so there's less jostling.

"Using the 'talk test' while running, you'll be assured that both you and the baby are getting plenty of oxygen. The increased circulation will be as beneficial as the continued muscular toning during exercise."

Dr. Shangold suggests:

- Do not get too hot. Body temperatures over 101 degrees Fahrenheit may not be good for your baby. Work out for a shorter time. Wear lighter clothing. Drink more fluids.
- Exercise only to the same perceived level, which you'll reach fast as you grow. Do no exercise to breathlessness.

Of course, before you run off, consult your obstetrician. Pregnancy is a much different physiological state than normal, and you may have complications that would make jogging inadvisable. Sadly, there are still many physicians who are anti-exercise. If your physician tells you not to run, you should ask the reason. If the answer is satisfying, respect the opinion. But if it isn't, seek other medical advice. Find a physician who will support your desire to maintain a healthy body.

The major changes in your body start occurring around the seventh month. The oxygen you need to run at a certain pace increases by 10 percent from the third through eighth months. Your resting heart rate also increases, and both conditions are related to increased weight. In fact, you may be working so much harder during the last two months that your anaerobic threshold can easily be exceeded.

Therefore, your running speed should be reduced to avoid going into oxygen debt. Nature will help you here. The heavier your fetus, the harder it will be to run. Many women in their ninth month find recovery difficult, and turn to walking or swimming.

When Pamela Mendelsohn Burgess became pregnant, she continued running with her child's father, Peter. "We had always enjoyed running together," she wrote in *Jogger* magazine, "and I had wondered whether we would have to start going separately because of my slowness due to the added weight. Peter began to carry rocks of increasing size to slow him down. His last rock weighed in at twenty-eight pounds!

". . . The day before Rebekah was born, we went for a long run on the beach in the fog. I felt like a huge friendly cloud about to burst as I lumbered along. Peter was doing circles around me, disappearing into the fog only to reappear seconds later. He said I looked like a voluminous pillow floating through space. We found a perfect sand dollar that day, jumped into the icy ocean, had dinner out, and went to bed early. The next morning labor began, and we were off and running."

Pamela's labor lasted twelve hours. "Running had helped to prepare me, having taught me endurance, pacing, acceptance of a little fatigue, and the discipline to push on to that marvelous second wind."

Your physician may want you to wait four to six weeks after the baby's birth before you start running again. Start slowly, stretch, and remember the walk-run method. You probably won't have the energy you did, but you'll have something more: One day at one of our fitness classes, I noticed a woman who had been pregnant and then didn't come in for a few weeks. She was back, jogging along with her friends—and pushing a baby carriage. She was delighted to be back, and so was baby!

MOTHERHOOD

Dr. van Aaken believes that motherhood may improve running performance. A German study of fifteen champion women athletes who bore children during their careers found that five gave up sports after childbirth, but that two of the remaining ten maintained their performances, and the other eight improved measurably. All of the women runners agreed that after childbirth they were "tougher" and had more strength and endurance.

Miki Gorman gave birth to a son at age 39, finished second in the 1975 New York City Marathon eight months later, and a year later ran her best-ever marathon, at 2:39. A study of women athletes who participated in the 1964 Tokyo Olympics showed that fully half the women who continued athletic training and participation after pregnancy improved their athletic performance within a year after giving birth. Another third bettered their performance within two years.

Nina Kuscsik didn't start running competitively until her thirties, when she had already given birth to three children. Since then, she has run six sub–3-hour marathons, and won the women's division of the 1972 Boston Marathon.

As Kathryn Lance writes, "In short, there is no more reason (other than lack of time) for a woman not to run after becoming a mother than for a man to stop running after becoming a father." Both need to run, and perhaps the only obstacle is to convince Dad to watch the kids while Mom works out.

MENOPAUSE

Regular exercise is even more important after menopause. With a diminished supply of the estrogen hormone—the hormone believed to make arteries more supple—women quickly become as susceptible to heart disease as men.

Further, menopause sometimes causes depression in women, for a variety of reasons. Running can provide a challenge and create goals at a time when a woman may feel her skills and value—especially as a mother with grown children—have diminished.

As we age, moreover, we become more susceptible to illness and disease. By being physically fit, we can overcome illness more quickly, and recover from surgery and other traumatic medical events more rapidly.

Furthermore, for women runners, studies now indicate that middle-aged women can maintain a more "youthful" sex hormone profile with aerobic conditioning. They are able to keep attributes that normally deteriorate with age, such as shape (keeping body fat from finding the hips and buttocks), increased facial hair typical of older women, increased incidence of skin pigmentation (those little brown age spots). Most impressive, exercise stimulates bone growth and slows mineral loss in women, and helps delay the onset of osteoporosis, the reduction of bone density and strength which is a serious problem among older women.

Clearly, our bodies are made for lifelong physical activity, and we should use them. Most women—afraid to sweat, convinced that their physical differences from men mean that they can't perform well athletically, or intimidated by husbands, boyfriends, or sour lovers—have stopped regular physical activity. If you are one of them, don't be cheated anymore. Start running.

and be a success, then imagine what I can do with my best aspects. The focus is on what I'm able to do rather than what I can't do."

Atalanta's national class masters runner, Patty Lee Parmalee, played an important role in helping the Achilles program get started. "In working with the disabled," she says, "I gradually have learned that any kind of disaster can be overcome, or, with the right attitude, turned to advantage."

Personally, I feel that the really disadvantaged people in life are those who could exercise if they wished, but prefer to live a sedentary life-style.

Beginning a Fitness Program

Generally, the physically disabled should compare themselves to able-bodied men and women of comparable age and fitness level. They should disregard their disability and realize that they are simply as out of shape—no more, no less—as any sedentary person. A disabled person has usually spent years being inactive. Much of the reason for being out of shape is psychological: You think you can't exercise. But you can!

Here are some guidelines for getting started:

1. *Check with Your Doctor* Find out what limitations he or she might want to place on your exercise program. If your doctor doesn't exercise, and is against your undertaking an exercise program, get a second opinion. Find a doctor who believes in exercise, and listen to his or her advice.

2. *Start Slowly* You may need to start with a walking program. Just get used to moving, alternated with rest. This is certainly enough for those who have been non-exercisers. You may need to learn to use a cane, or a prosthesis. Gradually develop a walking program for a longer period of time. Achilles Track Club member Janice Rehkamp is a good example. She lost a leg to diabetes and started exercising at age sixty. She walked with a cane for four months before easing into some running.

3. *Extend Your Walking Program* Gradually, after walking

for short periods, build up to longer exercise times. Move from 10, to 15, 20, 25, and 30 minutes of walking at one time with an increasingly faster pace.

4. *Alternate Walking and Running*   Follow the program of alternating running and walking, as detailed on page 40. You are no different from anyone else, but you may "run" slower and cover less mileage. A 20-minute workout that brings you up to your aerobic training heart rate (see page 7) is your goal. Put in 20-30 minutes of aerobic exercise within your heart range. Also, always walk/run at a pace that allows you to converse.

At first, you may not be able to exercise fast enough to get your heart into your aerobic range. Be patient. You must develop your muscular strength to exercise faster, and this will come with time.

Also, a weight-training program will help you, especially if you need to use your upper body to run with crutches or propel a wheelchair. See Chapter 8 for guidelines. Here are some more guidelines.

5. *Work Out in a Group*   You may find it encouraging to be able to share your gains—and your worries—with other similar runners. Dick Traum, the amputee marathoner, started at the West Side (New York City) YMCA, where he took my fitness class. Mort Schlein, a blind marathoner, began in our NYRRC beginner-runner class.

6. *Get Outdoors*   After you've started, be sure to set a goal of exercising outdoors. You may want to begin your training indoors, perhaps because you feel that your handicap will attract too much attention outdoors or you feel more comfortable being near "home base." Familiar surroundings make running easier. Going outdoors may mean overcoming hills, potholes, slanted surfaces, and so forth.

But you will find running outdoors a real pleasure. Dick Traum built up to running two to six hours at a time on the 23-lap-per-mile indoor track at the YMCA. He gradually moved outdoors, and now uses the track only in very bad weather.

As you gain confidence in yourself and your running, you won't worry about running outside. You'll find—as the Achilles athletes have—that other runners will cheer as you go by, and call out, "Way to go! Lookin' great!" Now you can show off your skills as a new runner. Be comfortable and be yourself.

Alternative Training

You may want to switch between running, walking, bicycling, or swimming. This will minimize the stress on your musculoskeletal system and give you a good aerobic workout. You might want to run two times a week, and bike or swim two times a week. Remember, swimming and bicycling are non-weight-bearing activities that don't require as much motor skill or stability. They are also good workouts indoors, near "home base," for those unable to find an exercise partner, if needed.

Even after you reach a minimal level of fitness—able to run 20–30 minutes—you may want to work out on a bike or in a pool as a change of pace. Dick Traum trained almost exclusively on an indoor bike for the 1979 New York City Marathon. His good knee had been bothering him, and this alternative training program paid off: he completed the marathon.

Training Tips for Outdoor Running

Start running outdoors in small loops, or in short out-and-back courses. This might be an outdoor track or around a block, or running out ten minutes and back home ten minutes. Gradually extend the distance as you feel more confident and start mastering the physical obstacles in your path.

Always tell someone where you are going, and about how long you will be gone. Take some money along for a phone call or a taxi in case you want to stop your run early. You can also use the money to buy something to drink if you can't find water. (Remember: Fluid intake is essential; drink often.) Finally, carry identification that includes any special medicines you may be taking or any special medical care you might require. This is good advice for *all* runners.

Run far from traffic. Try to avoid running after dark outdoors; this is the time for that indoor workout. If you must run after dark outdoors, wear reflector tape on your upper body and your shoes.

Be alert to the slant on roads and on tracks. You will be running "lopsided." Try to avoid such running conditions, but if you cannot, switch directions on an in-out route to adapt to the slant.

Equipment

Experiment. Talk to other runners for tips about a prosthesis, wheelchair, crutches, a cane. Like every other runner, all ambulatory disabled runners have one major and important investment: shoes (see Chapter 15). Go to a store that specializes in running shoes. These specialists, along with your doctor and sports podiatrist, can help you select the right shoes for you. Custom-made shoes or orthotics may help you.

Running Form and Style

Relax. Read Chapter 7 for guidelines. Our Achilles runners, through trial and error, find the technique that works best for them. Getting to the finish line with any form you wish is the goal. Here are how Achilles runners have overcome some common mistakes:

- Keep your head up. Don't lean forward too much. This slows you down, and may cause injury.
- Concentrate on hitting heel first, not toe first. This will also minimize the possibility for injury, such as shin splints.
- Don't tense up. Stay as loose as you can, and you will run more comfortably.

Competitive Training

You, like any runner, may enjoy the fun and spark of competitive racing. If you haven't started your training program yet, the thought of racing may seem very distant and even unattainable. But be patient. You can work toward that goal slowly, but with the determination of, say, Linda Down.

Participation is the key. All along this exercise path to fitness, you must keep firmly in mind the fact that you compete only against one person: the old you. If you reach the point of wanting to race, set two goals:

Increase the distance you can race (start at two to four miles); Improve your times for a set distance (for example, 10K).

The basics of competitive training are the same for all runners. Remember, you are an athlete! Beginner racers and marathoners should consult Chapters 5 and 6. More experienced runners will benefit from guidelines in *The Competitive Runner's Handbook*. Here are some specific tips for the disabled runner that we have learned from our Achilles athletes:

• Talk to race officials a day or more before the race. Tell them you are racing; ask them if you can start early.

By starting early, you will be passed by most of the runners, who will cheer you on. You'll see the leaders and most of your friends go by. You'll also be able to use the water stations late in your run. Carry water at the start in case the stations are not open early in your run. If you start early, be sure to have someone accompany you on foot or on a bike.

• Time your start so that you cross the finish line at about the middle of the pack or slightly later. You'll receive lots of support.

• Start using your own wristwatch so that you get accurate times at the mile markers. You'll also be certain to have your own finish time.

• Avoid starting the race with the other runners if you run very slowly. You will be on the course after most of the other competitors have finished. In a long race, water and medical stations have closed down. Traffic may be allowed back along the race course, and you'll have to deal with cars at the very time you are tired and fighting the course to finish. It may get dark, causing other problems. You'll miss your support group of other runners passing by and shouting encouragement. And you won't have a big crowd waiting for you at the finish.

In 1982 Linda Down started the New York Marathon with the pack and ran alone most of the way. She finished in darkness, running on the sidewalks to avoid the traffic. In 1983, however, she started three hours early, and finished with the five-hour marathoners. She really enjoyed herself, and got caught up in the race excitement.

• If you can't start early, line up at the back of the pack. Run with someone who runs at your speed, or is willing to escort you at your pace.

• Train by minutes, not by miles. Do not compare yourself to the able-bodied runner who runs 40–60 miles a week to prepare for races. You may in fact be running twice that in time since you train at a pace twice as slow and spend twice as much time on the road.

Balance is the key. You cannot log high mileage if you run slowly, but you can do some longer runs and balance them with easy days.

• Train on hills. One of the toughest obstacles all runners face is hills. These are a great challenge to disabled runners; they spend more time getting up hills, or, in the case of wheelchair runners, fighting gravity both up and down hill. Practice on small hills once or twice a week, after you are fit and ready for racing, and work up to hills similar to those you will encounter in a race.

Tips

Here are some tips for runners with specific physical handicaps. These are limited to my experience, so if you don't find your specific problem here, don't be dismayed. Talk to other disabled runners. Talk to your doctor. I'm certain that you can find a way to exercise.

Amputees When Dick Traum hopped into my office in 1975, I was shocked: "How should I treat this man who has only one leg to run on?" Dick, then 34, had found his weight and stress level growing along with his business, and had decided to register for my YMCA fitness program.

I was learning along with Dick. I decided that he should follow the same fitness principles that any beginner runner would follow whose handicap might be 20 pounds of excess weight and a sedentary existence.

"Can you run?" I asked him.

"Sure," Dick lied. He couldn't run a step. But he wanted to get started, and didn't want to get turned down for the fitness program, just because he had lost part of his leg. That evening, he practiced hopping along the hallway of his apartment building.

Dick Traum quickly progressed through the beginner, intermediate, and advanced levels of the Y fitness program. I challenged him to enter a five-mile race in Central Park, and he finished last, in 72 minutes, but as he crossed the finish line the other runners loudly cheered him. He has now run several New York City Marathons, with a PR of 6:44.

I wrote a story about Dick Traum that appeared in the January 1977 issue of *Runner's World.* A 22-year-old Canadian, who was about to have his leg amputated above the knee in an effort to hold off cancer, read about Dick Traum. Encouraged, Terry Fox vowed to run across Canada to raise money to fight cancer, and in 1980 logged 3,339 miles in a "Marathon of Hope." By June 1981, however, two-thirds of the way to his goal, Terry Fox died from the disease. He had raised millions of dollars for cancer research, and the books and television movie about his life inspired many men and women—able-bodied as well as disabled—to start a fitness program.

Running Style Dick Traum and Terry Fox used a style of double hop with the good leg, and a long step with the artificial leg. Fox also had a belt attached below and above the knee to pull the leg up faster on the back swing to increase his speed.

You can try running the normal way, but that will put too much stress on the stump. Most below-the-knee amputees can run with a near-normal gait depending on the exact type of disability and the quality of the artificial leg.

Adjusting to the Leg   Paddy Rossbach is an Achilles runner with below-the-knee amputation. One problem she had was that her artificial leg was made to adjust for wearing high heels. While she waited for a new leg, she worked out on an indoor bike and lifted weights to compensate for insufficient running mileage. She completed the 1984 New York Marathon in 6:52.

The first step for any amputee is to get fitted for a temporary leg, which may occur immediately following amputation or up to three weeks following the surgery. This is usually not a full-feature leg, but a "modern day peg-leg." You learn to walk with this leg. About six to eight weeks later, you will get a permanent leg and start more walking on it. Remember Paddy Rossbach: Get a leg designed for low-heeled shoes if you plan to exercise. The sequence, then, to adjusting to the leg and to running is:

1. Learn to move the leg. Begin walking.
2. Learn to walk on uneven ground, to play golf or some other mild exercise. Walk a little distance each day.
3. Select an alternative exercise to build up your cardiovascular endurance. This may be indoor stationary bike riding or swimming. You may also want to do some runner's-level weightlifting. (See Chapter 8.) This alternative training may be continued after you start running, as alternative training to relieve stress on your leg.
4. Take brisk walks of increasing distance.
5. Alternate running and walking, and alternate exercises. Walk, swim, bike, run in a pattern to minimize discomfort.

Running Legs   Chafing will occur, even with perfect fit. If you gain or lose weight, this will affect the fit. Experiment with ways to alleviate problems. Here are some tips from Dick Traum:

- Adjust the angle of the artificial foot by placing one- or two-inch squares of moleskin on various places of the foot to try and change the tilt.
- Change the height of the foot by placing a ⅛-inch or so pad under the whole foot. Put it under the natural foot to shorten, and under the artificial foot to raise.
- If you lose weight, tape a piece of moleskin to the inside upper front of the leg—where the leg meets your skin. For Dick, one pound lost equals four square inches of moleskin.
- To minimize blistering, use powder or petroleum jelly on the inside of the stump and in the back. Don't use it on all sides since it might cause the leg to slip off.
- Tape about a "Band-Aid-size" piece of moleskin to the stump at tender spots when running or when clearing up a welt.
- A special nylon "stump sock" in a total suction leg makes the leg more comfortable, but it also comes off more easily.
- Run every other day to allow welts to heal.
- Stop periodically when rain gets into the leg. Lift the leg and tilt it to pour out water.

If you have the time, money, and interest, you can purchase both a walking and a running leg. Terry Fox's running leg, for example, was more like a stick support; it saved weight. A suction-type leg, rather than one that holds on only with straps, is needed for serious long-distance running.

You may also need to oil and clean your artificial leg more frequently if you run, and the leg may wear out its hydraulic system earlier.

Here are some other suggestions from Dick Traum:

- When starting your exercise program, stay close to "home base." Run indoors, on a track, or on an out-back path. As you increase your confidence, experiment with runs over other courses, but stay where you can get help if you need it.

- As you increase your mileage, the "phantom limb" may return: a feeling of spasms in the leg you lost. Aspirin and rest will help, and the sensation will go away.
- Falling is part of running. Once, during a 25K race, Dick Traum stopped for water, walked a few steps, and his leg "took off" causing him to fall and knocking down his running partner, Linda Down, and her crutches.
- Bring along extra socks to change into if your stump sock gets soaked, and, if appropriate, extra parts for the leg.
- Ease into running on uneven terrain. Be especially careful on slippery surfaces. Downhills will be more difficult than uphills; tremendous pressure is placed on your legs as you go downhill. You may want to walk downhill, or use a cane to keep your balance on steep downhills. Or, try cutting back and forth at angles across the downhill slope to minimize the steepness of the hill.

There are many amputee runners today, including Governor Robert Kerry of Nebraska. Pat Griskus, from Waterbury, Connecticut, may be the fastest one-legged marathoner in the world. He lost his leg below the knee after being run down on his motorcycle by a drunken driver. For several years, he "kinda laid off doing much of anything. I was feeling sorry for myself, I guess. I started putting on weight and drinking too much—maybe a lot too much."

At age thirty-five Pat finally decided to get back into shape. He started with weightlifting, then swimming, then running. In the fall of 1982 he got a new artificial leg from marathoner Richard Press. The leg is unusual: it has a silicone insert to prevent pistoning—the up-and-down movement of the stump within the prosthesis socket that can produce sores and blisters. It also has a new SAFE (Stationary Ankle Flexible Endoskeleton) foot that mimics the movements of a natural foot.

Pat began secretly training for a marathon, and ran his first, the John W. English Marathon in Middletown, Connecticut, in

4:11:09. He has since broken the four-hour barrier, and his goal is to break 3:30 for the marathon and 40 minutes for the 10K. Pat is also an excellent swimmer, and competes in triathlons (swim-bike-run). In 1983, he placed in the middle of a field of 800 runners who ran in the grueling eight-mile road race up Mount Washington.

BIRTH DEFECTS

Peter Strudwick writes in the introduction to his book, *Come Run With Me:*

"In 1929, Germany was struck by an epidemic of rubella, commonly called German measles. My mother caught it.

"On the morning of January 30, 1930, I was born in Berlin. That afternoon, my mother was advised that I should be put away, either in an institution or (preferably) in an incinerator. In the atmosphere of growing Nazi values, doctors could foresee little use for a baby with legs that ended up stumps just past the ankles, a left arm that had only one thumb and finger, and a right arm ending at the wrist.

"My mother gave them a flat *'nein.'* As an American, she did not share the moral outlook that soon culminated in the idea of the Master Race."

Peter escaped Nazi Germany with his family, and came to the United States. In August 1972 he completed the tough Pikes Peak Marathon, and he has continued running marathons since.

John Cruz was a thalidomide baby born with one leg. Someone told him about the Achilles program, and he joined. Less than a year after he started training, John completed the rainy 1983 New York City Marathon on crutches. He later posed with marathon winners Rod Dixon and Grete Waitz at the White House as a guest of President Reagan. John, 22, says: "If I had been born with two legs, one of my dreams would have been to excel in sports. It is still one of my dreams. Finally I found a sport where I could compete. It's changed the way I look at life." It's also changed the way he looks: The NYRRC bought John his first fancy suit to wear to the White House.

BLIND RUNNERS

Mort Schlein has been blind since 1971, and started training in our first New York Road Runners beginner class in 1978 at the age of 45. He has since completed several marathons.

"Most people think it's incredible that a blind man can run," he says. "I don't know why. Blindness doesn't affect my feet, only my eyes. I move my feet like everyone else."

As a beginner runner, Mort's biggest problem was finding running partners willing to train at his pace. Later, he had to find runners willing to train at the distances he wanted. But now, he and other blind runners have a pack of training partners of similar ability who enjoy the fellowship of running. "I don't want anyone to feel that running with me is their good deed for the day," he says. And no one does.

Here are some techniques used by blind runners:

Rope-Holding Technique

Mort runs with a long (3½'–4') rope attached from himself to his running partner. He holds one end, the partner holds the other, and there is enough slack so that both can relax their arms. The partner tugs the rope to send directions; the rope is also a comfortable guide on straightaway sections. This technique is less restrictive than holding or touching elbows.

Elbow-Holding or Touching

The guide in this case runs close to the blind runner and touches the arm or elbow to help shift directions, or grasps one of them throughout the run.

Blind runners are ingenious about developing techniques so they can train. Joe Pardo, for example, is one of the fastest blind runners in the nation. At age 50, he ran a 4:40 mile. Joe lives in New York City, and trains by following the sound made by a bicycle with a card placed in the spokes.

Raoul Lugo started running in 1983 with the Achilles Track Club. He first tried to run using his white cane, but found it cumbersome. He then followed a training program alternating running and walking, using a rope to a sighted runner, and progressed well. When his guiding runner couldn't train, we put Raol on a stationary bike indoors several times a week. He also walked up the stairs of his apartment building. This is also Mort Schlein's technique: he runs the six flights of stairs in his apartment building, grasping the railing, as speed workouts; he walks down (or takes the elevator).

These methods, along with the treadmill, are some of the options available to blind runners. Like Mort Schlein, Joe Pardo, and Harry Cordellos (who has completed more than 50 marathons and has run that race at a sub-three-hour pace) there are excellent ways for blind runners to train and compete.

CEREBRAL PALSY

We have worked with four types of runners who have cerebral palsy, and who have joined Achilles for exercise. We have wheelchair runners and runners like Linda and Laura Down who get along on crutches. John Rose and Len Eaton have limited motor movement but walk and run without wheelchair or crutches. Rich Torres and Yvonne Myvette have only little loss of motor skills and run well on their own. They completed the 1984 New York Marathon in a little over six hours.

Runners with cerebral palsy, like anyone else, should start with a walking program and gradually progress to run/walk. Undertake this program only after consultation with your doctor, and begin with a group or a club, like our Achilles Track Club.

The United Cerebral Palsy Association encourages involvement in exercise by men and women who have this disability. One of the most memorable scenes in the annual Cerebral Palsy Telethon was of Linda Down finishing, alone and in the dark, her personal race in the 1982 New York City Marathon. She appeared on the TV program with Sugar Ray Leonard and Howard Cosell, who called Linda "the athlete of the century."

Dawn Cookler heard of Linda's accomplishment, and made a New Year's resolution to start a running program. "I figured if somebody else could do it, I could do it." But Dawn Cookler had spent ten years in physical therapy, and had gone through two operations. When she started junior high school, she could walk just 20 steps without the use of supportive aids. By the time she graduated from high school, she could walk 500 steps.

Dawn started her training on January 4, 1983. Just before her New Year's resolution, Dawn had been told that she would always need crutches for walking. Running was out of the question. But a few days later—depressed—Dawn Cookler buried her crutches in the snow. Soon after, she started an exercise program and started running with crutches. She promised herself to train for and complete a race. And in June, 1983, Dawn completed a five-mile race, with the temperature at 85 degrees, in 3:13. Who said it couldn't be done?

THE DEAF

Every year, the New York School for the Deaf, in White Plains, N.Y., puts on a track and field day. The event is organized by Tosh and Fred d'Elia. Tosh is Atalanta's world-class marathoner and the first woman in the world over age 50 to break the three-hour barrier for the marathon. She specializes in working with the deaf and hearing impaired at the school.

Deaf people may be in poor physical condition for two reasons:

1. They don't breathe well, perhaps because they haven't learned to breathe and vocalize.
2. They sometimes have been held back from physical activity.

Tosh has found that many of the children she works with are hyperactive and have behavioral problems. Running helps calm them down, and preparation and training for the annual track-and-field day also teaches the deaf that exercise is permissible, fun, and healthy.

Here are some starting tips:

- A deaf person's disability tends to affect the sense of balance. Start with fast walking to gain confidence, and gradually add running.
- Since many deaf don't talk, the concept of running at a "conversation pace" needs to be adjusted. Deaf runners, after reaching this level, should still run within their training heart rate range (see page 7). Those with limited verbal skills might be encouraged to frequently utter syllables such as "bah, bah, bah" to insure that they are running at a comfortable pace.
- Deaf runners should train with runners who have normal hearing capacity. While a track is generally safe, the roads are not. Cars and other vehicles are hard enough for the rest of us to hear. Deaf runners may wish to stay on a track or path, and keep off the roads when running alone or with other deaf runners.

There should be no limits for the deaf runner in terms of conditioning. I remember being run into the ground by Jim Carey, the Rome, New York, State School for the Deaf's top high school miler. His disability didn't hold him back, and neither should yours.

MULTIPLE SCLEROSIS

M.S. is an incurable disease of the central nervous system. It has no known cause, and the disease leaves its victims in varying stages of physical debilitation. Anne O'Malley was an active athlete before being stricken with M.S. in 1974. After a series of attacks, she was unable to stand for long periods, and used a cane for balance. She started following a special diet she read about in

Dr. Roy Swank's book, *The Multiple Sclerosis Diet Book*. "I began feeling better more often," she wrote in *Runner's World*. "I began to think about running. . . . I thought it might make me stronger and provide a support in the weak times."

Anne started running in 1978, and after a year she could cover a mile without stopping. In 1980, she ran a 10K race in San Diego, and, despite falling three times, finished. In 1981, she ran the same race again, and finished without falling once.

Now, to maintain her strength for running, Anne continues with the Swank diet, and runs 3.5 miles each day or 4.5 miles over two hills on Sundays. She also trains by doing yoga, sit-ups, and knee-strengthening exercises, and weight training.

"When I feel discouraged, become incontinent or feel the dread tingling numbness," she wrote, "I think of the good times and try to limit how much I dwell on my illness. I force myself to return to my wellness, because it is there that I may live and run and be free."

PARALYSIS

Many runners can exercise despite various degrees of paralysis. Some "run" in a wheelchair, while others get along on crutches or limping on their own. The causes of paralysis among the Achilles athletes vary and include those injured in car accidents, shot by muggers, etc.

Take the case of Scotsman Sandy Davidson, who works at the United Nations. Sandy was partially paralyzed by a stroke and now walks with the aid of a cane. Still, he trained for and then completed the 1983 New York City Marathon in 10 hours, 15 minutes, accompanied by his proud wife, Wilma. He ran with his own style of a brisk run-walk, using his cane for balance. He completed the 1984 marathon an hour faster than in 1983, and he no longer needed the cane.

We have found that the majority of paralyzed athletes in our program have amazed their doctors and themselves by not only increasing leg strength and endurance but also improving muscular strength and flexibility throughout their bodies, including their arms.

WHEELCHAIR RUNNERS

Millie Bardavid was crippled by polio at age three, and has spent her life in a wheelchair. One evening in the winter of 1983, Millie, now fifty-five years old, was returning from work when she saw a cluster of men and women in front of the New York Road Runners Club, across the street from her apartment. What caught her attention was the fact that many of these runners were on crutches or in wheelchairs. "Hey," she exclaimed to herself, "that's for me!" Millie decided to become a runner.

Millie's friend, Cathi Romano, used to push Millie in her wheelchair. Now, Cathi and Millie accompany each other on daily runs in Central Park, one on foot and the other in the wheelchair. Millie has stopped smoking. She gets around her neighborhood on her own.

A few weeks after she had started running in her standard chair, Millie got into a lightweight racing chair. "Feels great!" she said. "Let's go!" She set off on a five-mile race, and later completed a half-marathon. "It's changed my life," she says of her wheelchair racing. "I love it!" She was featured in a televised story about the Achilles Track Club on the *Today* show.

Here are some tips for wheelchair runners:

- Wheelchair running is easier, at first, than running on your feet. You can do about 20 to 30 minutes right away. Try this three or four times a week slowly, and then briskly for a few weeks. Thirty minutes of wheelchair running a few times a week has about the same aerobic value as running and meets the minimal fitness requirements. Don't coast too much!

- Uphills are hard! You have to push your weight and the chair uphill using your arm muscles, which are less powerful than your leg muscles. Start training on the flats, and gradually shift to small hills. Avoid long or steep uphills unless you plan to race on them.

- Beware of downhills. You can really roll downhill, which could be dangerous for you and other runners. Practice braking with your hands on small downhills. Avoid long or steep downhills unless you plan to face them in a race. Remember that coasting downhill means that you aren't benefiting aerobically from your workout at that point.

- A lightweight racing chair will make races a lot easier and more enjoyable. It may be essential for longer runs and races.

- Most wheelchair runners use gloves to protect their hands from the wheels.

- If you want to race downhill very fast—not a recommended idea—wear a protective helmet.

- If you must train at night, put reflectors and lights on your chair, and wear reflector strips on your clothing.

- Dress in layers. Your upper body will be working hard, and like all runners you may want to peel off some layers of clothing as you sweat, and add them back as you cool. The lower body, however, doesn't get much circulation, so wheelchair runners may want to wear extra clothing over the legs and feet on cold days.

- Be alert to crowned roads and slanted surfaces. They are hard to run on. Try flat surfaces or the middle of the crown—but never do this in traffic!

For racing, there are some other guidelines. Here are a few we've gained from our experience with the Achilles Track Club:

- Try to arrange with race officials to start early. You will get a clean start, and not interfere with the other runners.

- Persevere when going uphill. Keep moving and you'll make it. Going downhill, hold your chair at the pace of the runners around you. Don't try to zoom past runners. You risk injuring them and yourself.

- If you can get out of the chair to race, do so. You may go faster on wheels, but try to build up to running on your own, or on crutches.

Want more inspiration? Achilles Track Club's Andre Francis completed the 1984 New York Marathon in eight hours. He is a quadriplegic and hits the wheel with the heel of his hand to propel himself. Teammate Bob Greene lay in a hospital for 54 weeks after a car accident smashed both legs. A year later he used Canadian crutches to complete the 1984 New York Marathon in 10:45.

Remember, whatever your disability, you won't be the first on the road to fitness—or the last!

13 RUNNING AND THE HEALTH IMPAIRED

I have known runners with all sorts of handicaps. Not everyone simply buys a new pair of running shoes and starts off. Some people need running not only to get fit again but also to overcome physical and mental ailments. In this chapter, we will look at some of the problems I've encountered while helping men and women overcome their handicaps and run.

ALCOHOLISM

I know about a dozen dedicated runners who are abstaining alcoholics and now regular participants in New York Road Runners Club running events. One woman was hospitalized in an alcohol rehabilitation center; she was depressed and suicidal. She had been fired from her job and was going through a divorce. After her release from the center, she started our beginners class. Gradually, she built herself up to five miles a day, and running gave her release from her stress and a greatly improved self-image.

Running—combined with Alcoholics Anonymous or church groups—has put many men and women back on the road to healthy lives. A study reported in the *Journal of Studies on Alcohol* noted that almost 70 percent of those patients who undertake a fitness program with their alcohol rehabilitation become abstinent. The researchers believe that fitness training may make patients receptive to change, reorganize their leisure time, and help them deal with stress.

Not all treatment with alcoholics wins the struggle, however. Captain Joseph Pursch is a psychiatrist and director of the Alcohol Rehabilitation Services at the U.S. Navy Hospital in Long Beach, California; he is also a veteran marathon runner. The program at Long Beach has a 76 percent success rate, but Captain Pursch still sees runners who continue to drink uncontrollably.

"I see that pattern so often: the individual who denies his alcoholism because he can run two, or six, or 10 miles. I know one physician who ran the Boston Marathon. He was drinking a quart of whiskey a day, and he ran the marathon for years to prove to himself that he couldn't be an alcoholic. He finally got arrested for drunk driving and thought, 'Well, maybe I'm not an alcoholic when I run, but I sure am one when I drive,' and that got him stopped. Then he thought about this and he entered treatment. Now he's been sober for about four years and he realizes that he was an alcoholic all along."

Psychiatry has also often proven to be ineffective in treating alcoholism. Captain Pursch uses a holistic approach: he insists that his patients accept responsibility for their own well-being and physical health. One of his innovations is having his patients replace their negative addiction to alcohol with a positive addiction, like running.

On a typical day, his patients rise at 6:30, breakfast at 7:30, and clean up their living quarters and assigned areas. Then there are group therapy, lectures, films, AA meetings, and, at around three, running. Most of the patients are required to run a mile a day, seven days a week, as a minimum exercise. After graduation, in about two to six weeks, the patients are encouraged to become involved in their local AA groups, and to continue their running. "The object," says Pursch, "is to get these people moving again, and that will help them where it counts: in their heads."

ARTHRITIS

The causes of osteoarthritis remain a mystery, but they are not attributed to exercise. The myth that running places a great strain on the joints and leads to osteoarthritis is just that—a myth. Sedentary people are just as prone to arthritis, maybe more so.

A study, "Running and Primary Osteoarthritis of the Hip," published by Finnish researchers in *The British Medical Journal* in 1975, focused on 74 Finnish former record-holding runners. Their average age was sixty-five, and they had competed for an average of 21 years. X rays revealed osteoarthritis in only 4 percent of the runners, compared to 8.7 percent among those in a control group of nonrunners.

Lack of use may contribute to the onset of osteoarthritis. Proper exercise apparently allows the joint fluid to circulate, which is necessary for the nutrition of the various components of the joints. Running may prevent the disease, but it cannot cure it.

Osteoarthritis should be diagnosed by X ray, not by complaint. Runners who have it may have to take a few days off when it becomes bothersome, and perhaps substitute swimming or cycling for their workouts. Aspirin may help; heat also soothes. Moreover, a reasonable amount of movement of the affected joints may relieve the pain of osteoarthritis.

ASTHMA

Asthma is one of the most common respiratory diseases. It may affect as many as eight million Americans, many of them young children. Historically, asthma sufferers have been told to avoid exercise. Recent studies, however, suggest that avoiding exercise is unnecessary and perhaps even detrimental to asthmatic men and women. In the March 1981 issue of *The Physician and Sportsmedicine*, Alan R. Morton, Kenneth D. Fitch, M.D., and Allan G. Hahn wrote:

"Although exercise provokes bronchiospasm in most asthmatics, the severity of exercise-induced asthma can be reduced by several factors: control of exercise duration; less intense, intermittent exercise; warm-up; warmer, humid inspired air; aerobic fitness;

and drugs. Regular vigorous exercise increases fitness, enhances tolerance to attacks, and provides more social and psychological independence. The development of protective medication has made such activity possible for many asthmatics."

At least two-thirds of asthmatics have exercise-induced asthma. It is typically seen in runners, but not in swimmers or participants in other sports that have brief periods of exercise. In runners, it begins three to ten minutes after exercising and is characterized by increased wheezing and breathlessness. Presently, doctors believe that oral inhalation of cold air initiates the bronchiospasm.

Only a doctor can correctly evaluate asthma from symptoms such as wheezing, breathlessness, or coughing, since these can also indicate other diseases. Beware of medical advice that exercise must be stopped. Get a second opinion, preferably from a sportsmedicine physician.

Here are some guidelines for exercise for asthmatics:

Warm-up   Stretch and warm up much as any other runner. Gradually increase your body temperature with stretching, then walking progressing to jogging and running.

Duration   Exercise should last at least 30 minutes.

Frequency   Exercise four or five times a week.

Intensity   Exercise should start at a low level of intensity, and gradually increase as your fitness level improves. Begin with walking. If you experience a regular exercise-induced asthma, doctors suggest that you progress to low-level interval training using work intervals of 10 to 30 seconds, followed by rest intervals of 30 to 90 seconds. Then progress to high-intensity interval training. The purpose is short, intensive exercise that may avoid exercise-induced asthma attacks.

If you can "run through" your asthma, or if you have found a suitable pre-exercise medication, long-distance continuous activity—despite its tendency to induce asthma attacks—may be undertaken.

Cool-down Stretch and follow the same cool-down as other runners. Don't stop vigorous exercise suddenly. Walk and stretch for at least five minutes, or until your heart rate returns to within 20 beats a minute of your resting heart beat.

Medication Your physician may prescribe medicine to prevent exercise-induced asthma (such as cromolyn sodium or the B-adrenergic drugs). During activity, asthma may be reversed by the appropriate aerosol medicine.

Some asthmatics, however, are not helped by medication. They have several choices. They may exercise in an environment with 100 percent humidity: they can swim, or jog in place in a vapor-filled bathroom. Or, they can train their bodies so that when they develop asthma eight to ten minutes after they start to run, they are strong enough to continue to run, which will eventually stop the asthma. This level can be attained by running at least three miles or more, fast, at least once a week.

Because they are often pampered, many asthmatics have low fitness levels, lack motor skills, and sometimes have poor posture. They may view themselves as being nonathletic, since they are rarely selected to play with their peers on teams. We support the American Academy of Pediatrics position that the asthmatic child may participate in school and recreational activities and sports programs with minimal restrictions.

Almost everyone should have daily physical exercise, and rigorous activity has been shown to increase physical fitness, enhance tolerance of attacks, and bring greater social and psychological independence to asthmatics. By following the running program in Chapter 4, asthmatics have significantly improved their fitness level. They have slept and felt better, and lessened the impact of asthma on their lives.

ALLERGIES

Some 35 million Americans suffer from allergies, and the spring, summer, and fall are seasons of allergic rhinitis (inflammation of the mucous membrane of the nose). Many suffer from a combination of allergic problems. Respiratory allergens are most common, and may come from natural organic materials like pollens, mold spores, house dust, insect excrement, animal danders, and other airborne pollutants.

The allergic runner and exerciser can avoid airborne allergens by selecting when and where to exercise. You may decrease your reaction by working out in the early morning or late afternoon, avoiding dry and windy weather (by working out inside or alternating with another sport, such as swimming), and avoiding allergenic sources (dusty roads or trails near grass or meadows, not exercising on high-pollution days). Removal of offending foods and animals, and aggressive dust control may also help. The use of car and home air filters (air conditioners) can lower the allergens in your air. Oral and nasal medications may also help, but may cause side effects. Special filter masks (for example, 3 M's "Micropore Pollen Filter Mask") may be worn to minimize the amount of pollutants breathed into your lungs.

CANCER

Running will not prevent or cure cancer, but it has helped cancer patients feel and look better. Several cancer amputees run with Achilles TC, and if you are a runner who then discovers that he or she has cancer, you will indeed bring a healthy body to the crisis.

One member of the New York Road Runners Club running program was training for his first marathon when he learned he had cancer. A tumor was treated with chemotherapy, and he continued training by following the guidelines in *The Competitive Runners Handbook*. His excellent attitude and his energy surprised the doctors, and he shows signs of making a full recovery. One major boost was finishing the 1983 New York City Marathon in a little more than four hours.

Kay Atkinson set a 60–69 age-group world record for the 10K, and ran the tough Pike's Peak Marathon. But in 1982, her doctors discovered terminal cancer during exploratory surgery. Kay continued to run, however, despite radiation treatments, and formed a beginner runner group for cancer rehabilitation patients. Her last run—a send-off to other masters runners starting out on a cross-country run—was just 17 days before she died on April 24, 1984.

The Cancer Self-Help Program at Presbyterian Medical Center in Denver has since 1976 undertaken an innovative cancer program. The center supplements standard medical treatment for cancer with psychological counseling, biofeedback, and exercise. The hope is to combat the emotional stresses of cancer and to give patients a sense of controlling their own lives.

The Denver program originated with Carl and Stephanie Simonton, and T. Flint Sparks, who worked together in Ft. Worth, Texas. The Simontons observed that cancer patients who were active also did best fighting their disease. Sparks, the Denver center's director of counseling, started a self-help program for cancer patients. He suggests:

- Exercise for one hour, three times a week. Picture yourself getting well and being active.
- Set physical goals for yourself that are attainable, and work toward them. Add a block or a mile to your distance, which will give you a clear sense of making progress.
- Combine walking and jogging, or swimming and cycling on a stationary bicycle. Patients confined to beds should start with leg lifts, arm exercises, or short walks down the hospital corridor.

For the greatest benefit, of course, the patient needs to perform aerobic exercise for 45 minutes to an hour. Cancer patients may believe that they can never attain this level again. One of the mistakes they make is waiting until they feel better. They stay still, and the pain never disappears.

According to Dr. Paul K. Hamilton, a medical oncologist in Denver, half of all cancer patients receiving therapy could perform exercises like walking. Perhaps 25 percent could jog, play tennis, or swim vigorously. Yet, only a tiny fraction of cancer patients—even those in remission—exercise at all. Most see themselves as fragile, and worry about harming themselves with exertion. Of course, not all patients should exercise: those on chemotherapy should have their blood counts monitored before undertaking a running program; some drugs decrease the platelets (clotting cells) in the blood, and others may cause damage to the heart.

But the Simontons, in an article in the June 1980 *The Runner*, cite a patient who had cancerous kidneys and neck tumors removed, but also had secondary tumors in his lungs. He continued his running, and finished the Honolulu Marathon. Another patient, a woman in her late forties, had a bilateral radical mastectomy, and then completed the Honolulu Marathon. A few years ago, Robert Fisher was in the news when he pedaled his bike 3,700 miles across the United States—despite having incurable chronic leukemia.

Exercise won't protect you from cancer, but it offers one way of fighting back.

CARDIAC RUNNERS

Until the early 1960s heart attack victims were confined to bed and rest for months. The theme was "take it easy." The heart needed rest, and any exercise, doctors thought, might delay healing of the heart muscle or cause a rupture of the heart-attack scar.

This had not always been the case. In 1854 William Stokes, professor of medicine at Trinity College, Dublin, Ireland, had prescribed a walking program for his heart patients, and published his methods in *The Diseases of the Heart and Aorta*. But Stokes' observations went largely ignored until the 1940s, when a study in the United States showed that healthy volunteers, confined to bed for 21 days, experienced a reduction in the size and pumping capacity of their hearts, breathlessness, and even dizziness, sweating, nausea, heart pounding, and fainting when asked to stand suddenly. Most revealing, the study found that these characteristics could be reversed if the volunteers exercised in bed for an hour a day.

The lesson? Total bed rest over a long period of time may have devastating effects on the body. Today, patients with uncomplicated heart attacks are out of bed after a few days, and home within two weeks. They may even be moved gradually into a mild exercise program. And some, like Joe Michaels, who has suffered seven heart attacks since 1968, have turned to running.

Joe runs 7 to 20 miles a day. He started slowly: walking first, graduating to a slow jog after several weeks, then walk-jog-walk, and finally running full time. He has now completed 24 races, including two New York Marathons, 202 miles as a fund raiser for the American Heart Association, 581 miles (run/walk) from Toronto to New York for the AHA, and the Boston Marathon under the guidance of the American Medical Jogging Association.

Joe Michaels has several suggestions for men and women who have suffered heart attacks and want to exercise:

- Find a doctor who isn't overweight or a smoker, and work out some sort of exercise program.
- Start slowly, and build gradually.

"I want people to know that being sedentary is the real killer," he says, "and that they have to get out and get into shape."

Few coronary rehabilitation programs emphasize positive advice about what to do. One that does is the Toronto Rehabilitation Center Hospital, whose staff suggests exercise as a major component of post-coronary rehabilitation. Most patients start with a walking program, and progress to slow jogging. In 15 years, long-distance jogging has become the core of the Toronto program. Patients are screened, interviewed, examined, and carefully monitored before beginning the 20-minute exercise programs. The walking or jogging exercises are also carefully supervised, and include regular telemetry and Holter electrocardiograms. When the patient returns home, he or she is under the care of the regular referring physician. The patient works out four times a week, keeping a detailed log, and remains in contact with the Toronto staff and the home physician.

The success rate of the Toronto program is high, with decrease in angina and post-coronary depression. Those patients who have gone on with the program have formed the Toronto Rehabilitation Center Joggers, with its own macabre slogan: "The world's sickest track club." Some 50 patients have completed marathons wearing the TRC Joggers colors.

There are, of course, a list of warnings for the post-coronary exerciser:

- Rest, and do not exercise, when you have viral infections or flu-like symptoms.
- Be extremely cautious in exercising in heat.
- Maintain fluid intake and balance when exercising for long periods of time. This is especially important for marathon runners, some of whom have suffered heart attacks when running in heat without proper fluid replacement.
- Take very seriously any episodes of unexplained unconsciousness or blackouts or severe vertigo. Report them to your doctor, and have him or her monitor your heart rhythm. There have been reports of sudden death in healthy runners who had previously suffered these symptoms.

DIABETICS

Insulin is required by the body in order to store body sugars and to transport the blood sugar into cells for storage. Insulin is lacking in a diabetic, and must be injected or ingested. Also, the diabetic's diet must be regimented to maintain proper blood-sugar levels. During exercise the glycogen level is lowered and blood sugar drops. The diabetic athlete must take in sugar at regular intervals to keep from becoming weak and sick.

Running cannot cure diabetes or make insulin injections unnecessary. It may help lower blood sugar and lessen the amount of insulin needed, however. The complications from diabetes are best controlled by taking the right amount of insulin, eating the appropriate types and amounts of food, and getting regular exercise.

The best exercise for the diabetic is generally the same as for nondiabetic people. It should include the flexibility exercises from Chapter 2 to decrease the possibility of muscle injury, strength training from Chapter 8 to increase muscle size and tone, and 20 to 30 minutes of aerobic exercise to strengthen your cardiovascular system.

Diabetics with uncontrolled hypertension, coronary disease, or certain eye problems such as retinopathy should not perform strength training that includes weightlifting or isometrics. Walking, stationary cycling, stretching, and mild calisthenics are recommended instead.

Diabetic runners should coordinate their diet, medicine, and exercise under careful medical supervision. The diabetic runner needs to know how his or her glucose levels will respond to exercise, especially running. Now there are easy ways to monitor your own sugar levels; these allow you to exercise almost without restriction, as long as you alter your insulin program accordingly. Blood glucose self-monitoring kits are available commercially. You may also use these kits to determine the impact of carbohydrate loading on your body. Care should be taken, under a doctor's supervision, to monitor this technique of storing large amounts of additional energy in the liver and muscles.

Here are some further suggestions:

- Take several "teaching" runs after you are in condition and feeling like running long distances. Every 20 minutes during the run, then every hour or two for 12 hours afterwards, monitor your blood sugar level. This will help you determine how much to eat before and during a long run.

- You may need to alter your insulin injection schedule. Change your insulin regimen only after consulting with your doctor.
- You may need or want to increase insulin dosages during pre-competition days, and reduce insulin dosage on long-competition days.
- Most diabetic runners and doctors suggest injecting insulin into an area of low metabolic activity, such as your abdomen or arm.
- Dr. Norb Sander suggests that a diabetic carry a glucose solution in a small plastic squeeze bottle during all runs rather than take a chance of finding a supply along the route. During your long runs, you may wish to consume sugar every 15 to 20 minutes.
- Dr. Kris Berg suggests that diabetic runners avoid exercise during periods of peak insulin effect.
- Dr. Berg also suggests that the diabetic runner avoid eating a carbohydrate snack 30 minutes before activity.
- Finally, Dr. Berg recommends that diabetic runners reduce insulin dosages the day after long-run competition.

A guidebook, *Diabetes and Exercise: How to Get Started*, is available from the International Diabetes Center, 4959 Excelsior Boulevard, Minneapolis, Minnesota 55416.

DRUG REHABILITATION

Because of its well-documented physiological effects (see Chapters 20 and 21), running has also had a strong impact on helping drug abusers. Jim Little, a runner who is also executive director of New York City's Veritas, a drug rehabilitation center, came up with the idea of using exercise with drug abusers. Now he calls it "tremendously valuable. Apart from the benefits of physical fitness, running relaxes the anxious person and the addict who has the itch to shoot dope, while it energizes the depressed person, the barbiturate user." But Jim has found that running has another value: it teaches that you get out of something what you put into it. "Running requires effort," he says, "and when finished you feel you have accomplished something. For residents in the therapeutic community who have so few accomplishments, running becomes meaningful."

I organized and directed an experimental program for Veritas in cooperation with The New York Road Runners Club. The seven-week program, involving six people, was very successful: two members completed a four-mile race, and two others were able to run two miles by the end of the program.

George Williams, one of the class members, completed a four-mile race in Central Park, and was very proud of his achievement. Frank Martin, a Vietnam veteran, also ran well, and he and George cut down their cigarette smoking from two packs a day to just two cigarettes a day. They ran the four-mile race together in 36 minutes.

Joe Elluzzi "did alcohol, cocaine, reefers, and pills" before checking into Veritas. "Speeding in your sneakers," says Elluzzi, "is not unlike speeding with amphetamines. It's that same feeling that you want to do, do, do—and that you can." Williams, at first, worried that the up-scale running community would look with dismay at the "dope fiends" jogging alongside them. "They treated us like *runners*," he exclaimed.

I found that people who are depressed—such as heroin and Valium addicts—and who turn to running gain energy and often overcome their depression. Hyperactive people use running to relax. As Sharon Hogart, clinical director at Veritas, says: "Running is a sport in which everybody who follows through is a winner. Addicts have chemically numbed themselves so they don't feel. They've built psychological defenses, particularly the women, who tend to have no sense of power over their own bodies. This is also a population that's afraid of competition, and as odd as it sounds, terrified of success. With running, you're essentially competing with your self, and there's no big ego loss."

THE EMOTIONALLY DISTURBED

Scientific research has established that vigorous exercise does convey a wide range of benefits, from alleviating depression to improving self-image. Another area where aerobic exercise is proving beneficial is with emotionally disturbed children and adults. (In Chapters 20 and 21, we discuss some of these studies.)

One interesting report comes from research at the San Diego (California) Center for Children. The center is a residential treatment facility for children ages six to 13 who have severe emotional and behavioral problems. Just what effect can running have on emotionally disturbed children?

In studies over the span of two years, the center followed two groups of children, one doing a running program and the other practicing non-aerobic skills like tumbling and long jumping. Both groups were training for a Special Olympics. Each group practiced three mornings a week for 12 weeks.

The center found a sharp decrease in the daily aggressiveness of the children in the running group. The runners previously had been disrupting classes, throwing supplies, punching other students. By the end of the experiment, however, these children showed far less aggressive behavior, even on non-running days, supporting the theory that the benefits of running may be cumulative and persistent. Further, the majority of these disturbed children were taken off all medication after they began their running program.

Another encouraging example is Chuck Eisele, who set a United States record for nine-year-olds when he ran the 1983 Marine Corps Marathon in 2:56:57. Chuck started running when he was six, in an effort to overcome hyperactivity that was so severe he had to be treated with drugs. He couldn't sit still at the dinner table, and had almost no attention span in school. "He used to look drugged," says his mother. "He didn't look like my little boy." That changed with the running. "His grades have gone up, and he has an attention span now." Chuck sees his physician before every race. "He's just like a car," his mother notes. "We take him in for a checkup every 500 miles."

EPILEPSY

This disorder is characterized by recurrent convulsions that range from body-jerking seizures (grand mal) to milder transient spells (petit mal). Epilepsy is believed to be caused by some brain cells which, instead of putting out normal electrical discharges, put out abnormal ones, causing the seizure.

Anyone can have epilepsy anytime, but most cases begin before age 20. The tendency may be inherited, or may result from cell damage, a head injury, infection, drug abuse, or alcoholism. The major cause of epilepsy in adults is automobile accidents. Some 70 percent of epileptics control their seizures with drug therapy under a doctor's care. Surgery is sometimes a solution for those patients whose electrical abnormality is in an area of the brain that can be treated.

Epileptics, like asthmatics, have been unnecessarily sheltered and protected. They are often prevented from participating in sports or exercising in a normal, regular way.

In 1977, a young woman named Patty Wilson decided to do something about this attitude. Patty had suffered her first seizure in the third grade. Her friends had teased her, and were afraid to play with her. Even her father was scared of the affliction.

On her own, Patty Wilson had decided to become a runner. Her doctor encouraged her, and she always ran with someone. Patty won several high school cross-country races, and then ran some ultra-long distances with her father: 300 miles from her home near Los Angeles to Las Vegas, and 500 miles to San Francisco.

In the summer of 1977 Patty Wilson and her father set out on a run to publicize the fact that epileptics can be runners, and can run with the best: They decided to run from Los Angeles to Portland, Oregon, some 1,300 miles. For most of the run, Patty and her father averaged 31 miles a day. When they reached the Oregon border, high school track teams and local track clubs ran with them. People with epilepsy stopped and talked with her. "She was a light for them," said Patty's father.

Patty Wilson's story is dramatic, but underscores an important message: Epilepsy—or other handicaps—shouldn't stop anyone from exercising.

THE MENTALLY HANDICAPPED

Benefits have also come to the mentally handicapped who have taken up running and other aerobic exercises. I have worked with the Special Olympics in both Rome, New York, and New York City. I urge runners to volunteer and work with these young men and women; you'll find that both of you benefit.

The physically handicapped have means to overcome their obstacles. The mentally retarded need our help. Some six million Americans are mentally retarded, and most live isolated from the "normal" world. Special Olympics and other athletic organizations for the mentally handicapped work to expand the circle of friends the retarded person may have, while also breaking the cycle of isolation and improving physical health.

The Special Olympics train the mentally retarded in some 16 sports—including track and field, swimming, Alpine and Nordic skiing, and wheelchair events. The training may take place at schools, institutions, or within recreational and residential programs. It is open to anyone who is at least eight years old, who is not involved in regular interscholastic or intramural sports, and who has an IQ of 75 or less. There is no upper age limit.

The Special Olympic games are held annually, with international games every four years. The impact on these young men and women is profound. There are measurable increases in self-esteem and independence, and in parental and community support of these athletes. At least seven Special Olympians have run official marathons in the U.S., and more than 100 have completed 5K and 10K races outside the Olympics. Loretta Claiborne trained for three years, and completed marathons in Washington, Baltimore, and Harrisburg, Pennsylvania—all in under three hours. In the 1981 Boston Marathon, Loretta finished in 3:09:25.

The goal of the Special Olympics—like the goal of most runners—is "to finish the race." The physical, social, and emotional benefits from this training and participating are almost beyond comprehension: a 55-year-old woman who takes up cross-country skiing in Colorado; a Tennessee high-school student, who trains for the Special Olympics, wins a gold medal in the 220-yard dash, and then returns to his school to coach other handicapped boys and girls training for these games.

How can we help? Experienced, nonhandicapped runners are needed everywhere: in the Special Olympics, with physically handicapped runners, wherever other runners want to share their knowledge and skills.

PRISON RUNNERS

One of the newest areas of running involves runners who are also prisoners. Several prisons in the United States have formal or informal running programs, usually centered on a track. Running helps prisoners relieve boredom, control weight and fitness, and create a balance to their daily lives. Moreover, running may be part of healing, for the incarcerated as well as the handicapped.

Bob Buchanon, a senior corrections analyst with the Western Research Institute in Kansas City, Kansas, argues that rehabilitation is changing to reintegration—the gradual adjustment of prisoners back into the community. "It seems that through a combination of recreation and counseling, one can improve the self-image of prisoners. I don't think that running *per se* can solve the problem, but as part of a larger program of physical and mental fitness I think it can be a vital tool."

Some 99.2 percent of all prisoners in the United States are ultimately released; the rest die in prison. Preparation for leaving makes sense, and running is something a prisoner can do after he or she leaves. Running may be part of healing. Prisoners are now running marathons. The maximum security prison in MacNeil Island, Washington, has sponsored marathons, and the California Men's Colony at San Luis Obispo has featured 10K races.

I believe that one of the opportunities for healthy, nonprisoner runners is to give help to less fortunate runners, and to running prisoners. In 1983, I was asked by the New York Road Runners Club to help start a running program at the Rikers Island (New York City) Prison. Under the direction of Milena Krondl, Bob Wynn, and Joe Sciarrone of the New York Road Runners Club staff, I visited Rikers twice a week to lead workouts. The program started with 30 inmates and grew to several hundred. We ended the first year with the Rikers Island Olympics, for which the inmates had trained for several months. We had the prisoners doing calisthenics, stretching, and running up to five miles; all workouts were confined to the grassy areas and track in the prison courtyard. Charter members of the Rikers Island TC got copies of *The Runner's Handbook.*

Running may not be a single solution to any problem or handicap. For all of us, it is a tool: Many prisoners asked me for running tips to help them continue after leaving prison. Other handicapped runners, too, have started new lives by running.

14 SUITING UP TO RUN WITH MOTHER NATURE

Mother Nature provides us with seasons for running—from the brisk snappy weather of autumn to winter's sometimes windless mornings with light, fresh snow, or summer and spring's flowers, green hills, fresh gardens, and new breath of life. She is a runner's greatest friend—and teacher.

Runners go out in every season, in every environment, in clothing invented and selected to protect us, and to please our demanding Mother. As we expose ourselves more and more to running, we also expose ourselves to the vagaries of the environment. We need to know the challenges, and to prepare for them.

CLOTHING

One of the greatest strides made during the running boom of the 1970s and 1980s has come in runners' clothing. Designer styles, colors, and new materials have changed the way we look on the road. Companies now offer runners' clothing for both men and women in a wide variety of materials and colors. Previously, women had to buy men's-style shorts, singlets, and warm-ups. There's no excuse now for looking like a reborn high school jock, although Shepherd adamantly refuses to discard his old torn sweatpants.

In this chapter, we briefly list the old and new fabrics, and articles of clothing recommended by Mitch Maslin, owner/manager of New York City's Athletic Attic. Then, when we discuss

Mother Nature's seasons, we also report on the appropriate clothing.

The Old Fabrics

Cotton This standby is still popular because it is soft and cool, even though it absorbs moisture and may become abrasive. T-shirts and mesh singlets may be 100 percent cotton, which is very soft and also expensive, or a cotton blend, which is cheaper, doesn't shrink, and lasts longer. Blends include polyester and nylon.

Wool This is a cold-weather favorite because it keeps you warm even when wet. Some runners find 100 percent wool "itchy," but not a wool blend. Wool will shrink, and must be hand-washed and dried carefully.

Nylon This well-known fabric is lightweight, dries fast, holds body heat, and washes easily. It protects against wind or rain. Nylon is, however, a hot fabric; it doesn't "breathe" like wool or cotton. Windbreakers and singlets should be replaced with a cooler fabric as temperatures rise.

The New Fabrics

Polypropylene This is a new-old fabric, which has been popular among cross-country skiers for years. It is now found in thermal underwear, socks, hats, gloves, and fancy rainsuits. Why? Polypropylene is an extremely lightweight, excellent insulation. It traps warm air next to the skin while also moving moisture away from it. As a result, your skin holds a constant balance of heat and humidity, without the dampness of other thermal fabrics such as cotton. To be effective, polypropylene must be the first layer next to the skin.

On mild days, you need no fabric over polypropylene, which "wicks" moisture away from your body. On cold days, a loose-fitting cotton or wool layer over it will keep you warm and absorb the moisture. But this synthetic fabric is not waterproof or windproof. It is meant to be worn under a protective outer garment. It cannot work alone to keep heat next to your body.

Gore-Tex   Another popular, and expensive, synthetic of the 1980s, this is actually a film, not a fabric, but is bonded to a fabric, usually nylon. It allows water vapor (sweat and heat) to pass through it but holds back water droplets (rain and snow). It is almost completely waterproof. It insulates your body without letting you overheat, or get wet or cold. Gore-Tex works because it consists of millions of pores of "film" per square inch. Vapor and heat escape, but larger water drops cannot enter. The little holes also stop the wind.

Gore-Tex may be used for hats, gloves, and running suits, and is especially effective on rainy or cold days over wool or polypropylene.

Articles of Clothing
Socks   Most runners wear socks all the time, but others wear them only in winter or during races, while a thick-skinned few never wear them at all.

Socks are supposed to protect your feet from rubbing against the inside of your shoes, which can cause blisters; absorb sweat, which can hurt your feet and cause your shoes to deteriorate; and provide warmth and cushioning.

There are three types of athletic socks: tube, anklet, and regular. Tube socks have no shaping at the ankle or toe, and they tend to move around as you run. We do not recommend them for running. Anklet socks cover your foot up to your ankle. Some runners like them in summer, because they are cooler, or for racing because they are lighter than a full sock. Regular socks are cushioned and formed in the toe and ankle, and reach to mid-calf.

Socks may bunch and fold during long runs or when they get wet, causing blisters. For this reason, I prefer anklet socks for racing and during rain. Always wear clean socks; dirty socks may also cause blisters, and they wear out sooner. Also, when buying socks look carefully for deformities or rough spots that might irritate your feet.

Socks come in various fabrics, with distinctive characteristics.

Cotton, or a cotton blend, are most common. They are comfortable, cool, and durable, especially in warm weather. But cotton also absorbs and retains moisture, and feels uncomfortable on cold, wet days. Wet cotton is abrasive, and can cause blisters. Orlon in a cotton sock helps wick away moisture, and doesn't get as wet or abrasive. Acrylic or orlon also increase the bulk of the sock and its sponginess. Nylon added to cotton makes it more elastic; the sock stays up better. I use cotton socks year-round except when running in cold rain, snow, or slush. Then I switch to wool.

Wool is warmer than cotton, and doesn't lose its insulating properties when wet. I think wool socks are best in cold weather, or on wet, slushy, or snowy days.

Polypropylene sock liners with a wool sock on the outside will protect you on cold or wet days. This combination, or a polypropylene-wool blend sock, will keep your feet dry and warm.

Some socks have extra cushioning in the heel, toe, and ball of the foot. If you want these types of socks, be certain that your running shoes will still fit well.

Underwear For men, the cotton athletic supporter, or "jock," is a thing of the past. Most male runners now prefer running shorts with built-in briefs, or separate sports briefs made from a soft, seamless, absorbent stretch fabric. These briefs are not as supportive as a jock, and a compromise between the two is a spandex jock with a one-inch band. A special polypropylene brief with a windproof front panel will keep you warm and supported where you need it most.

Women runners can also purchase shorts with a built-in brief and a cotton panel for comfort and absorbency. Some women prefer cotton underpants or women's sports briefs under their running shorts. Women may hear from male doctors that they should wear a bra while running to avoid "sagging breasts." Dr. Joan Ullyot, in her book *Women's Running,* argues that sagging breasts are not the result of bouncing while running, and that the only reason for wearing a bra is comfort (most women, however, develop soreness after running braless). Sports bras are available for those women who prefer this undergarment, and they offer support without the conventional seams, hooks, and metal parts that cause abrasion when running.

Running Suits All-weather suits (tops, pants, and hood) are made from Gore-Tex or nylon. They are available in a variety of colors and styles.

Shorts Many runners' shorts are made from nylon weave, which is light, porous, soft, washes easily, and dries fast. It won't chafe when wet, like cotton. They are worn in warm or cold weather.

Most runners prefer shorts that are loose in the thigh or crotch. In Europe, however, "bunhuggers" are popular among some women. These shorts are made of stretch nylon, and are supposed to offer freedom of movement.

One of the advances in runners' clothing during the last ten years has been the development of shorts designed only for women. Previously, women runners had to make do with men's shorts. Now, companies like Pantera and Moving Comfort are designing shorts, singlets, and warm-ups exclusively for women. Manufacturers such as Nike and New Balance offer clothing for both men and women.

Shirts Most runners prefer cotton blend T-shirts or singlets on hot days because they are comfortable and cool. T-shirts are also in demand among runners: any race offering free T-shirts attracts a crowd.

Get your T-shirt a size too large. On cold days, try wearing a T-shirt under a warm-up jacket or nylon shell and over a polypropylene undershirt, which will draw moisture off your skin. Make sure that the undershirt is not too tight, or moisture will not be wicked away by the inner layer of polypropylene and will be held against your skin. Some prefer a cotton sweatshirt over an inner T-shirt layer. On hot, sunny days, some runners prefer a training T-shirt which covers their shoulders, but is mesh on the lower half—a combination of T-shirt and singlet. Singlets are made of nylon (which dries fast but clings to your body on hot days), cotton blends, or a combination. T-shirts with mesh holes for greater air circulation come in nylon and cotton blends. A favorite combination is a cotton blend singlet with a nylon panel across the chest, which eliminates the problem of chafing your nipples.

Gloves/Mittens Many runners, including me, prefer gloves, although mittens may be warmer since the fingers heat each other. White cotton garden gloves have been popular on cool days ever since Bill Rodgers started wearing them in the early 1970s. But cotton gets wet (from sweat or rain) and doesn't retain heat. Wool is better on cold days because it is warm even when wet. There are gloves and mittens with wool-polypropylene blends, or half cotton and half wool. On very cold days, you might prefer wool over the new special liners like polypropylene or silk. On windy days, Gore-Tex mittens or a nylon shell over an inner glove will protect you.

Never throw your gloves away during a run. Tuck them into your shorts, or stuff them into a pouch or pocket somewhere. If your hands get wet, or you turn and run back facing a headwind, you'll want those gloves. Your best bet, therefore, is a pair of gloves (or mittens) that will keep your hands warm even when the gloves get wet.

Head Gear/Face Gear To keep warm, keep your head covered. More than 40 percent of your body heat is lost through the top of your head. A hat or cap traps that heat.

For cold weather, the most popular headgear is the wool cap. You can roll it down to cover your ears, roll it up to let out some heat, or take it off and stuff it easily into your shorts, pocket, or pouch. Caps come in wool or synthetic blends, and all colors.

Shepherd wears a bright orange knit cap during hunting season in Vermont, and another wool cap (complete with bobbing pompon on top) during the winter.

Some runners prefer just to keep their ears warm with a wool earband. On extremely cold days, I wear an earband under my wool cap to keep my ears warm. You may also prefer a hood for your running top: a sweatsuit hood, or Gore-tex over a polypropylene or wool cap for extra protection.

On extremely cold days, some runners wear face masks of wool, polypropylene, or silk to protect against windburn, frostbite, or chafing. These masks have openings for the eyes, and some have slits for your mouth. Some extend to cover the neck. A balaclava comes as a cap, a cap and face mask, or a wrap for your neck.

If you dislike all of the above suggestions, go to a ski shop and check out the special products for skiers. There are ointments which are rubbed over the face and lips to protect them. Vaseline will also protect exposed skin during cold weather; some runners like to rub it on their legs since it seems both to protect against the wind and to hold in heat.

Sweatbands keep sweat from dripping down your face or neck. Most running stores sell headbands, or you can fashion your own from colorful bandanas. Steve Stack, my friend from Rome, New York, wears the elastic band off discarded underpants as a cheap headband.

Rubberized Clothing   Some runners wear a rubber suit—either the jacket or pants, or both—because they think this will help them lose weight. They are wrong! The weight loss is temporary, due to a loss of fluids, and will quickly return. Permanent weight loss comes from burning calories with exercise.

Plastic or rubberized clothing is dangerous: it prevents evaporation of perspiration, which cools your body. Running in a rubber suit prevents this natural cooling from taking place, builds your body heat to a dangerous level, promotes dehydration, and may lead to muscle cramps, fatigue, or even heat exhaustion. We do *not* recommend rubberized or plastic clothing for most runners. The only exception is to use such clothing to acclimatize the very well-conditioned runner in a cool climate for an important race in a hot climate.

Other Items   Some runners seem to carry a lot of little items with them. You may need keys, an extra Band-Aid, money, subway tokens, identification, or medical information. These may be tucked into various pockets, shoe purses that tie into your laces, or wrist pockets worn like a wristband. Or you can thread your apartment keys with your shoe laces, and tie them in a double knot. Who needs a fancy $15 runner's purse? Pin money to your clothing; spare change can be wrapped in a small plastic bag and pinned on. Safety pins can be used to pin your keys to your shorts, too.

I also recommend always carrying extra toilet paper—and this suggestion alone earns me the undying gratitude of thousands of runners. Try paper towels—they won't disintegrate when wet (from water or perspiration)—and tuck them folded into your shorts or pockets.

Some runners like to wear watches that keep track of their time during a race, or splits, or help in their speed workouts. Some have a beeper that you set for a specific pace to keep you running at a predetermined speed. These may not be accurate, and sometimes upset other runners running with you. Pedometers are another frill: They seldom work, and you can estimate your distance from your average pace. A 30-minute run at a 10-minute pace would cover about three miles, and that's close enough to put in your diary.

One of the setbacks to running in the 1980s has been the use of headphones attached to a radio or small tape deck. These little buggers block out most of the noise around you, and reduce your ability to react quickly to any sudden danger. Also, when you "tune out" you may be less aware of what your body is telling you about exhaustion or injury. You can also become distracted and run into things. Mitch Maslin saw a man running with head-phones and "grooving right along" until he ran into a traffic post in Central Park. He wasn't grooving in the ambulance.

If runners aren't putting things over their ears, they are strapping them on their ankles. Leg or ankle weights cause you to hit the ground with greater force, and may injure you. Hand weights, if you can carry them comfortably, may improve your arm action, but they may also keep you from learning proper running form. In any case, you can build leg and upper body strength with regular weight training (see Chapter 8). You'll get much more benefit by hitting the weights for muscle tone and strength, and hitting the road for running.

If you wear glasses, you may want to buy an elastic band that slides onto the earpiece and adjusts around the back of your head. Don't hold the glasses on too tight; the pressure on the bridge of your nose during a long run may cut you or give you headache. "Croakies" is a one-piece elastic retainer which slides over the bows of your glasses and is very popular with runners.

WEATHER

Heat and Humidity

Heat threatens everyone who exercises, no matter how well conditioned. A stroll on a hot day doubles the body's heat production, and even a day that feels cool when you are walking may be disastrous for the unprepared runner.

There are three types of heat disorders:

- Heat cramps are painful, sudden involuntary contractions of specific muscles or muscle groups.
- Heat exhaustion occurs when the cardiovascular system is overworked. Symptoms include an increased heart rate, palpitations, nausea, vomiting, and, finally, fainting. The skin remains moist and cold as the runner continues to sweat.
- Heat stroke occurs when the heat regulatory system sup-

presses sweating. The skin will be hot and dry, and the runner may develop convulsions, collapse, or go into a coma. Heat stroke is an extreme emergency and can be fatal. It can hit without warning, but most often the symptoms are evident. Warning signs include

—not sweating although very hot

—flushed red skin

—a burning feeling in the legs

—difficulty breathing

—burning in the chest

—headaches

—feeling dizzy and delirious

—inability to think straight or run a straight line

—a chilling sensation

—suddenly finding yourself on the ground.

Treatments are different for heat exhaustion and heat stroke. With heat exhaustion (pale, clammy skin), the immediate treatment is fluid replacements and rest. After heat exhaustion, the next critical condition is heat stroke (skin dry, red, and hot). A common—and wrong—first-aid treatment is to cover the victim with a blanket: This drives up the temperature even higher, and could be a fatal move. Body heat must be reduced immediately. Dr. Gabe Mirkin says: "Forget about giving the victim fluids by mouth. It is worthless. You are interested in cooling him off immediately. His temperature may be 110°F. Place the victim in the shock position: legs up, head down. Evaporation is the key. Pour anything you can on the victim immediately (water, milk, Coke, Gatorade, etc.). Rub his skin vigorously to open up the surface blood vessels. Hose water on him. The best thing to do is rub ice cubes all over his body. Get him out of the sun. Above all, keep pouring something wet on him. If the patient is not lucid and able to communicate with you intelligently, get him to a hospital immediately."

Heat exhaustion can occur as a delayed reaction. I was one of the speakers at the National YMCA's Cardiovascular Health Conference in 1976. Early in the morning, I ran 20 miles in warm, humid weather, then took a quick shower and went off to the lecture without eating or replacing fluids. The room was warm and stuffy and held more than 400 people, mostly doctors, who listened intently as I delivered my slide presentation. Suddenly, I was having trouble remembering my carefully written speech; I began asking the slide projectionist to please focus the slides. The next thing I knew, I was on the floor. I was okay, and finished my lecture with an important added message: Always eat and drink plenty of fluids after a long run.

Dr. David Costill, an exercise physiologist, says a runner faces four physical limitations to performing well in a race on a hot day. First, he or she must understand that a runner can only partially adjust to heat. You cannot run faster in heat, so the next choice is to prepare yourself to be more competitive in the heat than the other runners. Second, when running, your muscles produce eleven times as much internal heat as they do at rest, and thus require more blood. But on a hot day more blood is also demanded by the skin. The result is that the runner involuntarily decreases his or her pace because of reduced circulation to the working muscles. If you ignore these restrictions and continue to push the pace, you face a third limitation: Under any heat stress the skin can only eliminate body heat at a limited rate. If heat is produced by the muscles faster than the heat is removed from the skin, an unfavorable balance results between internal heat gain and heat loss. The fourth physical limitation is the runner's heat tolerance. If the runner forces himself or herself to perform despite a critical imbalance between heat gain and heat loss, his or her body temperature may exceed 105° F., and heat exhaustion may be closely followed by heat stroke.

Air temperature is one factor to consider when running. Humidity is another. The key to body heat removal is sweat evaporation, which accounts for as much as 90 percent of heat removal.

Under very humid conditions little sweat can vaporize; it is difficult for the body to lose heat. An air temperature of 60° F. with 95 percent humidity could be more dangerous than a 90° F. temperature in a dry climate.

A head wind facilitates evaporation, but a tail wind eliminates most of the air flow over the skin and therefore reduces sweat evaporation and heat loss. The position of sun and clouds is also a factor. Direct sunlight at high noon results in a rapid rise of body heat; cloud cover, of course, shields the runner. Running on an indoor track with little ventilation could be a concern on hot days, or even on cool ones if the gym is overheated.

The following guidelines to running in the heat apply to all runners, regardless of level of ability:

1. Avoid the heat. If you don't plan to race in it, don't train in it. Run during the cool of the early morning or late evening. Look for running paths that are shaded, and run on the shady side of the road.

2. Be in shape. An unconditioned runner places an extra burden on his body by running in heat.

3. Acclimate yourself to the heat. Allow 10 to 14 days of slowly progressive training to get used to new heat conditions. Your body needs time to improve the efficiency of its sweating mechanism, and its ability to reduce salt and mineral loss.

If you live in a cool area, you can "heat train" by running three or four times a week for several weeks in double sweats to create an artificial heat stress. Buddy Edelen trained in double sweat suits in cool England and won the 1964 Olympic Trials Marathon at Yonkers, New York, by more than 9 minutes. It was 90° F.

Ron Daws, an Olympic marathoner, suggests leaving on your winter wraps when spring arrives. Training in rubber suits and jogging in steam rooms are also effective. But these methods should only be used by highly conditioned athletes and plenty of liquids should be consumed before, during, and after these "heat training" workouts. A slightly more human method is to train for summertime races by running during the hottest part of the day.

4. Run on cool surfaces. I once ran a 15-kilometer race on an airport runway at Griffis Air Force Base (Rome, New York); the surface temperature of the asphalt was 115° F.! Hot pavement burns your feet, and the heat from the road pushes your temperature up. Try running on the dirt shoulders. Search for dirt or grass surfaces, or even a wet beachfront, on hot days. Pavement sprinkled with water is cooler.

5. Adjust your pace. Start out slowly and run a steady pace in both workouts and races. During workouts, take periodic rest breaks.

6. Keep your body wet. During races, pour water over your head, and allow helpers to spray water on you. Accept sponges offered to you, and douse your body with water. Be warned: I once unexpectedly doused myself with ice water and discovered agony and ecstacy. During workouts, dunk your shirt in water where you find it, and drape it over your head and shoulders. Ice is great on hot days. Put it under your hat, and just let it melt. Or, rub it across the base of your neck and under the arms. Chew it. Carry it in your hands.

7. Drink plenty of liquids before, during, and after your workouts.

8. Dress carefully. In direct sunlight, provide the body with shade. Wear white or other bright colors that reflect the sun. A hat should protect your head and shoulders. It should be white, lightweight, and well ventilated.

Cotton hats with small visors, made for bicyclists, make excellent hats for running in the sun. On hot, sunny days, runners may wear a white painter's cap or terry cloth hat; on milder days I like my cotton-blend painter's or biker's cap to provide some heat retention. There is usually room to tuck an ice cube inside during a summer race for extra cooling.

For those runners with a full head of hair, a cap will only trap heat and make you warmer. Try a terry cloth or cotton hat that you can soak in water or wet with ice to keep you cool.

During the 1976 Boston Marathon, with temperatures approaching 100°F., I wore a white painter's cap with a white handkerchief attached, white shorts, white T-shirt, and I carried a small towel to wet myself with along the course. Often handkerchiefs are pinned at the back of the hat to protect the back of the neck, one of the key areas of heat absorption.

Wear a full T-shirt on sunny, hot days, not a singlet, to protect your shoulders. Cotton is preferred to nylon because it absorbs water and "breathes" more readily. On the other hand, nylon shorts may be preferred to cotton ones, which tend to droop when doused with water. The best shirt may be an old cotton T-shirt with holes cut into it. It should fit loosely and not be tucked in. Some runners cut off the lower half of the shirt to aid air circulation. You may want to eliminate socks and insoles on hot days if you expect to get doused with water; they'll get wet and bunch up on you. Also "Spenco" insoles may make your feet become very hot.

Dehydration may cause a 6 to 10 percent loss of body weight, which can be very dangerous. Respect the elements on hot muggy days, but remember, you can also suffer from heat disorders on cool days, too, if you overdress.

Cold

Too many runners stop running when the weather turns cold. The greatest obstacle to winter running is really just getting out the door. Those who fear the cold, however, cite two reasons: "freezing of the lungs" and frostbite. Freezing of the lungs is a myth. The air we breathe is warmed by the upper air passages; thus cold air never reaches the lungs. Frostbite, however, is a very real danger; it can result in the loss of fingers or toes, and has even caused death. To prevent frostbite, keep covered, keep dry, keep moving, and avoid strong head winds, especially when wet. Frost-bitten skin is cold, pale, and firm-to-hard to touch. The first step in treatment is to warm rapidly without excessive heat. Use water about body temperature. Do not massage or, in the case of toes, walk on the injured area. Do not rub with snow. Take the frost-bitten runner immediately to where he or she can get medical aid.

Then get yourself properly bundled, back on the run. You shouldn't miss the fun and excitement of running in cold weather. Dressing properly is the key. The danger of cold includes the wind, which when combined with air temperature produces some-thing called a windchill factor. The chart from the *Encyclopedia of Sports Medicine* (see page 189) will help you find the true temperature before setting out. Running into the wind creates a lower windchill factor, while running with the wind may speed you along enough to produce a sweat.

Plan your workouts in the cold carefully. Warm up properly indoors (good advice even if you're going to shovel snow), and prepare the body for the sudden change in temperature. When running an out-and-back course, always begin running into the wind. Otherwise, you'll build up a good sweat with the wind at your back, and then turn into the biting wind for the return, which may cause frostbite or at least extreme discomfort. Be sure to remove wet clothing immediately after running to avoid getting chilled. Winter runs, also, should be shorter and slower. But they are very important in building up an endurance base for warmer weather racing, or just maintaining a fit body.

Use your own body heat to protect you from the cold. Even a slow run on a cold day produces enough internal body heat to warm up comfortably. The key is to trap this heat with insulating clothing, yet allow enough of it to escape before overheating.

Runners can overdress, especially on cold but windless days. Several layers of lightweight clothing, rather than one bulky win-ter coat, are best. The layers of clothing trap warm air between them. Also, as you heat up, you can unzip or remove (be careful

WINDCHILL FACTOR CHART

Estimated wind speed (in mph)	Actual Thermometer Reading (°F.)											
	50	40	30	20	10	0	−10	−20	−30	−40	−50	−60
	EQUIVALENT TEMPERATURE (°F.)											
calm	50	40	30	20	10	0	−10	−20	−30	−40	−50	−60
5	48	37	27	16	6	−5	−15	−26	−36	−47	−57	−68
10	40	28	16	4	−9	−24	−33	−46	−58	−70	−83	−95
15	36	22	9	−5	−18	−32	−45	−58	−72	−85	−99	−112
20	32	18	4	−10	−25	−39	−53	−67	−82	−96	−110	−124
25	30	16	0	−15	−29	−44	−59	−74	−88	−104	−118	−133
30	28	13	−2	−18	−33	−48	−63	−79	−94	−109	−125	−140
35	27	11	−4	−20	−35	−51	−67	−82	−98	−113	−129	−145
40	26	10	−6	−21	−37	−53	−69	−85	−100	−116	−132	−148

Green   Yellow   Red

(Wind speeds greater than 40 mph have little additional effect.)

LITTLE DANGER (for properly clothed person). Maximum danger of false sense of security.

INCREASING DANGER Danger from freezing of exposed flesh.

GREAT DANGER

about this) layers, replacing them as you cool off. Shepherd, running in cold Vermont winters, wears (from the skin out): athletic supporter, T-shirt, long underwear—both shirt and pants in temperatures below zero—bulky turtle-neck sweater, warm wool socks, sweat pants and shirt (with turtle neck pulled high), insulated U.S. Army gloves, knitted watch cap, running shoes, and a down vest. His arms are free, and the vest can be unzipped.

If you get too hot, first remove your gloves (fold them together and carry them in one hand, or tuck them into your pocket). Next, loosen your collar, and if you're still hot, pull back your hood. A zippered top is preferred because you can unzip and zip it as you wish, to allow heat loss. Your hat or cap comes off as a last step; this results in a major loss of body heat. Reverse these steps to re-warm yourself as the temperature drops. Be careful not to discard any clothing early in a winter workout, or wait too long to get warm again. Better to be slightly too warm than slightly too cold.

Your feet are sure to be safe and warm as long as you keep running. But if you stop to rest, walk, or chat, be alert. Nylon running shoes will cool off quickly. Wool socks are warmer than cotton; one pair will usually suffice. A plastic bag may be tied around each foot to keep it warm and dry.

The legs usually stay warm with one layer of clothing. If two layers are needed, try tights, long underwear, or old pajamas under sweat pants. Tights or long underwear are preferred by many runners to sweat pants as a single outer layer because they are less bulky. They are covered with shorts, which will help keep your privates toasty.

You might want to try tights made from a thermal cotton, wool, or nylon blend, or from polypropylene. A popular tight is made of Lycra Spandex which hugs the body like a second skin— these even come in bright colors and racing stripes. You may wear shorts over the tights, although some runners now wear tights without shorts, like speed skaters.

Cover the upper body with as many as four layers. The first should be an absorbent and nonirritating T-shirt or other undershirt, preferably polypropylene to keep you dry. The second layer should be a good insulator, like a long-sleeved turtleneck that protects both the arms and the neck. Soft, doubleknit ski turtlenecks are terrific. The high-tech option would be an inner layer of long-sleeved turtleneck polypropylene covered by a T-shirt or sweatshirt. The third layer—if needed—could be a wool, hooded sweatshirt, wool sweater, or the tops of your longjohns. I combine the second and third layer by wearing a hooded thermal sweatshirt with built-in layers—the outer layer (third or fourth) is usually nylon or Gore-Tex. In extremely cold weather, when it's windy, a down vest or a windbreaker of nylon is effective. Nylon won't let sweat evaporate, so be careful you don't overheat. Gore-Tex is effective as an outer layer in cold and wet weather.

Mittens are warmer than gloves, although I still prefer gloves for an unknown reason. Wool gloves are warmest, but if you have a habit of wiping your nose with them as I do, they can be abrasive. Thus my cotton gloves serve double duty as a handkerchief, and no one ever borrows them, either. When buying gloves, be sure that they cover your wrists. When it's really cold, I wear my G.I. woolen inserts covered with leather gloves. They have a pull-cord over the back of the wrist that traps warm air. Extreme cold also brings out my ski gloves, or even a plastic bag wrapped around my gloves. Some runners prefer to wear old socks as gloves. They can be tossed away at no great loss if they become a problem. Fancy new gear includes polypropylene liners and Gore-Tex mitts to keep you dry and warm.

The most important area to keep protected is your head, from which a great amount of heat can escape. A wool ski cap that pulls over the ears does the job in most weather. A single wool band across the ears can replace a hat, or be worn with a hat for double protection of the ears.

To protect your face against stinging cold a pullover ski mask is good. I prefer models with single eye slits that cover the bridge of the nose; I also like a mouth opening because I spit a lot while I run. Still, ski masks without a mouth opening protect the lips and help to warm the inhaled air. Some runners tie a woolen scarf over their mouths for the same reason. Ski goggles will protect the eyes, which sometimes get so cold you can barely see out of them.

When racing into cold winds, I smear Vaseline all over my face to cut down on windburns. In very cold weather be careful about touching your face with water, or even with your snow-covered gloves. The result could be frostbite. Ice forms on beards and moustaches, and according to my bearded teammate Jerry Mahrer, the ice formations on his beard serve as air cushions and actually warm the face. However, ice can be troublesome. Frequently when running in snowbound upstate New York I had to take a warm shower with my hat on until the ice melted so I could remove it.

A good cold-war story comes from Dr. Melvin Herskowitz of Jersey City, New Jersey, who wrote the following tongue-in-cheek account, warning about the danger of frostbite for the inadequately dressed male runner. It appeared in *The New England Journal of Medicine* (January 20, 1977):

To the Editor: A fifty-three-year-old circumcised physician, non smoker, light drinker (one highball before dinner), 1.78 meters tall, weighing 70 kg with no illnesses, performing strenuous physical exercise for many years, began a customary 30-minute jog in a local park at 7 p.m. on December 3, 1976. He wore flare-bottom double-knit polyester trousers, Dacron-cotton boxer-style undershorts, a cotton T-shirt and cotton dress shirt, a light wool sweater, an outer nylon shell jacket over the sweater, gloves, and low-cut Pro Ked sneakers. The nylon shell jacket extended slightly below the belt line.

Local radio weather reports gave the outside air temperature as −8°C, with a severe wind-chill factor.

From 7:00 to 7:25 p.m. the jog was routine. At 7:25 p.m. jogger noted an unpleasant painful burning sensation at the penile tip. From 7:25 to 7:30 p.m. this discomfort became more intense, the pain increasing with each stride as the exercise neared its end. At 7:30 p.m. the jog ended, and the patient returned home.

Physical examination at 7:40 p.m. in his apartment at comfortable room temperature revealed early frostbite of the penis. The glans was frigid, red, tender upon manipulation and anesthetic to light touch. Immediate therapy was begun. The polyester double-knit trousers and the Dacron-cotton undershorts were removed. In a straddled standing position, the patient created a cradle for rapid rewarming by covering the penile tip with one cupped palm. Response was rapid and complete. Symptoms subsided 15 minutes after onset of treatment, and physical findings returned to normal.

Side effects: at 7:50 p.m. the patient's wife returned from a local shopping trip and observed him during the treatment procedure. She saw him standing, legs apart, in the bedroom, nude below the waist, holding the tip of his penis in his right hand, turning the pages of the *New England Journal of Medicine* with his left. Spouse's observation of therapy produced rapid onset of numerous, varied and severe side effects (personal communication).

Pathogenesis of the syndrome was assessed as tissue response to high air velocity at −8°C, penetrating the interstices of polyester double-knit trouser fabric and continuing through anterior opening of Dacron-cotton undershorts, impacting upon receptor site of target organ to produce the changes described.

The patient continues to jog, wearing an athletic supporter and old light cotton warm-up pants used in college cross-country races in 1939. No recurrences are expected.

Apocryphal? I'd hate to be the one to test it.

I know of runners who work out in a windchill temperature of −125° F. Now that's cold enough to frostbite any appendage! The coldest I've ever run in was −19° F. during the 1976 Jersey Shore Marathon. Three months later I was in Boston running when it was 119° F. Mother nature is an extremist.

Snow, Slush, and Ice
Snow affects your running while it falls and when it is on the ground. Running into a driving snow can be troublesome. Keep

your head down, and look only a few feet ahead. Ski goggles may help protect your eyes. Sounds will be muffled, so be careful to run on the edge of the highways, facing traffic. Listen for approaching cars.

Running in newly fallen snow, or during a light storm, can be a joy, with the silence broken only by your breathing. However, running on hard-packed snow is dangerous. You must run defensively, avoiding both the highway and the ruts. In a 1977 marathon at Newton, Massachusetts, Vin Fleming (fifth at Boston in 1977) held a sizeable lead at the halfway mark, but was knocked down (and out) by salt sprayed from a vehicle. Perhaps you should try running on paths away from roads; hard-packed snowmobile trails are excellent, but don't tell the snowmobilers I sent you.

Ripple or waffle soles seem to grip snow and ice best. Galoshes or plastic bags may be slipped over your running shoes to keep feet dry and provide better traction. Be sure to do stretching exercises. Snow running requires a higher knee-lift and pulls harder at the hamstring muscles.

Shorten your stride to prevent injury from slipping and sliding. Different muscles may be used when running in snow or ice, and may tire more quickly. Shepherd runs best when it snows in Vermont. Each step may be a treacherous one, and yet the concentration makes the miles pass. The woods are silent, the animals out, tracks crisscrossing in the powder.

Ice is another thing. Be careful turning corners. If you run smoothly, and hit flat-footed, you won't have a fall. I've never fallen while running on ice, but I have slipped many times walking across the parking lot after a workout.

Rain, Sleet, Hail, and Storm

I ran my first marathon during a tornado warning in Kansas. First it rained, then sleet followed and then hail. Thunder and lightning capped the act. I was beginning to think Mother Nature didn't want me to run the race, but it was exhilarating and I felt like a kid running under the sprinkler.

If you run in the rain, wear a light nylon shell over a T-shirt, and nylon shoes, all of which will dry fast. Take off wet clothing as soon as possible after your run.

If lightning begins, bolt for the nearest shelter. Do not seek shelter under tall trees. Get away from them if that is your only choice, and lie flat on the ground. Don't stand upright in an open area, but lie flat on the ground.

Wind

You can run for an hour into the wind, turn around, and run for an hour in the opposite direction only to find that it, too, is into the wind. I'll never forget the 1975 Skylon Marathon. We ran the first 6 miles full throttle into a strong head wind, expecting to turn around and fly along the Niagara River to the Canadian Horseshoe Falls in record time. When we turned, so did the wind, and we fought 30- to 40-mile-per-hour winds all the way to the finish. The 1975 Boston Marathon was a runner's dream, with 30- to 45-mile-per-hour tail winds that pushed runners to records they haven't come close to since.

A head wind of 10 miles per hour will slow your forward progress by five percent, while a 10-mile-per-hour tail wind will push you along at about three percent faster time. A head wind will cool you on a hot day or chill you on a cold one. A tail wind can substantially increase your heat stress. Dr. Peter Cavanagh, associate professor of biomechanics at Penn State University, told a clinic before the 1976 White Rock Marathon in Dallas that as much as 8 percent of a runner's total expenditure of energy goes into overcoming wind, and that running twice as fast results in a wind resistance increase of four times. A 10-mile-per-hour wind requires an 8 percent energy increase, while a 25-mile-per-hour wind requires a 44 percent energy increase.

When running into a head wind, lean into it to decrease wind resistance. If possible duck in behind another runner or group of runners, and let them act as a windbreak for you. If you're racing, take advantage of a tail wind, and really fly.

OBSTACLES: MAN-MADE AND NATURAL

Night

Running at night requires precautions. Try to work out on well-lighted roads; a business district may be best. If you must run on dimly lit streets or in the country, carry a flashlight, and wear white, reflective clothing. Another trick is to tape bicycle reflector tape to your clothes and shoes; wear one of the small, white/red arm bicycle flashlights; wear a bright orange reflector vest. There are also reflector headbands, leg bands, sashes, gloves, and hats. Be defensive in the dark. You may also want to purchase a pair of reflectorized running shoes if you will be doing a lot of night running.

Air Pollution

A lot of runners want to know whether or not they should run in polluted cities. The answer is mixed. Contaminants include sulfur dioxide, particulate matter (soot), various oxidants which irritate the eyes, and carbon monoxide. Studies by architects in New York City, and by doctors in several cities in California, show that the worst place to run is along a highway or busy city street, but the good news is that pollutants from cars dissipate quickly beyond fifty feet from roadways. If you run along a roadway, keep your distance!

Large cities publish a daily "air pollution index." Too often it reads "Air Quality: Unacceptable." Actually, city air is getting better on the average. Even so, runners with a medical history of lung or heart problems should not run during air-pollution warnings.

But what about the rest of us? Dr. George Sheehan, the running cardiologist, states, "People who worry more about air pollution than about attending to their physical condition are deluding themselves. They would feel much better running in the city and becoming fit than they would sitting around doing nothing in the pure air of the country."

If you're a country dweller and are planning to race in a city, it is wise to spend several days acclimating yourself. Shepherd, the Vermont runner, finds it takes two workouts in New York City before he can run there without thinking his arms and legs have turned to concrete.

Some runners wear filtered masks to warm and moisten the air, or to protect them against air pollution and pollen. These may be used in any weather, but usually in the spring to fall. One type is the "Micropore Pollen Filter Mask" manufactured by the 3 M Company.

Hills

Without hills, we wouldn't appreciate the flat stretches. Any workout, like almost any race, should include uphill and downhill runs. Only beginner runners, especially if overweight, should stay on level ground, because the extra work of carrying the body up a hill places severe stress on the cardiovascular system and the legs.

Many runners do hill training at a vigorous pace because it is really speed work in disguise, and it increases your anaerobic capacity and leg strength. Downhill work will improve your stride, although fast downhill running should be saved for races since it puts a severe burden on your legs and back.

Some people actually enjoy hill running. I often run from my parents' home in Dansville, New York, to my grandparents' home in South Dansville—an 8-mile run from a valley to a hilltop where the view is spectacular. After hills there is the challenge of running mountains. Along with several hundred others I ran the 1976 Mount Washington (New Hampshire) Race to the top of the East's highest peak, 6,288 feet above sea level. The temperature was 90°F. at the bottom, and 52°F. at the top, with high winds above the tree line. It was torture all the way, and at times the grade was enough to make walking faster than running, but at the top we could extol the view and look down on the little red barn where we had started.

Exercise physiologists have proven on treadmills what hill runners have known all along. There is a large net energy loss when running hills compared to running flat or rolling countryside. There are ways to save some of that energy, to beat the hill before it beats you. I advise beginners on hills to run as far as they can comfortably and then alternate walking and running. But keep going. Pick a spot 50 yards ahead and run to it, then another goal and run to that. Shepherd runs the Vermont hills from farmhouse to farmhouse.

Also, follow this hill-running technique. As you approach the hill, shift into a lower gear and maintain a steady rate of effort and rhythm going up. Pick up the pace near the top, and maintain a steady rhythm going down. Use the hill to build momentum as you head into the flat beyond.

Uphill Going up the hill, pump your arms parallel to the plane of motion in an exaggerated fashion. Use them! Don't pump them across the body, but rather downward, like a cross-country skier. Your stride should be short, knees raised high. For short, steep hills you should get up on your toes, springing forward. You should lean slightly forward, back straight, hips in, chest forward. The head should be kept up. Avoid clenching the fists and tensing the upper body. Concentrate on pumping, running relaxed with a smooth, powerful, and even rhythm.

Downhill The arms should be kept low. The body should be tilted forward so that it is perpendicular to the slope of the hill. Now gravity will assist you as you fall forward down the hillside. Stretch out your stride, but don't overstride. Keep your stride close to the ground. Footstrike should be normal, but on steep downhills you should try to hit lightly, first on the ball then on the heel.

The key to downhill running is control. If you go too fast, you'll burn excess energy and risk falling, or straining the body. If you go too slow, consciously leaning back and "braking" as many beginners do, you'll place a severe strain on the legs and lose time in races. Running up or downhill it's important to hold yourself together, to stay relaxed while maintaining control of your movement.

Altitude
Beyond 3,000 feet above sea level, you will notice altitude changes as you run. If you visit a high-altitude area (Denver, Colorado, for example) you should spend two to four weeks adjusting to the change. If you're visiting for a short while, and want to run, do so slowly and at a shorter distance. The casualties at the 1968 Olympics, held at high altitude in Mexico City, demonstrated the dangers of all-out exercise under these conditions without preparation. Many world-class runners purposely train at high altitudes, although they race at lower ones, to improve their ability to transport oxygen.

Automobiles
Most of us have to run on roads, where we are second-class occupants. The auto owns the road—at least their drivers think so. I've had cars swerve at me, and drivers swing at me with their hands—and even with a car door. But I've also seen runners who thoughtlessly run in traffic lanes, or hit the road as though *they* own it. One of our runners, deep in meditation, ran smack into the side of a car—twice.

Here are some rules for road running:
- Always be defensive and expect the worst.
- Stay off high-speed roadways.

- Run on the shoulder of the road, or a sidewalk. Even then be on the alert. Three of our club's runners were knocked out of action one month prior to the 1977 New York Marathon when a drunk driver crashed into them as they were running on a sidewalk.
- On narrow, country roads, run in the center of the road. You can see cars easily, and they can see you. *Listen* for cars all the time. Move into the bushes quickly if you have to.
- Run facing traffic on paved roads.
- Be alert when approaching blind curves, and on hills.
- Run in an area you know, over a regular route. Eventually, you will develop a following of admirers, including dogs, who will watch for you, wave (or bark), and enjoy this craziness that brings you by their homes regularly in all kinds of weather.

Hecklers

They will test your patience. "Hut, two, three, four" and "faster, faster" will compete with "Want a ride?" and "Look at those legs!" Women running alone will hear much worse—mostly from men being boys. Kitty Lance would hear things like "If I catch you, can I keep you?" from fellow runners. One reply: "Only after fifteen miles." The witty rebuttal is one good approach. For "Where did you leave your pants?" I've enjoyed replying, "With your girlfriend. She likes skinny lovers!" However, if your reply is nasty, be sure that you can up the juice a little to outdistance angered hecklers. Always remember that if your hecklers are in cars, you can reverse directions, go up a path, or down a one-way street. If it gets bad, head for a well-lighted home.

Sometimes kids run out and mimick my actions. I invite them to join me, and mention that I'm running 20 miles. Before long, they drop out. But one persistent runner was a drunk who started chasing a group of us when we passed an outdoor party. His friends thought he was hilarious, and so did he. Amazingly, he ran with us for 2 miles before he stopped to vomit.

Dogs

I've stepped on snakes in Vietnam, tripped over rats along the Hudson River, been stung by bees, swallowed bugs, and was barely missed by a bear in Yosemite Park. But dogs can be the worst.

Some wary runners plan routes to avoid passing the houses of certain dogs, and others, in their anger at being chased and snapped at, have almost fulfilled that great journalistic reversal: man bites dog.

Not all dogs are interested in runners, but any dog that comes out to check on you as you run is a potential danger. Never take your eyes off him, especially as you pass by. Dogs bite from behind. Shepherd was jogging in Riverside Park when he passed two well-dressed ladies talking and letting their little poodles sniff and scratch. Just as he got by, Shepherd heard the growl and snap. One poodle had lunged at him, and missed only because it was on a leash. The owner said, "My, my, Tootsie, it's only a silly man."

Always talk to dogs in a soft, but firm voice. Say things like "good doggie" over and over (most owners address their dogs in this tone), and tell him to "stay home, stay, stay."

Try to anticipate a dog's intentions. If the tail is erect, ears straight up, lips curled open, hair raised on the back of its neck, he means business.

If you find yourself confronted with such a dog there are four techniques you can use to deal with it:

1. You can run. This works only if you are challenged by a Dachshund, or a dog on a leash (do not rely on a rope). If you run, a dog will sense your fear, and chase you. Or, imitate the fleet Masai of East Africa, who know that if they encounter a lion they must face him and stand still. To run is to die.

2. You can stop, and try to make friends. This, too, contains risk. Some dogs are trained guard dogs. That hand offered for a

sniff will appear to be a threat. If this tactic doesn't work, at least your arm gets the bite, not your legs, and you can still run.

3. You can threaten the dog. Shouting or growling—and some runners are excellent growlers—sometimes works. Often, dogs will retreat if you bend down and pick up a stone. (Be sure not to let the dog come too close before you bend down; in that position, you are vulnerable to a fatal bite.) If you grab a stone, and the dog halts, *slowly* raise your arm to throw it. He'll get the message, and retreat. But if he doesn't, begin to back off slowly, always facing the dog. Put some distance between you and the dog. To reinforce the threat of the stone, always throw it. Don't strike the dog, but the ground near him. He may even stop threatening you altogether.

4. Carry a stick or (better) a can of "Halt" with you. Some runners carry small water pistols with a half-and-half mixture of ammonia and water. That's effective, although the water pistols sometimes leak. Also, one time I tried out my trusty dog spray, but blew it into a strong head wind. I cried all the way home; the dog ran off laughing.

As a last resort, you might try my father's trick. He was out for his nightly walk, when a dog that had been bothering him for weeks came up. My father knelt down quietly, and when the mutt came within range, he punched him in the nose. He hasn't been bothered since.

Be especially wary of any dog whose owner loudly proclaims, "Oh, he won't bite." He will, you can be sure. Also, if you are bitten, remember what the dog looked like, and preferably where it lived. This will save you from going through the extremely painful and prolonged rabies injections.

Owners of dogs can be nuts. When two large German shepherds attacked and bit me, the owner said I had provoked the attack by throwing rocks at his dogs as they slept innocently on the front porch. Jack Cohen, a New York Road Runner, ran a favorite course in upstate New York where he was continually harassed by the same dog. He began calling the owner in advance so she could tie up the dog until he had passed. But when ole poochie howled, the lady got tired of tying him up. One day she suggested that Jack change his route, "After all," she told him, "the dog was here before you were."

15 ANALYZING RUNNING SHOES: IF THE SHOE FITS . . .

Each of your running shoes strikes the ground about 800 times per mile. If you run 10 miles a week, then each shoe strikes the ground more than 400,000 times a year. Marathon runners may find each of their shoes pounding into pavement, grass, and dirt as much as 3,000,000 times a year. Obviously, we should be concerned about the quality of these running shoes.

Inside our shoes are two of the most abused parts of the human anatomy: our feet. They absorb the initial impact of running and pass it upward to the ankles, legs, knees, hips, back, neck, and head. Most people have weak feet, which when pounded on the earth thousands of times a week, incur a wide range of injuries.

Dr. George Sheehan states in the *Encyclopedia of Athletic Medicine*: "The worst thing that ever happened to feet was shoes." Or perhaps the second worst, after concrete. These two products of urban civilization have finally conquered the human foot, which, in its primitive state, crossed continents, pursued wild game, and danced for days on end.

It's not quite that bad, for with the running revolution has also come a running-shoe revolution. When I recall the flimsy items my cross-country coach in college told me were running shoes, I shudder—and my feet ache.

Each fall, the major running magazines feature special issues that analyze all the top running shoes. These issues are valuable to you as a runner: There are hundreds of quality running shoes available, and companies are making shoes to fit the specific needs of each runner. Runners need a manual to sort out the good from the bad. We won't analyze brands of shoes in this chapter because the styles, prices, and even the manufacturers are changing too rapidly. Competition is intense between shoe companies, and the quality is improving constantly.

Running shoes have come a long way since the Dassler brothers of West Germany first took advantage of the growing market for good running shoes. Back then, profit led to greed, and the brothers fought. Adi formed one company (Adidas) and Rudi another (Puma). For years they dominated the American market until the Japanese (Tiger) introduced nylon uppers. Another dispute arose, and the Tiger people in the United States split from the parent company and formed Nike, manufactured in the United States. The big two became the big four: Adidas, Puma, Tiger, and Nike. For now, Nike and Adidas are the big sellers, but several American companies including Brooks, Converse, Etonic, New Balance, and Saucony also produce popular, quality shoes. The competition is good. Companies sponsor races and constantly seek to develop better running shoes.

One of the major innovations in running shoes since we first wrote this *Handbook* has been the increasing specialization. Ten years ago, runners had just two choices of shoe: training and racing. Today, a runner may select a shoe to fit his or her special characteristics. Shoes are made for light or heavy runners, heel strikers and toe strikers; for runners with high arches, flat feet, two feet of different sizes, extremely narrow feet; or runners with injuries; or runners who go in ice or snow, run short or long distances, cross-country or trails.

Further, almost every shoe manufacturer offers a model for runners seeking shock absorption, motion control, and flexibility. Some companies even customize their running shoes by offering insoles with removable plugs so a runner can adjust the shoe's firmness, or by in-store adjustments to vary the shoe's width. Companies like Nike and New Balance helpfully publish charts, which match type of runner with type of shoe.

The following guidelines for buying running shoes come from personal experience and the advice of three prominent advisors: podiatrists Dr. Richard Schuster and Dr. Murray Weisenfeld, and Mitch Maslin, who started in my beginner runner class in 1976. He now serves as an instructor for our New York Road Runners Club beginner classes and is owner/manager of New York City's Athletic Attic store.

WHAT TO LOOK FOR IN A RUNNING SHOE

A good running shoe protects the foot from the ground, supports the foot structure, provides traction, cushions the runner from shock at footstrike, and helps balance various foot deformities. In sum, it provides the runner with comfort and minimizes the chances for injury. According to Maslin: "The key factors are not how the shoe looks or how much it costs, but rather that it provides good cushioning, a firm and supportive heel counter to provide stability, a good arch support, adequate flexibility, and—if possible—is durable. And of course, it must fit your foot properly and feel comfortable."

The purchase of a good pair of running shoes is the one critical investment a runner must make. Does it fit right? Can I afford it? Does it give adequate cushioning and support? How heavy should it be? Behind most veteran runners you will find a whole closetful of discarded running shoes.

Not all models of a brand fit all feet. Take your time buying running shoes, and wear socks that you will use with the new shoes. Obvious as it seems, try on the shoes in the store before you buy them. Shepherd was buying running shoes at a very busy athletic store in downtown New York City when a furious customer stomped into the showroom and demanded to return a pair of running shoes.

"Why?" asked an innocent clerk.

"Because they don't fit," replied the irate customer.

"Did you try them on before you left here?" the clerk inquired.

"Hell, no," said the buyer. "I didn't have time."

They didn't take back the shoes, either.

The shoe you buy—and try on—should fit your needs and requirements.

HOW TO CHOOSE YOUR RUNNING SHOES: A GUIDELINE FOR BEGINNER BUYERS

There are six basic steps to follow when buying running shoes.

1. Choose a store that specializes in running shoes. A good local store will—or should—have experienced salespeople who are also runners, and who know about all the latest shoes. They should also hear about a shoe's performance from other runners. While you may order shoes through the mail, you may not get as good a fit as you will in a local store, nor will you get help if you have a problem with the shoe. Local runner/salespeople may also know of races, or coaches and fitness programs that meet your ability level.

2. Give your running and running-shoe history and running goals to the salesperson. Bring your old running shoes to the store. The salesperson may be able to tell from them what kind of new shoe will be best for you. Tell the salesperson how many miles you run a week, how often you run, how far you run, on what surface, and what your immediate running goals are. You should also describe any tendency toward injuries. Note: Don't tell the salesperson that you want the same shoe that superstar Alberto Salazar wears, or one that your runner-neighbor said is the best shoe. Also, don't pick a shoe because of the color, brand name, endorsements, or a magazine's enthusiasm. Buy a running shoe because it fits, meets your needs, and feels good.

3. Determine the proper shoe size. If you aren't sure of your size, have the salesperson measure your foot for length and width.

Your street shoe and running shoe size are often not the same; even your running shoe size may change from one brand to another. Shepherd, for example, wears a size 9 in Adidas and a size 10 in New Balance. If you wear orthotics or special arch supports, bring them with you and insert them into each pair of shoes you try on. (Remember to take the supports home with you!)

Most shoes are available in men's sizes 6–14, women's sizes 5–10. The width of the shoe varies from one manufacturer to another, and even from style to style by the same manufacturer. Few running shoes come in various widths; most simply range from narrow to average to slightly wide. New Balance, however, makes women's widths AA–D and men's B–EEEE.

Some women prefer a man's shoe because they feel more comfortable with the fit. In the past, however, women had to select from men's sizes. Only since 1980 have women had the same selection in running shoes as men. Now, almost all top-of-the-line shoe styles are available in both men's and women's sizes. Both women's and men's shoes are made from the same materials and constructed alike. The only difference is that women's shoes are constructed on a different last; the shape of the shoe reflects the difference between men's and women's feet. (A woman's heel is narrower in relation to the rest of her foot; this area gets special consideration from shoe manufacturers.)

4. Narrow your selection. Before entering the store, investigate the types of shoes you might wish to buy. Then invest in the best shoe you can find, and afford. Too many runners start out in cheap, poorly constructed shoes, get injured, and quit running. Imitation running shoes look like running shoes, feel like running shoes in the store, and act like running shoes—until you run in them. They don't have the same materials and construction.

Brand-name companies invest a lot of money in research on the mechanics of running. Nike, for example, operates a multi-million dollar, computerized research lab in Exeter, New Hampshire. While you may not need, or want, the most expensive running shoe, you shouldn't buy the cheapest. You can find a reasonably priced shoe that fits your needs—and your feet—as a beginner. Tell the salesperson your budget. Remember, your feet are important, and shoes are your only major investment on the road to fitness.

Ask the salesperson to select two to four pairs of running shoes in or close to your budget. Get various brands and styles. Put on your running socks, and try each shoe on.

5. Make sure that the shoe fits.

Length Choose a pair of shoes that fit both feet while you are standing. Shoe sizes vary from brand to brand, so don't be concerned if the shoe fits and the size differs from your street shoes. Also, try on two or three different pairs of the same size and brand shoe unless you feel very comfortable with the shoe. One will fit better than the others. Shoes are individually made and variations are not unusual; you may find a stitch seam, for example, in a sensitive place (like across a toe) in one shoe but not another.

Proper length will allow sufficient room to move your toes freely. Allow room for expansion; feet swell as you run. Shoes that are too tight in the toe box may cause cramping of the toes, black toenails, or blisters. Shoes that are too long may cause sliding that creates blisters, or even curling of the toes, which can lead to lower back problems. Generally, there should be about a thumbnail's width between your longest toe (not necessarily the big toe) and the end of the shoe. When in doubt about which shoe size to get, it is usually advisable to go with the larger size—and always fit for the larger foot.

Width The width should be snug, but not so much so that your foot bulges over the midsole material. A too-narrow shoe may not give you proper support. A shoe too tight in width may cause your feet to numb and cramp due to lack of circulation. If the shoe is too loose, your foot may slide, and the lack of support may lead to blisters or leg problems.

Be sure that the heel cup—the cup under the foot around the heel—fits firmly but not too tightly. If it is too loose or too tight, it may cause blisters, or Achilles tendinitis.

Try on your new shoes. Ask if you can run in them on a non-carpeted surface, preferably outside on the concrete sidewalk. Check for movement of the foot in the shoe, support, comfort, cushion, flexibility.

Heel Counter   The heel counter is the firm wrapping around the back of the shoe. It stabilizes the heel. A rigid heel counter that covers the entire heel is desirable. This is generally made from hard cardboard or plastic, covered with suede or pigskin or other material.

Squeeze the heel counter to see if it is firm and supportive. With your foot in the shoe, seat your heel firmly in the heel counter and try to move as in walking. (Be sure the shoes are laced.) Some movement is expected, but avoid excessive movement. Remember that as you break in the shoe, it will adapt to your foot.

Arch Support   In trying on your first running shoes, you will notice the support under your arches. Usually, your street shoes have no arch support at all. A good quality running shoe will provide adequate arch support. Many quality shoes now come with removable innersoles which provide support. Make sure you are comfortable with them.

Last   The shape of the last used to construct the shoe will affect the fit. A curved last turns inward from the heel to the toes, and conforms to the general foot shape of approximately 60 percent of the population. It is preferred by people with a curved foot shape, and runners who require more support of the outer portion of the foot, such as those with high-arched, rigid feet that tend to supinate. This shoe also generally feels better to those running a fast pace; most racing shoes have curved lasts.

A straight last has little or no curve from heel to toe, and provides greater support under the medial arch. A straight last is best for runners with a straighter foot shape and runners who require extra support of the inner portion of the foot—such as those with low arches or who tend to pronate excessively.

6. Hold in your hand the pair of shoes you select. Here is a list of things you may want to check.

Quality Control   Inspect your shoes closely and carefully. Check for poor construction. Place the shoe on a flat surface, such as a countertop. Look at the heel cup to see if it is perpendicular to the sole of the shoe. Look for loose threads. Feel the seams inside the shoe to make sure they are uniform, smooth, and well-stitched. Give the tongue a slight tug; some aren't stitched well, and pull off. Hold the sole in your hand, and pull on the upper part of the shoe with your other hand to see if it separates from the sole.

Shoe Weight   With the shoe in your hands, feel its weight. The beginner runner, attempting to increase mileage, should buy a well-cushioned, supportive shoe that may weigh a little more than the advanced runner's shoes. Concern yourself with protection. Most shoes are made from lightweight materials anyway, and the difference in weight will not translate into a difference in speed or time for the average runner.

Cushioning   A well-cushioned shoe will minimize road shock to your legs, and is recommended for beginner runners. Cushioning comes from three sources:

the outersole, which wears out from contact with the road;
the insoles, which come with the shoe or can be purchased separately to increase cushioning;
the midsole, between the other two, which provides additional protection.

There are several types of midsole materials, each with its own feature. Rubber compounds are heavier than other materials, but provide excellent cushioning and hold their shape and resiliency longer. EVA (ethyl vinyl acetate) is a synthetic foam widely used for midsoles; it is light, bouncy, and impact resistant. The air cushion is a third midsole form, pioneered by Nike, with channels of pressurized gas in polyurethane foam which provide spring and cushioning. Some runners, however, have had problems with excessive motion in an air shoe. Finally, the Air Wedge, a combination of EVA and air cushioning, improves the stability of the air shoe while providing air cushioning from the heel to midfoot.

Your running shoe should also include a wedge, which is a ⅜-to-¾-inch cushion under the heel, tapering to the midfoot. It provides extra shock protection under the heel, where beginner runners' feet strike the ground first, and heel lift to prevent strain of the Achilles tendon and calf muscles.

Soles   The outer sole must stand up to the friction of the road. The hardness and durability of a shoe range from soft and light (such as Vibram), to hard and durable (such as the Goodyear Indy 500 compound). The choice is softness versus durability. The best choice is probably a compromise.

There are many types of sole designs to choose, from waffle studs to flat rubber soles. Traction is usually not a consideration, unless you run a lot in mud, ice, or snow. Select an outer sole that feels best to your feet, and does what you want it to do. Waffle-type soles provide the best traction in snow—like snow tires. (Note: Don't automatically resole your running shoes; when the outer sole wears, check the midsole to see if it is losing cushion, and check to see if the heel counter is straight.)

Flexibility   Bend your running shoe. Keep in mind that as you break in the new shoes, their flexibility will increase. The shoe may feel stiff when new, but it should flex about 30 to 35 degrees as you push off your toes—about the same flex as your foot. If the shoe is not flexible under the ball of your foot, then the front and back of your leg may get stressed, with resulting injury to your Achilles tendon, calf or shin muscles.

A balance should be sought between flexibility and cushioning under the ball of your foot. Most quality running shoes are flexible, although you may want to buy a pair that seems less flexible than others in the store. Consult the salesperson for any special need of this kind.

Uppers   Most shoes are either nylon, nylon mesh, or a combination. Each is lightweight, soft, and dries fast, which minimizes blisters. The choice is yours.

Lacing   While the type of upper in a running shoe leaves little room for mistakes—don't choose leather—lacing systems do vary and should be checked. Lacing secures the shoe against the foot. Make sure that the tongue is well-padded, and that the lacing system (when tightly laced against your foot) does not cause a rubbing spot or constrict your feet too much.

There are three types of lacing available: conventional, with shoestrings through eyelets; variable width, with staggered eyelets to adjust width; and speed, with plastic rings. Speed laces allow you to lace up quicker, or unlace and open the shoe easier. The variable lacing allows runners with different width feet to adjust the lacing through the eyelets; this allows a runner like me to compensate for the fact that one foot is bigger than the other.

Inner Sock Liners   Sock liners cover the inside of the shoe to minimize blisters, absorb moisture, provide additional cushioning, and provide support. Many shoes come with removable sock liners. These may be a lightweight foam that will mold to the pressure-pattern of your foot for a comfortable, custom fit. Or, as in the Spenco liner, the liner may be inserted by the runner to provide cushioning and reduce friction (and thus blisters). The liner may also be a removable wedge or arch support—either a prescription or over-the-counter orthotic, that provides control against excessive motion.

Most sock liners can be purchased separately, so you can replace them when they wear out.

In sum, look for running shoes that meet your special needs. For example, heavy runners need more cushioning; forefoot strikers (who hit the ground on the balls of their feet) need more cushioning in the forefoot of the shoe. A good running shoe should be flexible, with good cushioning material under the heel and good arch support.

BREAKING IN SHOES

Breaking in your running shoes is easy. The shoes are flexible, and the nylon uppers are very soft. In general follow these steps:

- Walk around the house in your new shoes for a few days. If you discover a problem with the shoes, take them back to the store.
- Walk outside in the shoes for a few days.
- Run with them only for short runs for one week.
- Gradually switch from your old shoes to your new ones for your long runs. (Hold on to your old shoes; you may want them for running in snow or rain.)

CARE AND REPAIR OF YOUR RUNNING SHOES

Cut away any minor rough spots inside the shoe, particularly at the toe and tongue areas. Stitching flaws or tears can be repaired with dental floss and a needle. Vaseline any leather area inside to decrease friction and soften the leather.

Try to avoid getting your running shoes wet. Use your old pair for wet weather. If your shoes do get soaked, Shepherd, who lives in the snow and ice of Vermont, suggests pulling open the tongue of the shoe and stuffing in newspaper balls to dry the shoe out. Remove the innersoles so they dry faster. Avoid exposing them to heat like that from woodstoves, radiators, or hair dryers; let the shoes dry naturally. (Also, avoid leaving your shoes in the hot sun all day, or in the trunk of a car; the shoes can come unglued and warp.) Carl Eilenberg, president of the Roman Runners and now mayor of Rome, New York, warns that shoes get stiff after sitting overnight following a run in rain or wet snow, and should be flexed before you put them on.

With care, you can add miles to your shoes. Depending on your weight, the running surface, style of running, or type of sole, your range as a beginner runner might be 400–600 miles. If you run 15 miles a week or less, your shoes should last a year—if the heel counter and midsole hold up.

Beware of run-down shoes. A major cause of injuries is worn-down heels that allow the foot to hit the road at an unnatural angle. Normally, the sole under the ball of the foot and at the outside edge of the heel will wear down first if you are using the proper footstrike pattern. Some world-class runners wear out the toes from their powerful drive at push-off.

Look for a breakdown in the heel counter, your foot sagging off the last, excessive heel or ball wear. When in doubt, replace the shoe. Shoes with a colored "heel wedge" have a built in safety system to let you know it's time to get new shoes or repair the heel. When the inner coloring starts to show through the black sole, it's not safe to continue using the shoes. The "uppers" often outlast the soles. If you wish to resole or reheel your shoes to save money or to maintain the "broken in" comfort of miles of running, you have several options.

1. Various substances like "Shoe Goo," "Sole Saver," "Liqui-Sole," and "Sole Patch" come in a tube and can be spread over the heel. They need to be applied frequently, and wear down quickly, but a thin, even layer of any of these materials is effective in preventing the wearing of the heel of the shoe. They can be applied before the sole shows signs of wear.

2. Many shoe repair people will reheel your running shoes for a reasonable price. They simply cut out the worn part and replace it. Be sure that the new heels aren't too hard or too soft. A friend once told a cobbler to put an extra-hard rubber heel on his running shoes so that they would last longer. The result was a stress fracture because the shoe didn't absorb enough shock.

3. Shoes can also be rebuilt. Many companies will rebuild any make or model shoe for about half the cost of a new pair. They will put in a new sole—but probably not the same, since many soles are patented—and repair various tears and stitching, even replace the shoe laces. It's great not breaking in new shoes. I know runners who get three or four "lives" out of their "uppers." Note: Be sure that the shoe remains mechanically correct.

Make sure that the heel counter and midsole are still good.

CIVILIAN SHOES

"Fashionable Shoes" are almost worse than cigarettes, cars, and concrete. Women and men who wear platform shoes, high heels, or other faddish styles place great strain on their legs and shorten their Achilles tendons. Beware of walking around in thin-soled shoes afer spending lots of time in thick-soled running shoes. Many men and women now wear running shoes to and from work, and change into more acceptable, less supportive "work" shoes.

I almost always wear running shoes, or soft suede shoes with thick, well-cushioned, flat soles. This type of shoe helps my run-weary legs make it through the day at the office. Dr. Kraus even has running shoes dyed black and wears them with comfort at work.

Various shoes, like the Earth Shoe, with the heel lower than the toe, are advertised as helpful for runners because they correct defects that cause back pain, and stretch the backs of the legs. These shoes have indeed been helpful to some runners, but harmful to others.

The best shoe to wear when you aren't running may, in fact, be no shoe at all. You should walk barefoot on grass or at the beach, and as much as possible elsewhere.

"SHOE STUFFINGS"

Insoles

Running shoes now come with various types of insoles. These insoles are removable, and can be replaced by other inserts like orthotics, or discarded if you wish. In most cases, the insole should be removed if you wear custom-made orthotics. The insoles that come with most running shoes are usually constructed of plastic foam which molds to the shape of your foot. It may also provide some protection against over-pronation. Check with your podiatrist or shoe salesperson for advice about shoes and types of insoles that may help prevent injury and increase comfort.

Replaceable Insoles

Flat insoles are designed to absorb moisture, reduce blisters, and absorb shock. They may also adjust your shoe size if the shoes are too big. They are not designed to support or control your foot. Insoles can be purchased at most drug stores or running shops. Insertable insoles are simply put in the bed of your shoes, either over or in place of the insoles that came with the shoes. They also may be worn under orthotics to increase cushioning.

Dr. Scholl's Pro Comfort Sports Cushions are perforated to allow more air circulation and shock absorbtion. Spenco insoles are treated chemically to prevent blisters and calluses and provide cushioning. Sorbothane insoles are used only to absorb maximum shock. But these insoles are heavy (three ounces each), and you might want to wear them only for warding off impact to an injured area. Sorbothane also makes a heel pad, which is shorter and lighter and supplies a full cushion that is 40 percent lighter—but doesn't absorb as much shock—as the original heavier model. You might also wear the full-length Sorbothane insole for distance training, and replace them with lighter insoles, or remove them completely, for speed work and races.

Whatever you do, don't overstuff your running shoes. You may lose support at the heel, or cause your toes to jam.

Heel Lifts and Heel Cups

A heel lift may help you continue training even when troubled by shin splints, Achilles tendinitis, or calf soreness. By raising the heel of the running shoe, you are reducing the strain on the Achilles tendon and the lower leg muscles, thus minimizing the discomfort and helping prevent further strain. A "lift" of ¼ to ¾ inches will help absorb impact shock and spread your weight over a greater area of the heel. This may ease discomfort from heel bruises or spurs.

Heel lifts or pads may be purchased over-the-counter, or you can cut them out of surgical felt or sponge rubber powder puff pads. Make sure that the lift isn't so high that your foot no longer fits the shoe. Wear the lifts in both shoes, or you may cause an injury due to imbalance. Continue wearing the lifts several days after the problem subsides. Build the lifts to a height that gives relief, and then gradually reduce the lift until you no longer need it.

Heel lifts may ease your discomfort and keep you out of a doctor's office. Heel cups are also available in drug and running stores. These devices control movement of the heel, and distribute weight over a greater surface, thereby relieving pain.

Commercial Orthotics

There are over-the-counter inserts made from material like plastic or leather. They are contoured to the shape of the average foot, and modified to reduce excessive pronation. Runners thinking they may need professionally fitted orthotics may wish to use one of these devices first. They may help with mild pronation problems, or cushioning. Shepherd, for example, developed a slight knee problem, and acting on my free advice he purchased a pair of over-the-counter orthotics, wore them until the pain went away, tossed them in the back of his closet, and never needed them again.

If your running pain lessens using commercial orthotics, but doesn't go away, or if your symptoms return with an increase in mileage, you may wish to consult a sports podiatrist to see if you need custom-made orthotics. Commercial orthotics are sold by shoe size, and may produce results if your foot size is close to the model used. But many runners have slight differences in arch height, leg length, and range of motion not adequately corrected by these standard devices.

Prescription Orthotics

Most runners find comfort wearing a quality, commercial orthotic, but others need custom-made supports, designed by a podiatrist. These inserts are fashioned from a plaster mold of your foot, and are corrected to adjust to structural weaknesses of your foot. The range of problems is large: your heel may roll the wrong way; the front of your foot may need supporting in its natural position; your arch may need support; you may have a leg-length discrepancy.

Orthotics are not a panacea for all running pain or injury. Yet a survey of more than 1,500 runners at the 1980 New York Marathon revealed that 23 percent wore orthotics. This does not mean that 23 percent of all runners need orthotics, although many runners who increase their mileage develop problems that may be helped by wearing orthotics. Dr. Richard Schuster advises those who insist on orthotics despite the fact that they have no injury or symptoms: "Don't fix it if it works."

Orthotics are over-prescribed. Some injured runners demand them; some doctors will try anything to satisfy demanding runner/patients. If the podiatrist doesn't find any imbalance or other malfunction, there is no reason to prescribe orthotics. Dr. Schuster, a pioneer in the development of these devices for runners, warns: "Not all runners need them. Unless there are severe imbalances, or pain related to imbalances, the indiscriminate use of orthotic foot devices could stir up a hornets' nest" of other problems.

Orthotics, necessary or not, can indeed cause problems. They are difficult to mold and may not fit properly. They may impair a runner's flexibility. They often need adjusting, but runners don't have them changed; other runners don't properly break them in. Yet, a study by Dr. James Eggold, a Long Beach, California, podiatrist, points out that 40 percent of 146 runners reported total relief from symptoms after treatment with orthotics.

The most common orthotic is a flexible leather model with a cork-like bottom that can easily be adjusted by sanding off or building up areas. Rigid supports made of hard plastic are favored by some podiatrists. When breaking in orthotics you should first wear them while walking, and gradually increase your use when running. An insole may be used over the support at first to prevent blisters.

One problem of "shoe stuffing" is that you can over-stuff your running shoes in your search for perfect foot comfort and pain-free running. This is like looking for the perfect wave; it doesn't exist. Do remember that when trying on new shoes, bring whatever you may stuff into them. You might take a half size larger than usual.

Remember, too, that if 23 percent of all marathon runners put something in their shoes, that means 77 percent don't. Like Shepherd, perhaps you can take all that shoe-stuffing out, put it in the back of your closet, and run free.

16 INJURIES: DISEASES OF INACTIVITY, DISEASES OF EXCELLENCE

In 1955, Dr. Hans Kraus presented a theory, based on his studies, to the annual meeting of the American Medical Association. It was a radical idea for the time, and one for which he was widely criticized. Dr. Kraus proposed that underexercise was the cause of a large number of illnesses. He reported that 57.9 percent of 5,000 healthy American children between the ages of six and sixteen failed one or more of the Kraus-Weber Minimal Muscle Tests, while only 8.7 percent of 3,000 children in Austria, Italy, and Switzerland had failed the same tests. Dr. Kraus was accused of being unpatriotic!

When Dr. Kraus presented his report to President Eisenhower, however, it became the catalyst for the establishment of the President's Council on Physical Fitness. In 1960, President John F. Kennedy, a patient of Dr. Kraus, wrote in *Sports Illustrated*, "The harsh fact of the matter is that there is an increasingly large number of young Americans who are neglecting their bodies—whose physical fitness is not what it should be—who are getting soft."

Even today, the disease of inactivity is still with us. To the automobile, which Ulick O'Connor likens to a plague killing middle-aged men, we can add the elevator, golf cart, fast-food chain, and other conveniences. All are mechanisms of twentieth-century life that either rob us of activity, or fatten us. The result is "hypokinetic disease"—the disease of inactivity. The results of this habitual physical inactivity are heart disease; nervous disorders such as ulcers, headaches, and insomnia; and such musculoskeletal deficiencies as lower back pain.

In 1955, the medical profession laughed at Dr. Kraus's suggestion that underexercise was a cause of disease. Heart patients and those with back pain were ordered to remain inactive. Now, however, the American Medical Association has its own American Medical Jogging Association, with hundreds of members who run anywhere from a few miles a week to marathon events.

All runners overcome two physical obstacles: the diseases of inactivity, which are discovered when one is getting into shape; and then the diseases of excellence that sometimes come from running too well.

Injury is part of an active life, but it can also be avoided, or minimized. The rush to get into shape, the tension in our society, the lack of knowledge about relaxing, stretching, and running can all lead to a variety of frustrating injuries. A *Runner's World* poll, for example, showed that 34 percent of the sub-25-miles-a-week runners suffered injuries, but among runners covering 50 miles a week or more, 73 percent developed injuries.

What gets injured? In just the past decade, as the number of runners has increased and both knowledge of running and its equipment have become more sophisticated, injuries have changed. In 1980, doctors at St. Elizabeth's Hospital Sports Medicine Runners Clinic in Boston conducted a survey of 1,000 runners and compared their answers to those of a *Runner's World* survey ten years earlier. The results: Knee complaints had increased (from 25 percent to 30.5 percent); heel spur and *plantar fascia* complaints had increased (10 percent to 13.4 percent); and shin splints and related stress fractures had increased (10 percent to 20.6 percent). Achilles tendinitis, however, had decreased (from 18 percent to six percent). A 1979–80 study in California corroborated the findings: Injuries to the knee, shins, heels increased, while Achilles tendinitis had decreased. The most prevalent concerns of runners were foot and knee injuries.

Two basic factors have caused these changes. First, most runners stretch both before and after their exercising, thus minimizing the chance for some injuries. Second, running shoes have changed and improved, and this has decreased some injuries, but increased others. The increased flexibility of the shoes and the use of heel lifts have diminished complaints about Achilles tendinitis and about shin splints in the front of the legs. But as runners put in more mileage, and attempt to go faster, they have somewhat offset the benefits of improved running shoes. Complaints have increased about injuries to the forefoot and heels, about stress fractures, and about shin splints on the inner side of the leg. It seems that the most common complaint from excellence focuses on the bones and joints, and the anti-gravity or "pushing" muscles—which do most of the work in running—rather than the "pulling" muscles.

TEN REASONS WE GET HURT

In my work, I have found ten basic causes of injuries that occur to the runner who is moving from being underexercised to reaching a level of running excellence.

1. *Biomechanically Weak Feet* A distance runner's foot strikes the ground 800 times during every 7- to 10-minute mile. The force of impact of each foot is approximately three times the runner's weight. Surveys now indicate that 35 to 60 percent of all runners have weak feet. If the feet are weak, then the force exerted upon footstrike causes an abnormal strain on the supporting tendons and muscles of the foot and leg. The result is muscular or skeletal damage.

Further, the abnormal stress may cause a twisting of the foot at the ankle, the leg, or the knee. The result may be a stress fracture or "runner's knee." Commercially made or custom-fitted orthotics may help runners with weak feet.

2. *Unequal Leg Length* Perhaps 15 percent of all runners have this problem. In many cases, unequal leg length causes no injury, but in other runners, the problem may force the shoulders and scapula out of alignment; the spine to curve, causing nerve irritation; and the pelvis, knees, ankle, and foot to rotate abnormally. The result may be a whole variety of back, hip, foot, and leg injuries. Dr. Richard Schuster finds that most injuries first occur on the long side of the leg. Structural shortages may occur anywhere in the leg: the upper leg, the lower leg, and below the ankle. Heel lifts or orthotics to balance the leg-length difference may help, and should be placed inside the shoes, never exceeding half an inch in height. Exercises to stretch and strengthen the affected areas are also beneficial (see Chapters 7 and 8). *Caution:* According to Dr. Schuster: "The general rule relating to the management of leg shortage in runners is to do nothing if the runner is pain free."

3. Poor Flexibility Tight or shortened muscles can be more easily injured than stretched muscles and cause a variety of biomechanical problems. Stretching both before and after running is essential for the Achilles tendon, calf, and hamstring muscles and the back and hip. This is the only way to gain and retain adequate flexibility.

4. Weak Anti-gravity Muscles The back and leg muscles become overdeveloped and tight with running. Therefore, strengthening exercises for the opposite muscle groups are essential. These include exercises for the abdominal muscles (easing back pain), shin area muscles (shin splints), and quadriceps or thigh area (knee pain).

5. Stress and Tension As mentioned in Chapter 20, stress and tension may cause a variety of injuries, including lower back pain and injuries related to tense muscles forced into action. Relaxation exercises before and after workouts will help alleviate this problem.

6. Overuse Syndrome Overtraining, or packing too many things into your life in addition to running, can make you susceptible to musculoskeletal injuries as well as illnesses. Early symptoms of overexertion such as fatigue, chills, frequent colds, insomnia, and diarrhea should be recognized, and avoided. Listen to your body. Ease back in your running schedule, decrease your speed, time, and/or distance. Run slow, run easy, but if symptoms continue, see a runner-doctor.

7. *Improper Training Habits*   Sudden changes in intensity, duration, or frequency of your runs should be avoided. Work into changes slowly. Also, if you are running on dirt and switch to hard pavement, or from flat surfaces to hills, watch for signs of stress or injury. Run slower, or shorter distances at first. Proper running style should always be observed. Stay off your toes, run tall by standing more erect.

8. *Environmental Factors*   Good running shoes are vital. Since running costs so little, treat yourself to a solid, comfortable, well-made pair of shoes. (See Chapter 15.) Keep your shoes in good repair. If possible, avoid hard and uneven surfaces.

9. *Injury Rehabilitation*   Take your time! Allow any injury to heal before running hard, far, and long again. Recover slowly from illnesses as well. Relapses are common if you don't take the time for recovery. Many serious injuries result from ignoring a minor injury.

10. *Poor Advice*   Sedentary doctors used to be blamed for many of our ills. They favored "staying off it" or "don't do anything strenuous" prescriptions. There are still too few sports-oriented, exercising doctors, and the medical profession has been slow to acknowledge the value of exercise as preventive medicine.

Be wary of nonathletic, out-of-shape doctors who prefer inactivity and pills as cures. Also be very skeptical of poorly trained physical educators or boot camp drill instructors who believe in getting you into shape at any cost. The price may be your health. Unfortunately, the most dangerous "expert" of all is your fellow runner. Give some runners a few miles in their training diaries, a new warm-up suit—and suddenly they're experts.

Your best bet is to seek advice about running and injuries from running-oriented physicians, competent and cautious physical educators and physical therapists, and veteran, level-headed runners. Finally, remain skeptical.

Runners can run without injury. But like any one of us, runners tend to jump in and start out without a thought about *preventing* injury. The warm-up, flexibility, and cool-down exercises are excellent ways to prevent injury on the run. If you are increasing your mileage beyond normal maintenance, for example, don't increase it by more than ten percent per week.

The next section, and the chapters that follow, may prevent unnecessary injuries. I learned the hard way; they happened to me. But I also know from runners I work with that most of us don't worry about preventing injury we haven't experienced. Thanks to the work of such people as Dr. Kraus, Dr. Sheehan, Dr. Schuster, Dr. Subotnick, Dr. Rob Roy McGregor, Dr. Murray Weisenfeld, Dr. Don Helms, and Ted Corbitt, we are learning more about ourselves as runners who battle first the "diseases of inactivity" and then the "diseases of excellence."

MY TEN MOST FAVORITE INJURIES
FROM HEAD TO TOE

Maybe I should call them "Infamous Injuries." I've had all of them, to my great displeasure. But I still want to emphasize: You can prevent injury by observing the ten warnings above. While you shouldn't be afraid of getting injured, you should run as defensively as you should drive.

1. The Black Toenail, and Other Toe Problems

Toenails may cause many problems. If the nails are too long, they can jam while you're running and cause a blood blister under the nail. After cutting the nails back, however, be careful to cover them or spread Vaseline over them before running; if not, the freshly exposed skin may blister. Or, tight shoes may cause your toes to jam and create blisters on the ends as well as under the nails. Shoes that are too big can cause slippage, resulting in blisters, too.

A blood blister under the toenail may cause several things to happen. The blister may go away by itself, and the toenail return to normal. A blister may force the nail away from its bed, leaving it slightly tender; the nail will grow back normally. Or, the blister will hurt so much that the pressure on the nail will have to be relieved. Hemorrhaging under the nail will cause it to turn black.

I used to develop painful blood blisters under my big toenail after long races. They were caused by my toenails rubbing against the top of my shoe. My foot rides high in the shoe because I wear orthotics and insoles. In treating this injury, which once resulted in a 4 a.m. ambulance ride to a hospital, I learned that a blister may need to be popped to relieve the pressure. A doctor may sterilize a needle and gently probe beneath the nail. A common procedure for a podiatrist is to drill through the nerveless nail to the blister, which bursts; the relief is instant. Once, in desperation, I heated a paper clip red-hot, and melted a hole into the nail. It hurt like hell for a moment, but worked! I told a runner-doctor, and he assured me that the medical profession had known this intricate method for relieving pain for years, and some people even find that it doesn't hurt them. The next day I was able to run comfortably. This technique is difficult to face a second time, even after several shots of brandy. In defense, I've discovered preventive measures which have, so far, ended the problem.

Dr. Schuster suggested that I cut a slit into the top of my shoe over the toe, and two smaller ones to either side, to allow the foot to expand during long runs and to eliminate friction above the toenail. After several months of questioning his sanity—What, cut up expensive running shoes?—I finally gave in. It worked, and my shoes haven't fallen apart either. If you're hesitant, try cutting up an old pair first.

Another effective preventive method for me is to wrap the toe with gauze. Tape it securely, forming a cup of gauze to protect the nail. Foam rubber caps may work, and can be purchased commercially. They sometimes fall off while running, however, and may turn into sponges in wet weather. "Sanding" the toenail with an emery board also helps prevent blisters.

Another problem may be "tingling in the toes." This is frequently caused by nerve pressure in tight shoes. "Curling of the toes" is another ailment on my long list. My right foot is smaller than my left, so I face the decision of whether to have one shoe very tight or one a little loose. Looseness is less dangerous. Since I have lots of room in the right shoe, I often curl my toes under, sometimes causing tightness in my calf. An extra pair of socks on the one foot, or a shoe length appliance under the foot may help. I found that after slitting my shoes, my toes were more flexible and the problem went away.

Ingrown toenails can also be painful. Small cotton balls can be placed under the corners of the nails to allow the nail to grow properly rather than cut into the skin. The cotton balls should be replaced daily, but used until the nail properly grows out.

2. The Crusty Callus

Calluses develop from the constant rubbing of the foot in the shoe and the pounding of the foot onto the ground. They are usually found on the bottom and back of the heel, and under the ball of the foot. Calluses can be helpful in protecting the foot, but they can also cause painful problems. Thick calluses protect the outer skin layer, but also increase pressure on underlying tissues and bone.

Although calluses are surprisingly rare in runners compared to the general population, according to Dr. Schuster, they do cause us problems. Calluses form by a combination of friction and shearing action. I develop thick calluses on the ball of my foot. This is caused primarily by the rubbing of my foot in the shoe and the resulting friction developed between the metatarsal bones and the underlying skin and shoe. As the callus is allowed to grow, pressure is exerted on the subcutaneous tisue and eventually it results in an infected blister deep under the callus. The area has to be lanced by a physician, and the callus surgically removed.

To prevent this, calluses should be sanded down regularly with pumice stone, although some calluses should be encouraged, to protect the foot. Vaseline or some other type of skin softener may be regularly applied to keep the skin moist. Inserts or metatarsal pads are sometimes required to eliminate the pressure on the foot that can cause calluses. Spenco insoles or a similar friction-reducing device will also help prevent calluses from building up.

3. The Bloody Blister

Blisters are caused by "hot spots" from shoes that are too loose or too tight, dirty socks, rough spots in the threading of your shoes, running on hot pavement, holes or seams in socks, and many other things. The best way to prevent blisters is to prevent the friction that causes them.

High-quality, thick-soled shoes will help. Avoid those with improperly placed stitching and rough edges. If a rough area does develop in a good shoe, soften it with Vaseline. Never wear new shoes in a race or long workout. The shoes must be broken in gradually, and the feet must become accustomed to them.

Many so-called experts insist that socks prevent blisters, and argue that two socks should be worn to minimize friction. However, modern running shoes are thick, and don't need several layers of sock for added cushioning. With socks, the runner risks creating irritating skin folds, bunching, and slipping (especially if the socks get wet) which cause blisters. Socks should be clean, dry, and snug-fitting.

Beginner runners tend to get blisters because their feet are tender and need to be toughened gradually. Avoid the commercial "skin tougheners"; they may be good for other sports, but not for the continuous motion of running. Foot powder or Vaseline generously applied to your feet before running usually prevents blisters. Special care should be taken prior to races, when your "blistering pace" may result in increased friction within the shoe.

I used to develop incredible blisters under the arch from the friction of my foot rubbing against my inserts—a common problem with insert wearers. Podiatrists can adjust inserts to minimize friction, and, frequently, they prescribe insoles that are specifically designed to reduce friction and can also be valuable in reducing foot shock. However, don't race with insoles in rainy weather because they'll absorb water like a sponge, slip around inside the shoe, and cause blisters. Also, remember that insoles go *over* your inserts. I had been wearing my Spenco insoles underneath for extra cushioning until one day, slightly hung over, I reversed them, and my blisters went away.

If you do get blisters, be cautious. Stubbornly training on them may chew up your feet and knock you out for days. Stop and treat the problem, and you may return to your workouts immediately.

Treatment   Small blisters should not be punctured immediately. Keep the area clean and protected; the skin may reheal itself. Taping, especially with Band-Aids, may only aggravate the blister further. You may want to cover the area with a protective product like Spenco's Second Skin. Dr. Sheehan paints the blister area with a tincture of benzoin and then applies a tape, such as a Zona, a standard product found in most pharmacies. The tape is left on for a few days, and reapplied if the blister is still present.

A blister that gets bigger and becomes painful to step on must be "popped" to relieve the pressure. Clean it with an antiseptic solution, and puncture it with a sterilized needle. Dr. Weisenfeld uses a sterilized razor blade. Be sure to wash the area with alcohol or antiseptic before puncturing the blister. Make as small an incision as possible, and gently squeeze out the fluid with a sterile gauze. Don't peel off the cap of the blister. An antiseptic, antifungal agent should be applied to the area, and the blister should be covered with a sterile gauze pad or a Band-Aid that will let air in around the blister. Avoid plastic Band-Aids. You may use a square of gauze and tape it around the edges, or a loose-fitting Band-Aid. You may take the covering off at night to air the area or keep the Band-Aid on until the blister heals. To prevent infection, be sure that all fluid is out of the blister, and no foreign matter remains. If redness and pain occur, you may have an infection, and should see a physician immediately.

Tinactin solution should be used for wounds on the bottom of your feet. Dr. Weisenfeld, whose podiatry practice handles both runners and dancers, notes that a favorite trick of dancers is to use Curity brand lamb's wool to cover a blister. A wisp of lamb's wool is wrapped around the blistered toe, not tightly. Wrap it around a few times, then give it a couple of twists so the fibers intertwine and stick together. This protects the toe, and prevents blistering. It is also waterproof. Another trick was discovered by Jim Rumsey, a physical therapist and former trainer for the Florida State University track team: Take a three-inch-wide strip of elastic by Johnson and Johnson, and wrap it around the foot. Be sure it overlaps, and cut off the excess beyond the toes. The result is a "toe sock" that protects blistered feet.

Treat blisters immediately. Otherwise, you will favor the blister by adjusting your footstrike, even unconsciously, and altering your posture, which may cause leg, knee, or back injury. I sometimes run on blisters as though they don't exist, but if they cause me to alter my running form, I stay off them for a day or two. Two weeks before the 1976 New York Marathon, Lauri McBride, our team's top woman competitor, told me she had injured her knee, and couldn't run without pain. After some questioning, I discovered that her knee began to hurt following a 15-mile training run during which she slightly favored a blister. The minor alteration in foot plant caused an abnormal strain on the knee. After resting a few days, she was able to run the marathon, but she had lost crucial days of training.

4. Our Arch Enemy

The arches in our feet commonly bring pain and discomfort. One of them traces the underside and top of the foot, extending from just in front of the heel to the base of the first long toe joint. This "inner arch" (on the underside) is the one most often strained. The metatarsal arch, across the ball of the foot, also causes problems. It is not a true arch but an off-weight arch that normally flattens under weight. Weight can be unevenly or excessively distributed and cause pain.

Tendinitis or capsulitis around the small bones of the foot can make these arches painful or weak. This may be caused by a weak structural foot which needs support. Many runners suffer from *plantar fascia* (arch pain), which is an inflammation of the fibrous tissue that runs from the heel to the heads of the metatarsal bones in the ball of the foot. It may be caused by irritation of this tissue (*fascia*) and separation from its attachment to the heel bone. It is characterized by pain at the breast of the heel or arch when you get up in the morning, or after long periods of sitting, or at the start of a run. Pushing off on your toes when running uphill or picking up speed aggravates this condition.

The pain from *plantar fascia* may be alleviated by icing the injured area immediately after injury, taking aspirin, and resting for a few days or as much as six weeks. You might consider an alternative exercise during this period. Supporting the arch or using heel pads may also help.

Flat feet or feet with high arches both require support. Flat-footedness, however, does not necessarily mean that the arch is flat. It can be a condition in which weak ankles allow the foot to roll medially, giving the appearance that the arch is flat. Not everyone with flat feet develops foot and leg injuries during running. According to Dr. Weisenfeld, the low arch may be normal.

Exercises to strengthen the muscles of the foot sometimes bring relief. Picking up marbles with your toes, rolling a Coke bottle under your foot, standing on a towel with your toes over the

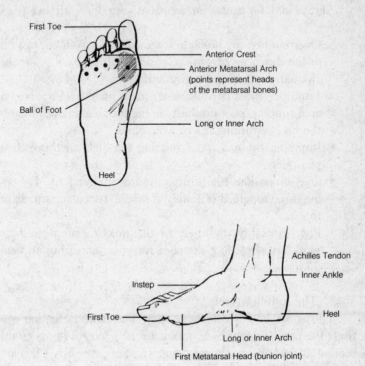

Anatomy of a Foot

edge and then picking up the towel with your toes, all help. Walking barefoot regularly, especially in sand, also strengthens the muscles of the feet.

When exercise doesn't give enough strength to the muscles of the foot, arch supports may be needed. Commercially made arch supports (for all types of arch problems) and custom-made inserts or orthotics may relieve arch pain and other foot and leg injuries as well. Immediate treatment of arch strain consists of rest followed by gentle exercises.

Always look for causes for your foot pain. Here are five possibilities:

- Overtraining: too much mileage on hard pavement or hills,
  or too much speed work. Consider cutting back or aerobic
  alternatives until the injury heals.
- Improper shoes or shoe wear: inadequate heel counter or
  arch support, poor flexibility in the toe area, uneven wear in
  the heels, "turning in" or worn shoes.
- Improper running form: running too high on the balls of
  your feet.
- Over-pronation: the turning inward of your foot. Try taping or commercial orthotics; if severe, try custom-made orthotics.
- Poor flexibility: tightness in the muscles supporting the
  foot. Try stretching exercises for your hamstring and calf
  muscles.

5. The Achilles Heel

This is our body's vulnerable spot. The Achilles tendon con-
nects the powerful lower leg muscle to the heel. An injury to this
tendon is painful and long-lasting. Dr. Schuster lists six major
causes of Achilles tendinitis.

1. The act of running tightens the calf muscles even more
   than normal, and most runners cannot dorsiflex their feet
   (bend them upward) to the ideal 10 degrees beyond the
   right angle. The result is added strain upon the Achilles
   tendon.
2. Many runners, especially beginners, neglect warm-ups and
   stretching exercises. Tight, tense muscles and tendons are
   more susceptible to injury.
3. Many runners, especially beginners, run on the balls of
   their feet, which causes strain on the Achilles tendon.
4. Bursts of speed by a runner who has not built up to it will
   also strain the tendon.

5. Running shoes, especially those with low heels or that don't readily flex under the ball of the foot, are inadequate.

6. Runners with narrow Achilles tendons have a higher incidence of tendinitis than runners with broader Achilles tendons, Dr. Schuster has found.

There are other causes that may precipitate an attack of tendinitis. Any sudden change in footwear (thick heels to thin heels), running surfaces (soft to hard), or training pattern (flat terrain to hill work, endurance to speed, increased mileage) may trigger tendon strain. If you overtrain a fatigued body, or run on worn-down heels, or stretch with fast or jerky motions, or force a stretch beyond the first point of discomfort, you may harm your Achilles tendon. High-heeled shoes for women and those funky platform shoes for men shorten the tendon. Earth Shoes and other similar brands with heels lower than toes may stretch the Achilles tendon. This may help some people, but it may also strain the tendon in some cases. Sometimes the problem is caused by a sharp bone cutting into the tendon, a condition which requires surgery. Finally, beginner runners must remember that their muscles are weak and tendons short. They need to be cautious, and work gradually on their running program.

Injury to the Achilles tendon may take two forms: tendinitis or rupture. Tendinitis is marked by pain and stiffness during and after workouts, as well as tenderness to touch. It may lead to partial or complete rupture, which involves a tear in the tendon accompanied by pain and swelling.

In cases of normal tendinitis, treatment consists of soaking in ice or cold water to limit inflammation and swelling. Cold tap water running over the Achilles is effective; or, pack the area in ice, or rub ice on it. Direct applications of ice as the foot is moved up and down for ten minutes immediately after running is a good technique. Later, heat should be applied before the workout and ice immediately afterwards until the injury has subsided.

Strain on an injured tendon may be lessened by placing heel

lifts in street and running shoes. As much as one inch of surgical felt should be added under the heel. As the pain subsides the height of the heel lift is gradually reduced. People with chronic Achilles problems may benefit from corrective inserts.

In the early stages of an Achilles injury, stretching should be avoided. The injury developed in the first place because the tendon was overstrained. After a couple of days of rest, mild stretching, massage, heat treatments, ultrasound and whirlpool treatments may help. Drugs such as cortisone injections may be an immediate help, but can also be dangerous and contribute to a more serious rupture.

Slow down immediately at the first sign of Achilles strain. This is one of the most dangerous injuries to run with because it can lead to a partial rupture, which in turn could lead to a complete rupture requiring surgery.

Hill work and speed work should be eliminated and mileage limited until the symptoms disappear. If there is pain and stiffness, stop running altogether for two to ten days. Remember, this is one of the slowest injuries to heal. When training continues, running should be on flat ground, and easy. The pace should be slowed down at the first sign of pain.

There are some preventive measures that every runner should take. Stretching exercises for leg muscles and the tendon should be done before running to prepare the tendon for strenuous activity. Exercises done afterwards will keep the muscles and tendons from stiffening and shortening. Flexibility exercises should be done often. Walking barefoot or in flat shoes is also beneficial. Exercises that help stretch the Achilles tendon include the standing Upper Back, Arm, and Hamstring Stretch (see Chapter 2), The Wall Push-Up (see Chapter 2), and Toe Raises (see Chapter 8). You may also want to try the following:

• Squat down, keeping your heels flat on the floor, feet shoulder-width apart and pointed out slightly. Slowly bend forward and touch the floor with your fingers for support. Hold for 30 seconds. Relax and repeat two times.

• Stand with feet parallel and hold onto something for support. Rise onto the balls of your feet without bending your knees. Hold for a few seconds, and return to the standing position. Do five repeats, and then another five with knees slightly bent.

• Sitting on the floor, lean forward toward your outstretched feet, grasp your toes (if you can), and pull them toward you slowly. If you can't reach your toes, loop a towel around your feet and gently pull your toes toward you. Keep your knees flat to the floor, if possible. Hold for ten seconds. Do five sets.

• Build or purchase a slant board with an angle of 15 or 20 degrees. Place the board eight to 12 inches from a wall, and stand on the board with your toes pointing "uphill." Lean toward the wall, resting your forearms on the wall and keeping your knees straight. Keep your hips forward and your heels down. Hold for ten seconds, and repeat several times. Do again with knees slightly bent.

You should stretch your Achilles tendons more than once a day, and always before and after running. I often do the "wall push-up" stretch against a wall while waiting for an elevator, or tug on my toes while talking on the telephone. I may look a little weird, but in New York City, who notices! One day while waiting for the bus I leaned against the shelter doing my stretching, and a couple of winos copied me for an impromptu fitness lesson.

6. Shin Splints

Abnormal strain and stress on the muscles and tendons that lift your forefoot (dorsiflex) and control your toes often result in shin splints. These muscles and tendons absorb shock and stabilize your feet during foot plant. The angle at which the foot strikes the ground and the ability of the muscles and tendons to withstand the force indicates your susceptibility to shin splints. If you get them, you know it. Shin splints are a painful swelling of damaged muscles and tendons along the front of your lower leg between the two bones, the fibula and tibia; the pain occurs noticeably during running.

There are two basic types of shin splints. The anterior tibial shin splints involve pain in the lower front of the leg. Posterior tibial shin splints create pain along the inside of the lower leg and ankle. Shin splints are common among beginner runners unaccustomed to the strain. I can determine the cause of at least 90 percent of their problems by asking three questions. Do you run on your toes? Do you lean forward when you run? Do you have good, well-cushioned shoes? When new competitors and veteran runners complain of shin splints, it usually means one of two things—either they have made dramatic shifts in their training programs, or they may have a strength-flexibility imbalance in the muscles of their legs.

Running style or training habits often cause shin splints. The following are to be avoided or corrected.

- Running on the balls of your feet and overstriding places strain on the muscle and tendons of the lower leg. Thick-heeled running shoes and heel lifts will help you land farther back on the heel at footstrike, and eliminate this problem.

- A forward lean of the body increases the strain on your leg muscles. Remember to run tall and concentrate on staying erect.

- A sudden shift from thick-soled shoes to thin, flat terrain to hills, endurance training to speed work, soft surfaces to hard, short mileage to long, may cause pain in shins. Thick-soled shoes are important for beginners and anyone running on hard surfaces.

- Some runners need arch supports or custom orthotics. Pain along the inside of the calf may be a type of shin splint related to weak arches.

- Poor flexibility, muscle weakness, and muscle imbalance between the front and back of the leg may cause shin splints. Tight calf muscles, weak arches, and shortened Achilles tendons also add strain to the shin area. Stretching exercises for calf, hamstring, and Achilles tendon are important, especially before and after running.

- Digging in with toes upon footstrike, and tension in the foot muscle during foot swing, also strain the lower leg muscles. Shoes that fit snugly in the toes, or the addition of anterior crests under the toes, may help prevent the former problem. The toes should also be allowed to "float" and relax during the forward swing.
- Bouncing on your toes on hard surfaces, stop-and-go running, and repeated pivoting should all be avoided.

Dr. Sheehan recommends taking positive steps to reduce or prevent the occurrence of shin splints. The following exercises, also noted in the shin supplemental exercises in Chapter 8, are suggested in addition to those for stretching the hamstring and calf muscles.

1. Sit on a table with legs hanging freely over the sides. Flex the foot to lift a weight (a bucket filled with pebbles or a sandbag or other weight suspended over the top of the foot).

2. Attach a rubber bicycle inner tube to a board; slip your toes under the tube and lift them against it.

3. Turn the feet inward while standing and make a rolling motion.

4. Stand on the edge of a towel and curl the toes to pull the towel under the feet.

If you do get shin splints, rest for a few days when the symptoms first appear. Running with severe shin splints may lead to a stress fracture. If the pain is severe, and you are losing power in your legs, see a physician. Otherwise, here is the recommended treatment for shin splints:

- Rest the legs and elevate the feet as often as possible.
- Take aspirin, or stronger pain-killers if your doctor recommends them.
- Ice-massage the area after each run. Continue to ice after all your runs until the pain disappears.

- Promote healing by elevating the heels of your running shoes, inserting arch supports or orthotics, or buying running shoes with a thicker heel. Also, use heat or ultrasound treatments, especially before bedtime. Strapping or taping by a knowledgeable athletic trainer or doctor may also help.
- Cortisone pills may also clear up the inflammation but shouldn't be taken for more than three days. The drug Norflex, a muscle relaxant, can relieve pain and doesn't make you drowsy. Both are by prescription.
- Run slowly on soft, flat terrain within the limits of pain. Gradually return to normal training.
- Avoid recurrence by following the principles of prevention listed above.
- Surgery, as a last resort, may be needed to repair injured tissue.

Look for causes. Overtraining (sudden changes in mileage, speed work, runnings hills) may be a problem. Cut back on your mileage, eliminate hills and speed workouts until the injury heals. During this time, consider a temporary alternative training program. Muscle imbalance (inflexible calf muscles or stronger hamstrings than quadriceps) may also be a cause. Do stretching exercises for the hamstring and calf muscles, and strengthening exercises for the quadriceps and the foot muscles.

7. Pulling Your Leg

A variety of muscular aches and pains in the legs affect the runner. These include muscle fatigue, tension-related pain, cramping, and muscle strains and tears.

General leg muscle stiffness is common among beginner runners. So, too, is pain in the calf muscles from running on the toes and causing constant tension on the calf. This is why I recommend that beginners run much slower and for less distance than their hearts and lungs say they can. Leg muscles that haven't worked in years will rebel.

- Gradually improve your flexibility and increase your leg muscle strength.
- Build up running distance or time *slowly.*
- Run only in well-cushioned shoes, and on soft surfaces if possible.
- Stretch before and after workouts.
- Take plenty of hot baths to soothe the muscles.

When the experienced runner suffers from leg fatigue, it is generally due to overtraining. Therefore, the rules above also apply to him or her. All runners must stretch, to minimize leg fatigue, prior to workouts and afterwards.

A condition that I call "concrete legs" is a variation of leg fatigue. After my first marathon, I had to be carried from the stadium to the car. I couldn't move my legs. I had never run farther than 10 miles before that day. Eventually I recovered, and as my training increased, my legs became stronger and after races, the recovery was faster. With lots of help from my friends, and a bit of experimentation, I've discovered a way to minimize concrete legs, or other leg pain:

- Don't sit down immediately after the race, and don't cross the finish line and fall into a heap. Keep walking or jogging for a while, and stretch for 15 minutes. Continue stretching on and off throughout the day. Don't lie or sit in one position for long periods of time. Don't force the stretch, but do force yourself to stretch some, even when your body protests.
- Soak in a warm tub as soon as possible, and follow that with stretching exercises as often as necessary.
- Exercise the next few days, but bike or swim instead of running.
- Applying various liniments before and after running to prevent or soothe muscle soreness can be of help. (Caution: Men, wash your hands thoroughly after using the "hot" liniments before going to the bathroom, or you may find

yourself with a burning desire to soak in a tub of ice water.)

Leg cramping is also a painful experience. It usually occurs in hot weather, when the runner's body fluid reserves have been drained along with key minerals. Dietary deficiencies in potassium, calcium, and magnesium can cause cramping. Other causes include tension, caffeine consumption, and the lack of warm-up.

The beginner runner may get a charley horse—a pulled muscle, usually the hamstring muscle in the back of the leg. This is actually a strain or tear in the muscle. It occurs because the muscles are either too weak or too inflexible in the beginner, or imbalanced in the experienced runner. Sprinters have powerful thigh muscles and comparatively weak hamstrings. Distance runners have strong hamstring muscles and weak quadricep muscles. The beginner needs to strengthen his overall leg muscles to prevent pulls; the veteran runner needs to do special exercises for the quadriceps to balance leg strength and to prevent a thigh muscle pull.

A muscle that is suddenly jerked by a sharp action, or one that hasn't been properly warmed up, or is tight and inflexible will pull at its tendon or connection with the bone. The distance runner who is inflexible will often develop a hamstring pull near his or her buttocks. Stretching exercises (see Chapters 2 and 8), are essential for minimizing hamstring pulls. At the same time, runners can hurt themselves while stretching if they jerk hard and fast, or force a stretch.

Hamstring pulls come with bursts of speed, or by jumping over obstacles. Cold weather also makes all runners more prone to pulls; they should warm up carefully and avoid speed work during these months. Running or walking on ice and snow may strain hamstring muscles that are unprepared.

If a leg muscle is pulled, ice should be applied as soon as possible. For forty-eight hours, the leg should be elevated if possible. Gentle massage, whirlpool, ultrasound and light exercise is the next step. Walking and swimming may be necessary before returning to running. Severe pulls should be referred to your physician.

8. The Battle of Wounded Knee

Knee problems combine stresses or strains on the knee joint with the inability of the knee to handle the stress. Abnormal stress many come from the fact that your foot strikes the ground 5,000 times per hour with the force of three times your body weight. If something in the supporting structure gives, the result is often pain, or the inability to run. Knee pain is the most common running injury. Dr. Schuster notes that 75 percent of his patients have some knee pain, although they may be in his office for some other reason.

The kneecap normally rides smoothly in a groove. It is attached to the large quadriceps muscle of the thigh, which is strong enough to pull the kneecap sideways if the angle of the pull is twisted. The result may be irritated cartilage, which is symptomatic of runner's knee, or tendinitis. A variety of factors may cause this faulty biomechanical problem.

When you have knee pain, avoid hill and speed work. Running with the toes consciously pointed slightly inward will help prevent the kneecap from moving out of place. Ice applied immediately after running and before bedtime reduces the pain. Ted Corbitt's favorite trick is to ice the knee before bed, and then place a damp cloth over it covered tightly with a plastic bag. As the moisture evaporates it keeps the knee warm and loose, and promotes circulation to the area to aid in healing. A similar benefit comes from wrapping the knee in flannel before retiring. Ultrasound and whirlpool may also help. Knee braces and supports are good temporary aids, but also tend to act as a crutch for muscles that need to be stretched and strengthened. It is often wise to bicycle or swim for a few days in order to keep the strain off a damaged knee.

A *Runner's World* survey indicated that more than 20 percent of all runners are sidelined with knee problems, and three out of four of Dr. Schuster's patients have injuries related to the knee. Our goal is to treat these injuries before they occur.

The following causes of and treatments for knee pain come from my own painful experience after injury in college, and information from the doctors who helped me return as a runner, Dr. Sheehan and Dr. Schuster.

• Structural instability of the foot. If you have a short big toe and a long second toe (Morton's Foot), weak arches, or an unstable heel, you may be prone to knee injuries. With Morton's Foot, it is not the toe that creates the problem, but the metatarsal behind it. The toe reflects this abnormality. These foot imbalances can be helped with arch supports, heel cups, or custom-made inserts.

Most runners have structurally weak feet that pronate (turn inward) or flatten while running, causing a tremendous torque action on the knee. I usually have my runners try a commercial arch support first, and if that doesn't work or at least begin to solve the problem, I refer them to a runner-podiatrist. Many runners are "saved" by commercial or specially made foot control products designed to neutralize the foot at impact.

• Short, tight calf and hamstring muscles and inflexibility in the supportive structures of the knee joint contribute to the problem. All the flexibility exercises in Chapters 2 and 8 will help with knee problems. The following are also beneficial:

—Lie on your back, knees flexed. Slowly raise one leg overhead, grasping the leg behind the heel with both hands. Pull the straight leg toward your forehead. Hold the position; don't force it. Alternate legs.

—Sitting, place your right foot sideways on your left thigh, and gently apply pressure downward on the knee. Alternate.

—Standing, grab your right ankle with your right hand, and bending the knee, slowly pull upward behind you. Alternate.

—Standing, legs about 3 feet apart, toes pointed ahead. Now

turn the left foot 45 degrees outward and, keeping the knee locked, hands behind head, slowly lower your forehead toward the left knee and hold for 15 seconds. Do not force it. Alternate.

—Standing, place one leg on a chair or table at a comfortable height parallel to the ground. Push the heel downward, hold for 6 seconds, relax. Then lean your body weight forward, and feel the stretch. Repeat twice, and alternate legs.

• Weak quadriceps muscles, or quads weak in relation to the hamstrings, can cause an imbalance which affects the pull on the kneecap and leads to pain. The solution is to exercise and strengthen the thigh muscles.

—Sitting in a chair, straighten the leg, and tighten it, holding the kneecap up. Hold for 10–20 seconds in isometric contraction. Repeat 10 to 20 times.

—Sitting on a table, lift any type of weight suspended from the legs, with legs straight, one leg at a time.

—Walk up several flights of stairs regularly.

—Walk in water, emphasizing knee-lift.

—Hike or run on hills or in soft sand.

Dr. Weisenfeld notes that guards in basketball rarely get knee pain, which he feels is due to their running backwards a lot. He recommends, in addition to the above exercises, running backwards occasionally to strengthen the knees.

• Unequal leg length causes an unequal distribution of weight, and can cause knee pain. Heel lifts, even homemade with surgical felt, can relieve the imbalance. Custom-made orthotics may be necessary.

• Shoes must be well cushioned with a solid shank. Shoes with a "cutaway" under the arch are structurally weak, and allow the foot to pronate, twisting the knee. Watch the wear pattern on the soles of your shoes. If they wear down on the inside of the heel rather than the outside, you may need inserts.

• An uneven running surface may also twist the knee and

bring damage. Avoid unevenness. Run on alternate sides of a graded road, being careful of traffic. Change directions, if possible, in a gym or indoor track to avoid running at a slant. Knee pain can result even from running along the slanted beach.

• Sudden changes in your running schedule may cause knee pain that may disappear when you ease off.

9. My Aching Back

To determine whether you are a strong candidate for back pain, take these four simple tests. Two are from the Kraus-Weber Minimal Muscle Tests, the third is used by Dr. Schuster in analyzing leg length discrepancies, and the fourth was developed by me after working with hundreds of people suffering from back pain.

Test One: Abdominal Muscle Strength Lie on your back, knees flexed, both hands behind your head, heels as close to your buttocks as possible (held by a friend or a heavy object). Roll into a sitting position. Incredibly, one out of every four people I test for beginner running classes or back classes cannot do one sit-up. My experience is that 10 percent of all runners cannot do sit-ups. You should be able to do at least 20 consecutive bent-knee sit-ups if you intend to run regularly. If your abdominal muscles can't support your erect body during running, then the pelvic girdle will tip forward, causing a swayback. The result is strain on the abdominal muscles and ligaments of the back.

Test Two: Flexibility Stand with both feet together, hands together, and slowly lower your fingertips toward a point on the floor beyond your toes. Keep the knees locked, but don't force it! If you can't touch the floor, have someone measure how many inches distant you are, so that you can later measure your improvement. More than 85 percent of back pain sufferers in my classes fail this test.

Flexibility decreases with age, and with running, which strengthens—and tightens—calf and hamstring muscles. Yet flexibility returns with practice and exercise. Three years ago I was seven inches away from touching the floor, and now I can touch it with the palms of my hands. Regular stretching before and after workouts does wonders. Also, attacks of back pain and sciatica lessen with improved flexibility.

Test Three: Unequal Leg Length   Sit in a chair with both feet flat on the floor. Put a carpenter's level, or a flat piece of wood, across the knees. Major leg length discrepancies will be obvious. Unequal leg length places pressure on the lower back, and is a major cause of back pain among runners. It can be relieved with heel lifts or inserts to allow for the shortness of one leg and to equalize the pressure at impact. However, Dr. Schuster emphasizes that if one leg is shorter than the other, but causing you no difficulty, it should be left alone.

Test Four: Type A Syndrome   The Type A personality is tense and jumpy. As a runner, he is recognized by his (or her) short, choppy stride, tense face and shoulders, clenched fists, high arm carry, and frequent compulsion for speed. As a result, he or she often suffers from back pain, and may need to learn to do relaxation exercises before running, and to run in a relaxed style at a slow to moderate pace.

Overcoming most back pain is merely a matter of flexibility and exercise. Studies show that more than 80 percent of all back pain is due to muscular weaknesses rather than pathological factors. Four basic types of people develop back pain:

- The sedentary, soft American who has weak postural muscles.
- The weekend athlete and the previously sedentary person who rushes into exercise without preparation.
- The experienced athlete who has developed a muscle imbalance by not strengthening his or her abdominal muscles, or stretching the hamstring and calf muscles.
- Tense people, whether sedentary or active.

If you suffer from back pain, you're not alone. More than 80 percent of all Americans are victims at some time in their lives. Within three days after appearing on a television show about back pain, I received 300 phone calls pleading for help. Sufferers are found everywhere. Both ultra marathon runners Gary Muhrcke and Dr. Norb Sander suffer from chronic back pain, as does Nina Kuscsik, a world-class marathoner. Yet, with all the suffering, no one knows for certain what causes back pain. We do know, however, that overcoming most back pain can be merely a matter of flexibility and exercise.

In addition to the probable causes found in the four tests, there are several other causes that will concern runners.

1. *Poor Flexibility* Stretching exercises for the hamstring and calf muscles will aid in limiting back pain. (See Chapters 2 and 8.) Exercises in which you bend slowly forward, backward, and to the side also loosen the back. "Hanging" from a bar for 30 seconds to 1 minute also helps stretch the back muscles.

2. *Weakness in Key Postural Muscles* Abdominal strengthening exercises such as bent-knee sit-ups are essential. Next to sit-ups the best abdominal exercise is the basket hang: Hanging from a bar, you slowly raise the knees up to the chest and slowly lower them. Sucking in the "gut" and holding it for an isometric contraction is also good.

The gluteal muscles (rear end), erector spinae (back muscles along the spine), and the abdominals can be strengthened with two exercises: Lying on your back, tilt the pelvis back, tighten the buttocks and stomach, and push the lower back into the floor and hold; or, stand with your back against a wall, push your lower back toward the wall as you tighten the buttocks and stomach.

3. *Structural Weaknesses* In addition to unequal leg length, structurally weak feet and back may cause back pain. Curvatures of the spine cannot be corrected in most cases, but the strength of the supporting muscle can be improved by exercise.

4. *Uneven Footstrike* Running on a slant or in worn-out shoes is risky. Change direction on indoor track; alternate side of

the road when outdoors.

5. *Impact Shock*   With footstrikes between 5,000 and 7,000 times an hour, you need well-cushioned shoes.

6. *Running Style*   Running in a constant forward lean will cause added strain on the back muscles.

7. *Pregnancy*   Additional pressure is put on the back during pregnancy because of the shift in weight distribution. The abdominal muscles are weaker after pregnancy. It is important to continue abdominal muscle strengthening both during and after pregnancy.

8. *Obesity*   Men and women who are fat place a greater burden on their backs, especially if the stomach protrudes. A swayback condition may occur.

9. *Bad Work and Sleep Habits*   Learn how to lift heavy objects. Don't lift with your back, but bend at the knees and allow your powerful legs, strengthened by many miles of running, to do the work. Sleeping on your stomach may cause a swayback condition, and strain the back. If you persist, place a pillow under your hips. Sleeping on your back may also cause problems, and placing a pillow under your knees will allow the lower back to flatten. Comfort is the key to sleeping correctly, but the preferred position is on your side, knees flexed—the fetal position. The bed should be very firm, and a bed board should be placed under the mattress. Dr. Kraus recommends a hard, horsehair mattress with no spring.

10. *Tension*   Back pain and tension go together. If you are going through a period of emotional tension, you may have to take it easy on your running. Something has to give; often it's your back.

11. *Sciatica*   The sciatic nerve is described by Dr. Sheehan as "the longest river of pain in the body." It begins in the lower back and extends all the way down to the ankle. Pain may occur in the back, hip, leg, or even the ankle and the two lesser toes. It may be a numbing sensation or a severe pain shooting from the back

down the leg. It is caused by a pressure on the nerve and can be the result of poor flexibility and weak postural muscles or a manifestation of a herniated disc. Not all leg pain is due to sciatica. Muscle pain sometimes mimics sciatica pain.

12. Herniated Disc Discs are located between each vertebra of the back and act as shock absorbers. If one is ruptured or damaged, it may be surgically removed and the bone fused together. Obviously, such an operation is a cure of last resort. By examining the possible causes for the stress on the disc, you may not need an operation.

13. Student's Disease Back pain may also be psychological. It is a well-known phenomenon, especially among medical students, that if you study a disease in great detail you begin to develop the problem yourself. I got back pain during an exhaustive study of that disease. Fortunately, I learned my lesson: I'll never do a paper on impotence!

If you've suffered back pain, you should rest a few days and return to running very slowly. Taking warm baths, as well as drawing the knees up to the chest, helps reduce a back pain spasm. Relaxation exercises, stretching exercises, and gentle running are the next steps. Sometimes running intervals of fast bursts of speed will stretch out the muscles. Be sure to intersperse the bursts with slow jogging or walking.

Exercise can help a lot. A television executive I know was told he would have to wear a girdle for the rest of his life, or undergo a disc removal operation. He took a back-pain class, followed by a beginner's fitness class which emphasized exercise. He threw away the girdle and told his sedentary, overweight orthopedic specialists where to go—go exercise. He's now running 5 miles a day and feels like a new man.

The National YMCA program, "The Y's Way to a Healthy Back," was developed by Dr. Kraus and Alexander Melleby. It is being offered at Y's across the country and is recommended for any runner who is experiencing back pain.

14. The Thick Head

Overcoming stubbornness and stupidity may be a major problem. I've learned how to identify and deal with most major injuries, but I still get them because I often ignore early warnings. However, I'm less prone to injury than I once was, so perhaps I'm learning. Joe Henderson, editor of *Runner's World*, suggests becoming an "experiment of one," learning through experience and common sense. Bill Bowerman, former University of Oregon track coach, preaches "train, don't strain," and Dr. Sheehan says "listen to your body"—it will warn you when you're pushing toward injury or disease. To these great prophets of the running world, I can only add the warning: "Do as I say, not as I do." I'm still learning.

This chapter may seem to indicate that running inevitably leads to injury. It is true that, as runners, we are subject to injuries of a wide variety, but that doesn't mean we shouldn't run, only that we should be cautious, warm up and cool down carefully, and be alert to signs of injury or pain. By knowing what injuries are possible, we can better avoid falling victim to them. What signs are significant? What does pain tell us?

OTHER PROBLEMS

Here are other problems I've had or heard other runners complain about. They are listed alphabetically, and the information here is not meant to replace a visit to your running physician.

The Ankle

Ankle sprains are caused by structural imbalance, improper foot gear, rough terrain, and improper conditioning.

The typical runner's ankle sprain occurs when a sedentary, overweight person runs in thin tennis shoes. It also happens to the overweight runner, whose weight puts great stress on the ankles, and the beginner runner who has been pounding on weak ankles that become inflamed and painful. Women beginner runners are most prone to ankle sprain, and a surprisingly large number of them complain of ankle swelling. Californian runner-doctor Joan Ullyot calls this a "beginner's pseudo-sprain." It is not caused by stepping in a hole and turning the ankle, but by weak supportive muscles. These runners haven't been using their leg muscles much, and the muscles and tendons around the ankles have become weak and are easily strained or injured. Women's ankles are further weakened by wearing "high-fashion shoes"—high heels, pointed toes—which shorten the Achilles tendon and hamstring.

Both men and women who begin running should wear well-cushioned shoes and work on the supporting muscles and tendons of their ankles. They need gradual strengthening, which can be done with exercise such as ankle circles (turning the ankle slowly in a circle), or walking on the sides of your foot. The ankles should always be loosened with these exercises prior to running. Swimming will also strengthen your ankles. Beginner runners should follow the Run-Easy Method that includes walking as well as running. Although ankle sprains are rare among veteran runners, the more experienced runner may suffer from a severe sprain that ruptures the tendons. But the most common sprain occurs when you've been running on uneven surfaces, especially during over-training. As Dr. Schuster notes, however, runners most often injure their ankles while they are walking because they are less alert to the change in ground surfaces than while running.

Once the damage is done, ice should be immediately applied to reduce swelling. The ankle should be taped or wrapped in an ankle support, and elevated. The elastic ankle supports should be worn all day until the swelling goes down. Later, whirlpool or ultrasound treatment and warm baths will aid in removing waste from the area. This may be followed by light exercises, but if the ankle hurts and is swollen, stay off it, even if that means using crutches for a few days.

Beware of doctors with needle and plaster. Cortisone injections may give temporary relief, but excessive injections can lead to joint destruction and perhaps tendon rupture. No more than one injection should be given per two months, according to Dr. Weisenfeld. Other doctors believe that the best way to keep runners off their feet, even if they promise to be good, is to slap on a cast. This probably is not necessary.

My ankles were very weak. I was in a cast many times, although I still managed to play in a championship basketball game while wearing a shell cast and an oversized shoe. In fact, I officially became a road runner two days after getting out of a cast on my leg due to another ankle injury: I turned it playing Capture-the-Flag with a group of kids. The more I ran, I discovered, the stronger my ankles became. Previously, I would feel pain in my weak ankles just walking across a field. Running actually strengthened them, probably because of the twisting and turning of cross-country workouts.

Another ankle problem is caused by one of our ankles' best friends: our thick-soled running shoes. It's easy to turn an ankle in these shoes in the beginning, when you're not used to having so much rubber under your foot. It's also easy to turn an ankle in these shoes when running fast around corners. Beware of speed work on tight-cornered indoor tracks. It may be better to use a thinner-soled racing flat.

Athlete's Foot

Athlete's foot is a fungus which causes two types of eruptions. One occurs between the toes—the skin turns white and soggy, often peeling off and leaving red, raw patches. The other occurs on the sole of the foot, where small blisters cover the affected area. Athlete's foot can be more than a nuisance. It can itch and burn and cause severe discomfort, and, left untreated, it can spread rapidly, causing large blisters, raw skin, and swelling. It can make wearing shoes unbearable, and walking or running impossible.

It is most often caused by improper foot care, wearing sweat-soaked socks or tight, airless shoes that create a climate for fungus to grow.

Good foot care is the best defense. Feet should be washed every night in warm water, dried thoroughly, and sprinkled with anti-fungus foot powder. Fungus also feeds on dead skin tissue, so it's important to clean the skin regularly with a nail brush or pumice stone.

It is also important to wear clean socks every day, especially in summer. This means both your running footwear and your "civilian" apparel. Don't try to get another run out of a pair of wet, dirty socks. Since nylon socks and rubber footwear don't absorb sweat, they can also contribute to athlete's foot. Wearing sandals in the summer to allow your feet to ventilate and keep dry is also a good idea.

The myth is that athlete's foot can be picked up in the locker room. But I spend half my life walking in and out of locker rooms in bare feet, and have never had more than a minor touch of athlete's foot. Lucky? I prefer to think that the condition is more a matter of your health care for your feet.

Ball of the Foot

Pain in the ball of the foot may have several sources. Pain under the head of the first metatarsal (the big knobby bone behind the big toe) is usually caused by trauma. It is also called sesamoiditis. Pain under the second, third, and fourth metatarsal heads (those behind the respective toes) are called stone bruises, or just painful bruised bones. A burning, stabbing, or numbing sensation may also occur in the metatarsal area and extend into one or more toes. This is caused by the impingement of a thickened nerve sheath. Pain on the top of the forefoot over a specific area is often the sign of a stress fracture of one or more metatarsal bones.

There may be several causes for these various, painful injuries:

Overtraining   Too much high mileage with pounding on hard surfaces; too much speed work or workouts on hills. Cut back until injury heals; consider alternative exercises.

Improper Form   Running too high on the toes, leaning

forward. Try running more erect, and striking the ground with a heel-ball impact.

Worn or Inadequate Shoes Thin-soled shoes, inflexible soles, shoes too tight or too narrow in fit. Select a shoe that overcomes these deficiencies.

Weak Feet Structural weakness. Morton's Foot, a condition in which the second toe is longer than the first, and the first metatarsal bone is short, can cause the second metatarsal to accept an abnormal weight load. Also, a large build-up of calluses can cause pressure on the nerves of the foot, resulting in pain or a feeling of numbness.

Common remedies include:

- *Icing* the injured area immediately after pain is felt. Ice after all runs until pain disappears. Take aspirin or a stronger medication if your doctor suggests.
- *Padding* the ball of the foot heavily at the point of pain. Actually, the padding should go behind the painful area to take your weight off it. Before the Boston Marathon I developed an excruciating pain over the metatarsal head below my second toe. The condition was instantly cured by Dr. Schuster, who merely added some extra padding to the inserts behind the painful area. Presto! I was running pain-free again.

If the problem persists, however, special orthotics should be obtained to distribute your weight at footstrike. A delay in proper treatment could result in the development of a stress fracture.

Blood in Urine

The first report of a runner's urine appearing bloody after "a severe run" was written by Dr. L. Dickinson of the Clinical Society of London; it appeared in 1894. Over 90 years later, this occurrence, still largely unexplained, remains one of the most alarming and most mysterious of athletic ailments.

After a hard run, the runner's urine may indeed appear bloody. It may be blood, or hemoglobin from the destruction of red cells in the body, or myoglobin from the breakdown of muscle fibers during exercise. Don't panic. Jack Shepherd passed blood while flying from Chicago to Denver during our 1978 author's tour promoting this book. He had been increasing his mileage, running on hard pavement, and undergoing the usual stressful routine of these tours. His blood was dark, stained a sheet of toilet paper, and the sight caused Shepherd to hyperventilate when he got back to his seat. His rolling eyes scared the hell out of me, and earned him a ride in an ambulance from the airplane to a Denver hospital. Stay calm. Try to remember the color of the blood, or collect a sample of your bloody urine for your doctor to examine. Do this right away, because your next urine, says Dr. Sheehan, may be "as clear as spring water." Shepherd's was, and he never passed blood again.

Most likely, bloody urine is hemoglobinuria, which occurs in cyclical patterns. It comes and goes in athletes, and may be triggered by an allergy, exhaustion, or other factors. Frank Shorter, the Olympic marathon runner, has had episodes of bloody urine—and keeps on running.

One form of treatment is rest: The condition cures itself within forty-eight hours. Or, switch from pavement to grass running, use shoes with good cushioning and additional rubber or inserts, and practice a lighter footfall and a gliding style. Also, avoid extreme fatigue, and add vitamin C to your diet in substantial amounts.

Blood Sugar, Low

Low blood sugar is frequently accompanied by feelings of drowsiness and fatigue. It may be a long-term condition (hypoglycemia) or only a temporary one, commonly called the mid-morning "blahs." By mid-morning your breakfast has been digested and your blood sugar is low. This is the time when many people feel the need for a candy bar or cup of coffee with Danish. But the best temporary way to raise your blood sugar level is with 10 to 15 minutes or more of exercise. This releases sugar from its storage spots in the muscles and builds up blood sugar.

Runners with hypoglycemia should follow a high-protein–high-fat diet, but should use high-carbohydrate dieting prior to long-distance efforts that may involve glycogen depletion. The runner with hypoglycemia should also be under the supervision of an athletically oriented physician.

Chest Pain

Chest pain, especially upon exertion or shortly afterward, can be a vital warning of heart disorder. The chest pain, or angina, is caused by ischemia—a lack of sufficient blood flow for the heart's need. Angina attacks may be mild to severe, described either as "crushing pain, like an elephant sitting on your chest," or as a "mild discomfort or ache."

The pain may start in the middle of your chest and radiate to the shoulders, arms, and even jaw, teeth, and ears. Sometimes, the pain may appear in only one area, such as the left arm, and not in the chest at all.

Angina need not stop a person from running *if it has been stabilized*; that is, a predictable pattern of symptoms in relation to the patient's activities has been established over a period of time. Cardiac patients may take nitroglycerine tablets at the onset of anginal pain. Obviously, anyone with anginal pain should exercise only under close medical supervision.

Most chest pain in healthy people is not due to angina. We all have occasional twinges, aches, and muscle spasms in the chest which are totally unrelated to the heart. Some pain is caused by your gastrointestinal tract, nerve pressure in the neck, gallbladder problems, ulcers, and the like. Overbreathing or hyperventilation may also cause pain. So will soreness in the muscles around the breastbone.

I once questioned my own health when I developed a severe pain on my left side during three successive days of running. Then

I remembered catching a sharp elbow during a basketball game. I was getting old. My ribs had been slightly bruised and were irritated by running, causing me to breathe deeper, and forcing the injured rib cage to expand and contract rapidly.

Chest pain should not be taken lightly; neither should any heart palpitations or irregular beats. Most of these pains or ectopic heart beats are benign, but you should immediately report them to your doctor, and have an electrocardiogram, preferably a stress test. We know of runners who have complained of chest pain and who then had positive stress tests indicating that they did, indeed, have a cardiac problem. Obviously, having a heart attack is not the best, or safest, way of documenting the course of chest pain. Runners who have had heart attacks, "silent" or not, or who have developed a cardiac arrhythmia, have been able to continue running. If symptoms appear, see your doctor without delay.

Colds and Flu

Running can help you get rid of colds, but it can also weaken you to infection. It's possible for us to run right through colds that would level our unfit friends. When runners overstress themselves, however, they are very susceptible to the common cold; I'm most vulnerable during the two weeks after a marathon, or the prerace build-up before one.

Exercise tends to break up the congestion of a cold. It also gives a psychological lift. But colds are a warning signal. Dr. Sheehan says, "I treat colds with respect. It is my feeling that they represent a breakdown of the defense system. The cold is an early warning symptom of exhaustion." There have been documented cases of sudden death in athletes who exercised heavily despite fighting a viral infection. If you have a cold, cut your mileage, slow down, and run within the limits of your energy.

To avoid colds: Obviously keep warm, keep your head covered in cold weather, and don't stand around in wet clothing after a race or workout. Doses of vitamin C may also help fight colds and flu.

Fever and flu are more dangerous. The body is in a weakened state. It doesn't need the additional stress of running, and it's best to rest completely, and then return slowly to a normal schedule. I once spent an entire summer bothered by flu, or perhaps a touch of mononucleosis. I was so intent on returning to my training program that I suffered three "relapses." It is wise to listen to your body, for your stubborn mind can lead you astray.

Diarrhea and Constipation

Diarrhea and intestinal cramps may be caused by a wide variety of things—change in diet, especially to a vegetarian one; increased exercise; certain foods such as milk, wheat products, chocolate, nuts, raisins, fruits, and vegetables. They may be caused by the onset of illness or the ingestion of new bacteria in a foreign country. Serious diarrhea will dehydrate your body, and may cause fever, uncontrolled bowel movements, and fainting. These symptoms should be medically treated immediately.

Diarrhea from diet or nerves is less serious, and can usually be prevented or controlled by taking care with foods and training before a race or a long run; proteins should be avoided. The worst possible combination would be a greasy hamburger and a glass of milk. The night before a race, eat carbohydrates. The morning of a race, fast if you can; if not, don't eat for at least three or four hours before the race (or long run). Always attempt a bowel movement before hitting the road. If you are planning a long run, or feel vulnerable, like the morning after downing lots of bad beer, be prepared by carrying along a wad of toilet paper. If the cramping becomes severe, stop and walk. Don't try to hold off too long; sometimes you can get away with walking into a restaurant and asking for a bathroom, but you can't count on this solution. The best bet is to look for a hidden spot, and go! Constipation is rarely a problem for runners, but if it is, add bran to your diet because it acts as an "intestinal broom." However, do not eat bran before racing or a long workout.

Prerace diarrhea is common, and it may even make us run faster. Bill Rodgers ran a 2:10:09 in the 1976 New York Marathon, only a few seconds off his American record. When asked what he thought about during the last few miles as he threatened the record, he replied: "I just wanted to get to the john."

Groin Pain

Groin pain appears to be most common among women, perhaps because of the wider pelvic girdle. It often is coupled with limited rear foot motion and unequal leg length. According to Dr. Schuster, "Patient files seem to indicate that some groin pains are related to the inability of the lower ankle to move from side to side—particularly outward. The only other structures that can provide this kind of in-and-out control are the adductor muscles (which pull the leg inward) of the hip—hence the possibility of groin pain."

An insert or heel cup will stabilize the heel and limit the pain. Stretching and strengthening exercises for the adductor muscles that pull the leg outward should also be included in the treatment. Here are two exercises that may help:

To stretch the groin muscles, sit with the soles of your feet together and gently push down on the knees, holding the position. Repeat.

Lie on your unaffected side, with your back and leg straight, and suspend a light weight from your foot above the base of the ankle with the strap. Lift the leg about 12 inches, hold for one second, and return. Repeat several times, but don't continue if pain develops.

Heel Pain

A heel bruise is generally caused by running on hard surfaces in shoes with thin soles. Running over sharp rocks and pebbles may also cause bruises, as will running too far back and too hard on the heels. A heel bruise may simply require a few days of not running to heal. Cushions under the heels will help you return to running sooner.

Heel bumps or spurs are more painful and can last longer. These are caused by pressure and friction over the top of the heel bone. Irregular movement of the heel bone caused by structurally weak feet, inflexible muscles, slanted running surfaces, or worn-down shoes cause the irritation of the tissue (*plantar fascia*) that extends in a fan shape from the toes to the heel. The bursa (fluid-filled protective sac) becomes inflamed, and the combination of bursitis and calcium deposits results in the heel bump. This bump is located between the skin and the tendon, or the tendon and the bone. Bumps may occur in the back of the heel where the heel bone and Achilles tendon meet, or on the bottom of the heel. The pain actually comes from the inflamed *plantar fascia*.

Cortisone injections may give temporary relief. Sometimes surgery is necessary to remove excessive bone or irritated bursa. This should be a last resort. Of special danger is a heel bump that could cause a rupture of the Achilles tendon.

A heel bump or spur on the back of the heel can be relieved by cutting out portions of the back of the shoe, and replacing them with soft elastic. On the bottom of the foot, the problem can be relieved by using heel cushion pads, three-quarter-inch sponge rubber, or plastic or rubber heel cups. You might also try to redistribute your weight away from the heel with taping, commercial orthotics, or custom-made orthotics.

Dr. Sheehan recommends the following:

- Wear well-cushioned shoes with a good heel counter, high heel, and solid shank.
- Use a commercial arch support or have custom inserts made to eliminate the cause of the rolling action on the heel and foot. Sometimes just the addition of a heel cup to stabilize the heel is sufficient.
- Do flexibility exercises regularly for the calf and hamstring muscles.

- Run on grass or other soft surfaces, keeping away from speed and hill work.
- Apply heat to the heel before running, and ice afterward.

Common causes of heel pain include: running too much on the balls of your feet, too much mileage on hard pavement, too much speed or hill work too soon, shoes without a good heel counter or flexibility or adequate cushioning, or shoes worn in the heels.

Recovery will take time. Rushing back into fast running or hard training after this injury would be unwise.

Hip Pain

Hip pain is almost always caused by unequal pressure upon footstrike. Worn-down shoes, unequal leg length, slanted running surfaces, and structurally weak feet are most often the culprits. The use of inserts, heel lifts, and well-cushioned and evenly worn shoes, and staying away from slanted surfaces like tracks and graded, paved roads are the most frequent cures.

Sciatica, resulting from nerve pressure, can also cause hip pain. Stretching exercises are an extra benefit if sciatica persists. Osteoarthritis is another cause of hip pain, and can be partially relieved in its early stages with aspirin. Triggerpoints (see page 268) are also frequently found in the hip area. Many times, hip pain results from running while favoring another injury.

The following exercises will stretch and strengthen the key muscles of the hip:

1. Lunge position. Right leg in front of body. Lean forward on the right leg, bending at the right knee, left leg to the rear on its toes, stretched out straight. Do not bob. Hold position for 30 seconds to a minute, then reverse. Repeat several times.
2. Side lunge position. Hands on hips, extend your left leg sideways as far as you can along the ground. Stretch the left leg by resting on the inside of the left foot and putting

maximum strength on the inside of the left thigh. Hold. Stretch for 30 seconds to one minute. No bobbing. Alternate legs, and repeat.

3. Stand sideways to a wall, one hand with arm outstretched to the wall for support. Allow hip closest to the wall to fall toward it. Do not move your feet. Hold for 30 seconds to a minute, then alternate sides and repeat.

Jock Rash

Also known as "jock itch," this horror is similar to athlete's foot: It involves a fungus growing in a damp environment. Wearing clean, dry athletic supporters and bathing regularly are important. I've also heard of a drastic precautionary measure: Swab the area with vinegar; the acid creates an atmosphere in which the fungus cannot survive. Perhaps this method is indeed effective, but I've not tried it.

As a preventive measure, you might try one of the commercially available powders. Sprinkle a little on either side of your groin and along the crotch both before running and after showering. This will dry the area, prevent chafing, and soothe whatever rash may have begun.

If you have jock rash, your doctor will prescribe an ointment (or powder) to get rid of it. Follow his directions faithfully. My co-author recalls one soccer season in college when he and his teammates watched a football player in the locker room who had jock itch. The rash first took the outline of his athletic supporter, and then, ignored, it slowly spread down his thighs and up his abdomen until it covered an area—Shepherd swears it's true—almost two feet wide. The player had no trouble finding a shower after practice—or locker space.

Many men use powder and also wear "jockey shorts" or even nylon bikini briefs to prevent chafing. Women, on the other hand, are turning from their nylon panties to cotton ones, which absorb moisture. European running shorts come with built-in supports. All of these garments should be washed after every run.

The Stitch

Runner's World always refers to this as "the dreaded side stitch." And it is. The stitch is believed to be a spasm of the diaphragm muscle, which separates the lungs from the abdomen. It strikes the runner just as suddenly and painfully as a charley horse attacks the sprinter or the sedentary, middle-aged man or woman who tries to run hard without warming up. The stitch may, however, begin slowly, and gradually intensify. Sometimes it feels like a knife stuck deep into the bottom or upper side of the rib cage. It usually occurs on the right side.

There are several possible causes. Running on a full stomach makes one more susceptible, especially after having had milk or grain products, which disturb the stomach. An improper warm-up can lead to trouble as the body rebels against the sudden switch from inactivity. A stitch often occurs after the runner starts the race too fast and thus may be related to oxygen debt. Generally, faulty breathing is the primary culprit.

Beginner runners and veterans are both susceptible. A beginner is often tense; when his tensed diaphragm becomes stretched by the rapid breathing during running, a stitch may occur. Experienced runners sometimes breathe improperly, which can also stretch the diaphragm and cause a stitch, particularly late in a race.

How do you fight the dreaded stitch? An increased fitness level helps. As the beginner gradually improves his or her overall cardiopulmonary endurance, and the strength and flexibility of his or her abdominal muscles and awareness of pace, the incidence of stitching decreases. In fact, it rarely occurs again until the runner increases his or her pace or begins to compete—in other words, reaches another stage of running development.

To avoid stitches, beginner runners should carefully stretch all their muscles during the warm-up and perform a variety of abdominal exercises. They should concentrate on proper abdominal breathing, or belly breathing. Prior to running, beginners should walk, raising their arms high overhead and thrusting the stomach outward as they breathe in deeply, and dropping their arms, and exhaling through pursed lips as the stomach is sucked in. Running is started at a slow pace never exceeding the talk-test level. Between running intervals, repeat the walking/belly-breathing technique.

At the first sign of a stitch, walk slowly and repeat the breathing exercise. Emphasizing the belly-breathing technique helps the beginner runner adapt it to his or her normal running pattern of breathing. If the stitch becomes extremely painful, stop and grab the knee on the side of the pain and pull it to your chest for a few seconds, squeezing hard. This can be done while either standing or lying on one's side. This modified fetal position takes the pressure off the diaphragm, which is undergoing a muscle spasm; it's the same technique used to relieve pain from a back spasm.

Runners who experience a stitch in a race have more of a problem. You can't just stop and do some exercises, although Tom Fleming did during one major race, and then went on to win. Most of us would find ourselves hopelessly behind hundreds of runners after only a few seconds' delay.

If you happen to be running the race of your life, the dreaded side stitch is especially annoying. More than likely you develop a stitch during a race because of a fast start, and tension. Dr. Sheehan says that a racer who is tense and draws the stomach in while breathing places a tremendous strain on the diaphragm as he or she stretches the taut muscles very quickly and forcefully. Runners may also "trap air," which further stretches the diaphragm. Concentrating on something else, like the shape and movement of the runner—male or female—up ahead, may help. Dr. Sheehan suggests that we breathe out against slight resistance, even if we must groan. Listening to him and Ted Corbitt during a race is almost unpleasant. They moan and groan, these cagey ol' aged sixty-plus running veterans, but they pass you by while you're grasping at your side. Super-exaggerated belly breathing has worked for me. I'll breathe in very deeply and noisily and exhale deeply with a huge groan. This has two side effects: Everyone thinks I'm a little bonkers—which may be true enough—and my noise-making startles runners about me, who then scamper ahead.

A more subtle on-the-run treatment for the stitch is to raise your arms overhead while breathing in deeply, expanding your stomach. As you lower your arms, exhale loudly and contract your stomach. Accompanied by a slowing of your pace, this may do the trick. Sometimes, however, you simply must stop and do some stretching exercises until the pain goes away. The ultimate treatment is just to tough it out and pretend the stitch has not happened, but there are few runners I know who can do this.

Stress Fractures

A stress fracture is a partial or complete break of a bone. It usually occurs in one of the metatarsals in the foot, or in one of the shin bones. The exact causes of stress fracture are not known and sometimes a runner may even have one without noticing it. Runners with poor footstrike due to improper running style or foot instability seem to be more prone to stress fractures. So are runners who sharply increase their mileage or the intensity of their workouts. High school and college track coaches who really drive their young runners, particularly indoors, ruin many good athletes by pushing them into stress fractures. Even runners who have never had problems may suddenly find themselves with a stress fracture. This may be because bone is a metabolically active tissue, and stress fractures may occur during a period of momentary weakness.

The fracture comes on very subtly. At first it may seem to be a case of bad shin splints, but if the pain persists, X rays should be taken. Sometimes, however, the fracture won't show up on an X ray for two weeks or so, and if the pain persists, more X rays may be needed.

Do not be careless: Treat the injury as a stress fracture until your doctor tells you otherwise. Beware: Some stress fractures are not always accompanied by pain, and may feel like a nagging inflammation. Runners are tempted to "work it through," and continue running on a stress fracture, which could lead to a very serious injury. Always check with your doctor.

Once diagnosed, the stress fracture may keep you out of your running shoes for a month or longer. You may be able to do some light jogging with shoe inserts to distribute your weight, but most likely, rest is your only option. Bicycling, swimming, and stationary rowing may help keep your conditioning. Obey your doctor's instructions; some physicians now slap a cast on stubborn runners to force them to rest. Running on a stress fracture could result in a fractured bone and should only be done with the permission of a podiatrist or physician. The common treatment for any bone injury is to slap on a cast. This often is unnecessary, and can lead to muscle atrophy. An athletically minded podiatrist or orthopedist is your best friend when a stress fracture sabotages your running program.

It is possible to return to heavy training gradually after a stress fracture. Millrose AA runner Mike Cleary lost ten weeks of training due to a stress fracture of the shin bone, and within three months of resuming training ran his best times for 2:54 and 2:39 for the marathon. The key to his success was in keeping off the injury, and then gradually building his mileage back to normal. Often, stress fractures will reoccur. It is therefore important, after healing, to investigate the cause by having a thorough biomechanical evaluation by a sports-medicine expert.

Triggerpoints

Triggerpoints are local tender spots of degenerated muscle tissue in the skeletal muscle. They can produce severe pain or muscle spasm. The pain may radiate down the extremities, head, neck, and back. Runners are most susceptible to triggerpoints in the legs and back.

Triggerpoints may be caused by faulty running style or structural weakness that results in an abnormal strain on a particular muscle group, muscular imbalance produced by weak or stiff posture muscles, or tension. The pain may come and go, but becomes most intense during periods of emotional pressure.

I was a victim of triggerpoints. Actually, I was a victim of my inability to slow down and do one thing at a time. During the summer of 1976, I was running 100 miles a week, and feeling great. Then came graduate school, long hours of pressure at my old job, the first edition of this book, the organization of the New York Marathon. I was in a self-spun web of pressure, and three weeks before the marathon, I broke down. My knee and back hurt in a whole new way. It wasn't pain from structural weaknesses or inflexibility. It was tension pain.

When I probed spots in the tendons above my knee, calf, hip, and back, pain radiated from them. Dr. Hans Kraus ordered point massage twice daily. It was sheer agony as the masseur pressed deeply on the tension-knotted muscles. It almost worked. I ran the first 10 miles of the marathon pain-free and very fast, but it was hell from that point on.

The treatment procedure for triggerpoints is to inject an anesthetic (Lidocaine, Procaine, or Novocaine) into the knot to break up the spots of degenerated muscle tissue. This is followed on succeeding days by electrical stimulation to relax the muscle. Absolutely no exercise or even prolonged sitting or standing are allowed during the treatments. Therapy is followed by a program of relaxation and stretching exercises, and a gradual progression back to a normal running schedule. I wasn't able to exercise for a month and a half, but I was able to return to competition. Treatment, however, only eliminates the symptoms, not the cause. The pain may very well return.

Varicose Veins

The veins in the legs carry deoxygenated blood back to the heart. Since these vessels must conduct blood upward against the force of gravity, a series of valves is employed to prevent the backflow of blood. In people who sit or stand a great deal, the valves of the leg veins tend to wear out, and in time the high pressure of the long column of blood that they must support overcomes the elasticity of the veins' walls and valves. Thus, the veins are dilated and become "varicose veins." The tendency to develop varicose veins is largely, but not exclusively, hereditary.

Dr. Colin James Alexander hypothesized in *The Lancet* in 1972 that Western man's habit of sitting in chairs could be the major cause of varicose veins. Primitive people without chairs rarely suffer from the affliction. Chair sitting places a high and constant pressure on the vein walls. Rocking chairs, however, promote circulation. Sedentary life, therefore, may increase the normal dilation of the veins that comes with aging, and the veins become more sensitive to other factors like standing, pregnancy, and tight clothing.

Medical studies show that people with varicose veins are bothered less if they follow an endurance conditioning program such as running. Running will not make varicose veins go away, but it will increase the strength of the supportive structures around the veins, and assist in the venous blood return from the legs to the heart. Actually, varicose veins may become more prominent as you run, but this isn't furthering the condition.

Superficial varicose veins are more a cosmetic than a medical problem. A surgical operation to strip the veins will improve the looks of the legs, but not aid in improving circulation. Sometimes surgery is necessary, however, if the condition becomes too painful.

Marathoner Nina Kuscsik often complained to her doctor about leg pains due to varicose veins, but the muscle tone of her legs from her marathon running hid the problem, and her doctor didn't think it serious. Not until she decided to have surgery and was relaxed under the anesthesia did the true condition of her veins become evident.

Swelling is common after surgery. Nina was instructed to wear an Ace bandage on her entire leg for three weeks to promote circulation and prevent pressure over the incision. Oddly, she was also told not to bother with the bandage while running, which naturally improves circulation. She said, "So I was out there running four days after surgery, before the stitches were removed. I had no swelling at all!"

Runners with a tendency toward varicosity should sit with their feet up, wear elastic support socks to assist circulation, and avoid tight pants and socks.

17 THE HEART-LUNG MACHINE

What happens to your body when you run? At the center of your chest—indeed, at the center of your life—is your heart. It's an extraordinary muscle about the size of your fist that weighs 8 to 10 ounces, beats an average of 70 to 80 times a minute while resting, or about 4,200 times an hour, 100,000 times a day, more than 36 billion times a year.

The heart is composed of muscle tissue different from any other tissue in the body: Cardiac muscle has its own distinct appearance under the microscope. The heart is also one of the best muscular structures of our bodies, ready to improve its condition if we exercise it in a proper manner. This muscle pumps your body's entire blood supply (about 5 quarts) through your vascular system in less than a minute; during exercise blood may travel through your arteries at speeds of 40 miles per hour.

The red cells in your blood carry oxygen to the muscles of your body, and return waste—carbon dioxide—to the lungs to be expelled. Exercise increases and enriches this exchange.

On either side of your heart are the lungs. These organs are light, porous, and spongy in texture and highly elastic. Inside your lungs are microscopic air sacs called alveoli. The lungs contain millions of them, tiny and balloonlike. Here, your blood becomes oxygenated. Each tiny alveolus is covered with a membrane wall one-cell thick. When air is breathed into the lungs, molecules of oxygen pass through the thin membrane of the alveolus (with its bronchi and bronchioles) to attach to the hemoglobin of red blood cells. The membrane is so small that each red blood cell must line up and pass through in single file to take in oxygen and give up carbon dioxide, water, and other wastes.

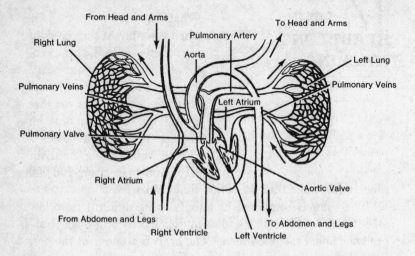

The Heart-Lung Machine

These organs—the heart and lungs—nourish your body, give it strength, and help remove some of its wastes. During low levels of activity, the heart and lungs maintain a steady rate: 70 to 80 beats, 15 to 18 inhalations per minute. The lungs fill with between 200 and 350 milliliters of oxygen with each breath.

As you warm up prior to running, your heart rate increases. Your muscles begin demanding more oxygenated blood. Your heart begins pumping harder. It is a double pump. It consists of layers of muscles in circles and spirals that tighten, contracting blood out of its chambers (systole) and relaxing to let blood in (diastole). As it contracts, expelling blood, the heart shortens, shrinks, and twists.

There are four chambers in this muscle: two at the top, called atria; two at the bottom, called ventricles. Each atrium is separated from the ventricle chamber below it by a valve; the right atrium and ventricle are separated from the left by a strong muscle wall. Each atrium is a holding chamber, each ventricle a pump.

Blood from your muscles, low in oxygen and dark red in color, arrives back in your heart by the veins; it flows from the right atrium into the right ventricle, which pumps it into the right and left pulmonary arteries, and through the bronchi and bronchioles. In the lungs, the exchange of carbon dioxide for oxygen by the red blood cells makes the blood bright red. It flows back to your heart through the pulmonary veins to the left atrium, which holds and passes it into the left ventricle. That durable pump ejects the oxygenated blood to your aorta, the body's largest artery, which branches and divides and reaches into all parts of your body. With every contraction, or beat, your heart receives back about 5 percent of the blood it has just rejected via the coronary arteries, for nourishment. Without oxygen, the heart muscle itself could not function.

The blood surges from the aorta to arteries throughout your body, then into arterioles and the smallest vessels, the capillaries, which carry blood to the individual cells. Here, oxygen and other chemicals are delivered, and waste like carbon dioxide collected. The blood begins its return trip to the heart by capillaries to venules to the veins.

As you finish your warm-ups and calisthenics, your heart is driving blood through your arteries to meet the new demands of your muscles. With this greater flow of blood to your tissues, as you begin your run, there is a corresponding need for increased oxygen delivered and used by your body tissues. Your large arteries, as they always do, are expanding and contracting in rhythm to your heartbeat and pushing the blood along. Your smaller arteries are opening wider to get additional blood flowing to the active muscles. Your blood actually thins so it will flow better. This is why warming up is important: It lets the body's myriad functions begin, so that blood can increase its flow to your muscles.

Now, the metabolic process of your entire body is being stimulated. The cardiovascular system reaches into every distant cell, and your cells are responding to the demands that running makes upon them. The kidneys are activated to carry off the biochemical wastes of muscular work. The liver's enzyme system works harder to purify the blood and replace enzymes lost in running. Other organs begin producing young white blood cells. Blood flow to the stomach and intestines diminishes (one reason for not eating before exercising), while the blood flow to the skin and muscles increases sharply. The brain, lungs, and heart are all being enriched and nourished.

As running becomes more vigorous, your blood pressure rises as the heart contracts and ejects blood (systolic pressure). Your body is demanding more oxygen; more blood must be pumped through the lungs, heart, and arteries to the demanding muscles, and returned. Your heart increases its stroke volume, placing increased pressure on the walls of your aorta and the arteries themselves.

If you're in good condition, the systolic pressure will rise during your run, level off, and may drop slightly. Continued long-distance running may produce a second gradual increase. Among people in good condition, the diastolic pressure during the relaxation phase of a heartbeat remains almost unchanged, or decreases slightly, during exercise; among the unconditioned, it rises.

Exercises with heavy lifting may in some cases put a dangerous stress on the blood vessels and cardiovascular system due to the sudden increase and decrease in blood pressure. Gradual endurance exercise allows your arteries and capillaries to open for better circulation; opening causes a decrease in their resistance. The heart doesn't have to work as hard to get blood to those demanding muscles. Further, endurance training increases the number of capillaries in the heart and skeletal muscles, which brings even more oxygen to the heart and muscles, and helps remove waste products more efficiently. There is also evidence that endurance exercises like running actually lower blood presure in hypertense people. Lowered blood pressure reduces the heart's need for oxygen.

In addition to increasing the rate at which oxygen is used by the cells, exercise also increases the rate at which carbon dioxide is formed. Changes in your breathing are essential, so that more oxygen is supplied and carbon dioxide is quickly removed. That exchange depends upon the rate and depth of breathing, the efficiency of your lung ventilation, and the condition of your blood and circulatory system.

Now, you are running. Your brain is receiving stimuli demanding more oxygen for the muscles. It sends nerve impulses to your chest muscles, which increase the rate and depth of breathing. Your breathing has increased from 18 to perhaps 50 breaths per minute. The tidal volume of air has jumped from 10 percent of capacity to 50 percent; oxygen intake has gone up to perhaps 20 times what it was. With the increase in respiratory volume, lung ventilation—the exchange between alveoli and your bloodstream—also increases. You are now breathing in larger amounts of air, and making more efficient transfer of it to your bloodstream and muscles, including your heart.

In a single breath the average trained runner can process a full liter of air more than the untrained person. The maximum breathing capacity per minute may reach 40 to 50 more liters than the untrained person. Your lungs have become stronger, able to move air in and out at a faster rate. Your blood is carrying more oxygen.

Your training has also increased your heart's efficiency. It grows stronger, and pumps more blood with each stroke. A conditioned person may have a resting heart rate 20 beats per minute slower than an unconditioned person. That means that you may be saving as many as 10,000 heartbeats during a single night's sleep. Even while running, your heart pumps blood and oxygen at a much slower rate than the unconditioned heart, which may beat dangerously fast.

Some studies have shown that running also increases the number and size of blood vessels that carry blood to your body. It has enlarged your arteries, and made them more elastic, better able to expand and contract. There are more capillaries in your active muscles. Studies find, for example, that active children, as adults, have larger coronary arteries than their more sedentary peers. So do runners who train for marathons. *The New England Journal of Medicine* reported on the autopsy of the seventy-year-old Clarence De Mar, who almost all his adult life ran the Boston Marathon each year and was considered one of the greatest marathon runners ever. His coronary arteries were so enlarged that they couldn't possibly have been closed by atherosclerosis.

The key to your endurance is oxygen. Your body needs oxygen for energy; it cannot store it. The lungs must bring it in and the body must deliver it to the organs or tissues that demand it. A runner's heart, grown in size and strength, pumps almost twice the volume of blood with each stroke (beat) than that of an untrained person. Moreover, myoglobin—the oxygen-binding pigment of muscle—has a strong affinity for oxygen. Exercise raises the levels of myoglobin to twice normal levels. This means that your muscles are better able to extract oxygen from the blood and also increase the amount of oxygen in the tissues. It may help delay the onset of lactic acid production, which causes fatigue.

As you slow down, and perform your cool-down exercises, other physiological changes occur. The rate and depth of your breathing return to normal, as do the heart rate and the stroke volume. As you become more fit, this process will take less time. An abrupt halting of all exercise after running can be dangerous because blood caught in the extremities may "pool" there. The muscles need a cool-down period to return the circulatory system to normal.

Some of the benefits of long, slow exercise to your heart-lung machine are well documented and not controversial. Jogging three times a week, 20 minutes a day, at aerobic levels, may reduce your resting heart rate on the average of one beat for every week of running up to 15 weeks. Postexercise recovery rates should improve at about the same pace. Cardiac output and your stroke volume will also increase as a result of your training. That is, your ventricle will produce a more forceful contraction. The results, then, are fewer but stronger heartbeats. Hypertensive people have shown a tendency toward more normal blood pressure after running at least three times a week, over a 15-week period. Long, slow running also increases oxygen delivery to your brain, liver, kidneys, skin, and genitals.

Here the controversy begins. There is a spirited discussion going on about whether or not running merely tones the cardiovascular and muscular system and improves the quality of life, or whether it actually prevents death caused by heart attack. Cardiovascular diseases are the major causes of death in men over thirty-five. Heart attacks rank number one, strokes, number three, and other blood vessel diseases, fourth. (Cancer is second.) Heart disease kills one of every ten people who die before age thirty-five, but one of every three over thirty-five.

The crucial question is whether or not vigorous exercise like running reduces the incidence or severity of heart attacks. There are few causes of coronary heart disease about which we can do nothing. We can control our diets to make them low in fat, we can lose weight, avoid stress, not smoke. And we can exercise.

There are some benefits of which medical science is certain. Cigarette smokers are less likely to suffer fatal heart attacks if they also exercise vigorously and regularly. Overweight men and women can reduce their heart attack risk by as much as 25 percent by undertaking a regular exercise program. People with high blood pressure who also exercise cut their risk factor in half. Clearly, vigorous exercise may improve your cardiovascular efficiency, lower your blood pressure, and modify your blood chemistry. It may also lower your serum triglycerides, and better the ratio of high-density to low-density lipoproteins.

Your blood contains two fats essential to life: cholesterol and triglycerides. Cholesterol is naturally a part of your body; it is synthesized in the liver and nearly every tissue and organ. It is an indispensable component of cellular structure. But there is a sharp difference between the cholesterol your body produces and that ingested from foods.

When too much lipid (cholesterol/triglyceride) is in the blood, a condition called hyperlipidemia exists, and deposits form on the inner walls of the arteries. This reduces their diameter, and bring about atherosclerosis. It is thought that other fatty deposits on the arterial walls may cause the formation of a thrombus which would also block the artery. Exercise might prevent the formation of a thrombus or, because exercise increase the blood's clotting time, it may assist in dissolving one.

Recent research, however, suggests that the amount of cholesterol in the blood is not as important as the ratio of high-density to low-density lipoproteins, the protein compounds that transport the cholesterol in the bloodstream. Low-density lipoproteins (LDLs) carry cholesterol in their core, and are the major mode of transporting cholesterol into our tissues, where it may form an atherosclerotic plaque. This plaque of fats and other materials clogs our arteries and will limit or halt altogether the flow of blood. High-density lipoproteins (HDLs), on the other hand, clear away cholesterol from the tissues and return it to the liver to be excreted. It is not yet established as a scientific fact, but HLDs are also thought to remove cholesterol from the artery walls and prevent it from being deposited there, thus thwarting the atherosclerotic process.

Research in California and Scotland suggests that HDLs may protect against heart attack by interfering with the cell's taking in LDLs and by stopping this buildup of fatty deposits that cause hardening of the arteries and heart attacks. "The higher the HDL cholesterol level, the better off people seem to be," says Dr. William P. Castelli of the National Heart, Lung and Blood Institute. Other studies show that people who are highly immune to heart disease have high levels of HDLs in their blood, and low levels of LDLs.

Further, doctors know that LDLs can be lowered by reducing the intake of cholesterol and saturated fats in our diets, or by drugs. HDLs, some evidence shows, can be elevated by drugs, or diets rich in fish and low in cholesterol. Further studies are indicating that vigorous exercise raises high-density lipoproteins while lowering low-density ones.

The Stanford Heart Disease Prevention Program studied forty-one middle-aged California men who ran 15 miles or more a week, and a similar group of nonrunners. The runners had half the triglyceride levels of the nonrunners and slightly less cholesterol. But perhaps most important, the runners' blood contained almost half again as many high-density lipoproteins as the nonrunners. Some sixty-year-old runners had HDL levels comparable to those of a teenage girl—the most immune group of all. In fact, women generally have higher levels of HDLs than men, which may account for the lower incidence of heart disease among them.

By removing the cholesterol that narrows the coronary arteries, HDLs help prevent heart attacks. A 1984 study headed by Dr. Basil M. Rifkind demonstrated conclusively that lowering levels of cholesterol in the bloodstream reduced the rate of heart attacks in a high-risk group of middle-aged men. Each 1 percent fall in cholesterol corresponded to a 2 percent reduction in the incidence of heart disease. Moreover, a study at New York Hospital–Cornell Medical Center indicates that runners have less viscous blood than nonrunners, which means that it flows easier and forms clots less readily than the blood of nonrunners.

Studies are also showing that regular exercise will lower and stabilize your weight. Dr. Grant Gwinup of the University of California at Irvine put eleven obese women through a year's regime of vigorous walking. No weight loss occurred until the women could walk 30 minutes a day, or more. Then, during the rest of the year, all of the women lost between 10 and 38 pounds.

Most of us gain weight when we stop regular exercise, usually within a decade after we leave school. Few school programs develop exercise skills that carry over into adult life; even playing tennis once a week cannot be considered adequate. Consequently, most of us notice the first roll of fat by our late twenties. One pound of fat equals 3,500 stored calories. If you are 20 pounds overweight, that means you've eaten and stored as fat 70,000 calories. If you had walked 10 minutes a day for 5 years, you probably wouldn't have gained any of that useless and dangerous weight.

Running burns as much as 100 calories per mile. Further, regular runners find that their weight drops to a steady level, and that regular workouts depress appetite. That is, the workouts, instead of increasing your demand for food, stabilize it.

Regular exercise can also help smokers quit. If you are still smoking, and trying to run, the next few paragraphs may—literally—save your life.

Smoking has been linked to cancer, poor nutrition, ulcers, increased resting heart rate, high blood pressure, and coronary heart disease. For one thing, tobacco smoke contains nicotine. If you took the nicotine from an average cigarette and injected it into your veins, it might kill you. Inhaled, you merely get the poison in smaller amounts, not immediately fatal.

Smoke from tobacco contains 500 to 600 known poisons. Among them are carbon monoxide, hydrogen cyanide (a respiratory enzyme poison), pyridine, phenols (known cancer-causing agents), aldehydes that irritate the lungs, acrolein (used in World War I as a gas), and seven different polycyclic hydrocarbons also known to cause cancer. This smoke, and its accompanying poisons, is absorbed by your lips, mouth cavity, throat, nasal passages, and esophagus, and is drawn deep into your lungs. Nicotine, if swallowed, irritates your stomach and intestines. Chew a cigar, and your lips and mouth get poisoned; smoke a pipe and the tars from the stem are sucked into your mouth and throat.

Your body's nervous system alertly tries to combat these poisons. Saliva flows, your heart rate speeds up, your blood pressure increases. The peripheral blood vessels contract and the skin chills slightly. Your fingertips and feet may get cold, caused by the constriction of your veins from tobacco substances. Laboratory tests show that sometimes blood actually stops flowing in places like the fingernail fold—your fingers may die a little with each cigarette.

The constriction of your veins gives you a "slowed-down" feeling. Slowed circulation leads to the belief that cigarettes "calm the nerves." Actually, the body is undergoing terrific stress. Studies first performed in 1909 prove that one cigarette increases your heart rate by 20 beats per minute. This condition persists for about 25 minutes after you finish smoking—about the length of time between cigarettes—and also increases your blood pressure. Yet your veins have constricted, and the heart now is being forced to pump harder to move blood through veins that are smaller.

Moreover, those small air sacs, the alveoli, so vital to the exchange of oxygen and carbon dioxide, suffer widespread destruction when you inhale smoke. At the same time, the small arterial blood vessels delivering blood to the lungs for oxygenation are narrowed. Now the heart is forced to beat still harder to get blood to your lungs where it absorbs oxygen from damaged air sacs. The smoke in your lungs adds to the heart's load, and the oxygen entering your bloodstream is not clean, but contains tars, nicotine, smoke compounds, carbon monoxide.

The heart strains in its effort to push blood through constricting vessels; the blood itself contains contaminants instead of vitally needed oxygen. If your arteries are partially blocked by cholesterol deposits, you're in further trouble. But at least now you understand some of the reasons behind the fact that if you smoke (and don't exercise) your chances of dying from a heart attack are twice those of the nonsmoking runner.

Smoking causes a multitude of other problems as well—to both smokers and nonsmokers. For example, a medical report in England indicates that the children of smokers have two to three times the incidence of pneumonia and bronchitis than children of nonsmokers. In 1975, the medical journal *Lancet* reported that after smokers and nonsmokers had spent an hour in a closed room, the nonsmokers ended up with more nicotine in their lungs than the smokers. Their healthier lungs and higher oxygen uptake capacity helped them absorb the greater amounts of nicotine.

Like running nonsmokers, newborn children have lungs that are also particularly receptive to nicotine in the air. One smoking parent exposes his child to 60,000 hours of "passive smoking" by the child's twentieth birthday. A long-distance runner with smoking parents, says Dr. Thomas Bassler, loses 6 minutes from his potential marathon time for each month of the first 6 months of his life spent indoors with cigarette smoke. There is even a noticeable difference between runners born to smokers in the months of spring and summer; they have a better chance because, as babies, they were more often outdoors and away from cigarettes.

Clearly, runners and other nonsmokers have a right—an obligation—to tell smokers to blow it in some other direction.

If you don't smoke, and you exercise regularly (and aerobically) and enjoy all the accruing benefits we've discussed, what are your chances of suffering and surviving a coronary attack? There are no clear proofs that exercise protects. And the research itself contains well-documented contradictions.

One of the most comprehensive studies of cardiovascular disease and exercise was published in the April 1970, issue of *Circulation*. This study covered 12,770 men between the ages of forty and fifty-nine in seven countries—the United States, Japan, and in Western Europe. A review of this study in 1971 by the National Heart and Lung Institute Task Force reported that there was no difference in coronary-disease risk between sedentary and active men in this age category. "If physical inactivity is indeed a risk factor," the Task Force concluded, "it is of much smaller magnitude than hypertension, cigarette smoking, and elevated serum cholesterol."

A five-year review of two groups in west and east Finland, with high levels of activity and also high serum cholesterol, found that among the active men the rate of coronary heart disease was the same as that among sedentary men.

But before you sink into your easy chair and give away your running shoes, you might be interested in other research. In 1953, Dr. J. N. Morris of the Medical Research Council of London Hospital reported that London bus drivers who sat all day had 1.5 times as much heart disease and twice the coronary death rate as the bus conductors, who climbed up and down the stairs of the double-decker buses collecting fares. In 1956, however, Dr. Morris published a paper titled "The Epidemiology of Uniforms." When he examined the records of the uniforms issued to these London drivers and conductors, he found that the drivers had been consistently issued larger uniforms than the conductors. The fact that the drivers were fatter, not more inactive, may have caused their higher number of coronary attacks. Or, the thinner and less coronary-prone men may have preferred the more active work of conductor.

More conclusive support for exercise is found among workers in kibbutzim in Israel who were studied by Dr. Daniel Brunner of the Government Hospital at Jaffa. He reported that while the lives, diet, stress, and other factors of these workers seemed identical, the sedentary workers had 2.5 to 4 times as much heart disease as more active workers.

A long-term study of San Francisco longshoremen, published in March 1975, reached similar conclusions. Once again vigorous activity was significant. Among the 6,351 men studied over a twenty-two-year period, those who did the heaviest labor had a lower incidence of heart disease, and only one-third the rate of sudden death from heart attack than men in less strenuous work. The researchers concluded that vigorous exercise was "a critical factor in cardiovascular well-being, especially as it would prevent sudden death from coronary heart disease." They reported similar findings in a follow-up study in March 1977.

By far the most conclusive study on exercise and heart attack was first reported in November 1977 and updated in 1984 by Dr. Ralph S. Paffenbarger, Jr., of the Stanford University School of Medicine. Dr. Paffenbarger questioned 16,936 Harvard University alumni aged thirty-five to eighty-four about their health and exercise. He reported that strenuous exercise, like jogging for at least three hours a week, has a "definite protective effect" against heart attack—even if the man has other medical liabilities like overweight or high blood pressure. The study revealed that fatal heart disease was found to be nearly twice as common among the most sedentary subjects as it was among the most active.

Furthermore, Dr. Paffenbarger found that as men exercise more, the risk of attack decreases. That is, men who expend fewer than 2,000 calories per week showed a sixty-four percent higher risk of heart attack than those who were more energetic. Those who played "light" sports like golf, bowling, baseball, or biking were no better off than those who were inactive. But men who walked regularly were better off than those who didn't, and men who exercised vigorously were better off than those who walked.

Dr. Paffenbarger measured the incidents of heart attack versus energy expended in exercise. By doing so, he showed that about three or four miles of running per day was the minimum amount of exercise that will significantly reduce the risk of heart attack. Running between 20 and 30 miles a week—or the exercise equivalent—makes you 64 percent less likely to have a heart attack than a sedentary person. Beyond 40 miles a week, you may have some small increments in additional protection. Periodic hard running also adds to your health benefits.

Dr. Paffenbarger's research also holds out hope for men and women who start to run long after they have left college (or college-age level). He has determined that active college students who stop exercising after they graduate have no more protection than their inactive peers. But men who, whether active in college or not, took up strenuous exercise later had a clearly reduced risk of heart attack.

As more data are gathered, other conclusions are becoming known. One area that supports the proposition that exercise protects against heart disease deals with men and women who have already suffered from heart attacks. Their rehabilitation offers some convincing arguments.

Since 1967, Dr. Terrence Kavanaugh, medical director of the Toronto Cardiac Rehabilitation Center, has been encouraging his post-coronary patients to exercise. The program includes no smoking, special diets, and jogging; some also run marathons. Most of his patients run three miles a day in 36 minutes, five times a week if they are older than forty-five; those under forty-five run three miles in 30 minutes. The results are impressive. "We have a 1.4 percent-per-annum mortality rate from 1967 to last October [1976]," Dr. Kavanaugh told *The New York Times*. "In groups that don't exercise, the comparable rate is 6 to 12 percent. And we get those results with 780 patients—probably the biggest exercise coronary rehab group in the world."

Dr. Herman Hellerstein of Case Western Reserve University, a co-speaker with me at the 1977 New York Lung Association dinner, is also an advocate of exercise for post-coronary patients, although he doesn't believe that running alone—without giving up smoking and eating a proper diet—offers much benefit. Dr. Hellerstein found in his experiments during the last decade that post-coronary patients who exercised regularly had much less chance of suffering a second, fatal heart attack than sedentary post-coronary patients.

In 1956, Jack Shepherd was a camp counselor at Camp Becket, a YMCA camp in the Berkshire Hills of Massachusetts.

Dr. Paul Dudley White, then President Eisenhower's cardiologist, was an alumnus of Becket who frequently returned to the camp to extol the virtues of exercise. Dr. White would talk with small clusters of young Becket men, urging them to continue their exercise beyond high school and college. "If you want heart trouble," he later wrote, "be inert physically. The general warning to stop all exercise at forty seems to me to be ridiculous and more likely than not actually to lead to an increase in coronary attacks and hardening of the arteries."

Medical science, and hundreds of thousands of runners, have since that time corroborated Dr. White's warning.

18 DIET AND RUNNING

Runners understand that old saw, "You are what you eat." They are forever in search of food, drink, and vitamins that will increase their stamina, energy, strength, performance, and recovery.

However, diets promoted for runners are confusing. Overload with carbohydrates? Maintain a high-protein diet? Restrict sugar and salt intake? Drink beer to gain weight or strength? Swallow megavitamins plus protein supplements? Little wonder that one nutritionist says, with some exasperation, "American athletes have the most expensive urine in the world."

To understand what diet might be best for you, let's make several points clear. No one diet regimen is suitable for any large number of athletically active people. What works for one may not work for another. The best diet is also the most balanced and nutritious. Proper nutrition means that essential nutrients—carbohydrates, fats, proteins, vitamins, minerals, and water—are consumed and used for optimal health. A runner's basic needs aren't very different from those of other healthy people. Finally, and most importantly, diet and exercise go together. Many people who start running do so because they are overweight, or they want to hold their weight in check. They may already know that unused muscle tissue becomes fatter—even though they may be eating less. No one can lose weight, and hold that loss, without exercise. Vigorous exercise increases your metabolic rate, and that rate is sustained for more than 15 hours, burning calories at a higher rate than without exercise.

In fact, runners soon learn that if you exercise vigorously and regularly you can ignore going on a diet. Your weight will stabilize. Food you eat will be burned up, nutrients absorbed more readily and efficiently. A study by Dr. Peter Wood of the Stanford University Medical School indicates that people who run six or more miles a day eat about 600 more calories daily than nonexercising people, but weigh 20 percent less.

Dr. Jean Mayer, an internationally known nutritionist and president of Tufts University, notes that when rats exercise moderately (less than two hours a day), they actually eat less than unexercised rats. When the rats exercised more than two hours a day, putting extra energy demands upon their bodies, hunger was indeed stimulated and food intake increased to match energy output. The same mechanism, Dr. Mayer theorizes, keeps the weight of humans who exercise regularly on a constant level.

Moreover, researchers at Cornell University have learned that exercising within two or three hours after eating consumes more calories than identical exercise on an empty stomach. In addition, vigorous exercise suppresses hunger for several hours.

"Diet and exercise go together," says Dr. Clayton Myers in his *Official YMCA Physical Fitness Handbook*. "If you diet without exercising, the result may be a thin weak person in place of a fat weak person. Muscle tissue that is not used will atrophy and proportionately become fatter even though the intake of calories has between reduced."

WEIGHT

Statistically, when America's predominant way of life was manual labor, before the turn of the century, adult weights on the average remained steady. Since 1900, as we've become more and more sedentary, the average American caloric intake has decreased, and obesity has increased. Even our health charts seem to encourage us to be overweight! According to Dr. Irwin Stillman, the normal average weight for men over age twenty-five is 110 pounds plus 5.5 pounds for each inch over 5 feet. (A man 5 foot, 10 inches would weigh 165 pounds.) Women start at 100 pounds, and add 5 pounds for every inch above 5 feet. These calculations have become the subject of some debate. *Runner's World*, for example, has written that men and women should weigh at least 10 percent below these norms. Dr. Ernst van Aaken suggested 20 percent below.

But many runners, especially competitive runners, weigh as much as 20 percent less than the average person of the same height. Your bone structure and metabolism will dictate what is too much or too little weight for you. If you err, err on the side of being too light. Dr. Edward Colt, an endocrinologist at New York City's St. Luke's Hospital, says, "The lighter you are, within certain limits, the less likely you are to become injured. The limits are set by your own constitution—each individual has an optimum weight below which he or she feels tired and becomes susceptible to infections." Women are especially prone to anorexia, and should not place too much value on thinness and loss of weight while sacrificing health and strength.

Overweight is a well-known and well-documented problem. If you are 20 percent or more above your "ideal" weight, get your weight down before you attempt any racing, to prevent injury. The overweight runner puts stress on the cardiovascular and skeletal muscle systems, and doesn't handle heat well. He or she also pounds the ground with greater force. Start with a walking program and add running after losing some of the excess weight.

To determine your best weight, consider the following points and then consult the charts estimating the best weight for you. Remember that estimates are just that; you, perhaps with your doctor, can determine your best weight.

What did you weigh when you were eighteen to twenty-five? During those years, most of us were too active to get fat. Accord-

1983 METROPOLITAN HEIGHT AND WEIGHT TABLE

MEN

Feet	Height Inches	Small Frame	Medium Frame	Large Frame
5	2	128–134	131–141	138–150
5	3	130–136	133–143	140–153
5	4	132–138	135–145	142–156
5	5	134–140	137–148	144–160
5	6	136–142	139–151	146–164
5	7	138–145	142–154	149–168
5	8	140–148	145–157	152–172
5	9	142–151	148–160	155–176
5	10	144–154	151–163	158–180
5	11	146–157	154–166	161–184
6	0	149–160	157–170	164–188
6	1	152–164	160–174	168–192
6	2	155–168	164–178	172–197
6	3	158–172	167–182	176–202
6	4	162–176	171–187	181–207

Weights at Ages 25–59 Based on Lowest Mortality. Weight in Pounds According to Frame (in indoor clothing weighing 5 lbs., shoes with 1″ heels).

Source of basic data: *1979 Build Study,* Society of Actuaries and Association of Life Insurance Medical Directors of America, 1980.

ing to Dr. Irwin Maxwell Stillman, author of *The Inches-Off Diet,* no one should weigh more than he or she did at age twenty-five. Life insurance weight charts—which show that people weigh more as they age—reflect what is happening, not what should happen. As we age, our metabolism slows. To counteract this slowdown, we should eat less and exercise more, thereby leveling off our weight rather than continuing to gain. Your weight at age twenty-five, therefore, should be a first goal.

A HEALTHY DIET

To be fit and maintain a healthy diet means discriminating be-

1983 METROPOLITAN HEIGHT AND WEIGHT TABLE

WOMEN

Feet	Height Inches	Small Frame	Medium Frame	Large Frame
4	10	102–111	109–121	118–131
4	11	103–113	111–123	120–134
5	0	104–115	113–126	122–137
5	1	106–118	115–129	125–140
5	2	108–121	118–132	128–143
5	3	111–124	121–135	131–147
5	4	114–127	124–138	134–151
5	5	117–130	127–141	137–155
5	6	120–133	130–144	140–159
5	7	123–136	133–147	143–163
5	8	126–139	136–150	146–167
5	9	129–142	139–153	149–170
5	10	132–145	142–156	152–173
5	11	135–148	145–159	155–176
6	0	138–151	148–162	158–179

Weights at Ages 25–59 Based on Lowest Mortality. Weight in Pounds According to Frame (in indoor clothing weighing 3 lbs., shoes with 1″ heels).

Source of basic data: *1979 Build Study,* Society of Actuaries and Association of Life Insurance Medical Directors of America, 1980.

tween foods, understanding the basic value to you of carbohydrates, fats, proteins, minerals, vitamins, water and other fluids. All foods we eat contain some of these nutrients. They provide the body with heat and energy, the materials for growth and repair of body tissues. They assist with the regular body processes. Each nutrient has its own special function and relationship to the body. No nutrient is independent of others. We all need them, but the amounts we need vary according to age, sex, body size, environment, exercise level, and nutritional condition.

Our cells obtain and use nutrients through the three-step process of digestion, absorption, and metabolism. Basically, the foods we eat are broken down in the body to simpler forms, taken through the intestinal walls, and transported by the blood to the cells. Food intake is measured in calories: A calorie is "the amount of heat required to raise the temperature of one gram of water one degree of centigrade." A pound of body weight averages 3,500 calories of energy. To gain a pound, you must take in and store that amount, to lose a pound, you must get rid of that.

All carbohydrates, fats, and proteins contain calories; water, minerals, and vitamins do not. The normal caloric intake is 18 per pound per day for men, and 16 for women.

As all of us know, it is easier to feed calories to the body than to burn them up. One chocolate soda, for example, equals a week-and-a-half's office work. Calories, in the form of fat, also build up easily.

This is one more reason why we need more, not less, exercise as we grow older. Dr. Ralph Nelson of the Mayo Clinic shows that a 154-pound man at age thirty who maintains a constant exercise level and eats the same amount will weigh more than 200 pounds by age sixty. To remain the same weight on the same amount of exercise, he must reduce his caloric intake by 11 percent. Professor Per-Olof Astrand states that "a person's weight should not increase after his or her twenties. Since muscular tissue declines [with age], a loss of a few pounds is actually good proof of no increase in fatty tissue."

Running is a high continuous energy burn-off: Some long-distance runners burn calories at the rate of 1,000 an hour. Just by running and eliminating all sugar where you now use it, you might lose as much as 25 pounds a year. (Four extra teaspoons of sugar a day will add 5 pounds of fat a year, 52 pounds in ten years.)

Knowing this, there are certain foods you should avoid.

Junk Foods These foods are any edible thing that contains no essential nutrients—except perhaps calories. Eating them creates two hazards: You ingest chemicals and unessential ingredients harmful to your body; and junk foods replace more nutritional foods that your body needs. Eating junk food is also an excellent way to put on fat—lots of it.

My friend Carl Eilenberg weighed 273 pounds when he was thirty-three; he was 5 feet, 10 inches tall and his waist was 46 inches around. His heart rate was 90, and his blood pressure 160/80. "I used to get out of breath just ripping open the pretzel bag or sucking up a milk shake," he says. "I'd skip breakfast, then down martinis, soup, sandwiches, fried clams, beer, and banana splits for lunch. Well, sometimes I'd skip the soup. I'd eat crackers and popcorn after dinner."

Carl played golf on weekends, bowled once in a while, but never walked anywhere. "I honestly thought I was a pretty typical, reasonably healthy, in-shape adult male." Then he saw himself on television. "My head and neck looked like a watermelon. I was thirty, looked fifty. I was a big, fat slob, a very big fat slob."

He began running, a little at a time. He also cut the junk foods. Today, in his fifties, he looks more like twenty, and weighs 155. He has a pulse rate in the 50s, low-normal blood pressure, a greatly reduced cholesterol level. As he says, "Most important, I really like myself."

If you're in the junk food habit, try switching to Herbert Shelton's simple diet of fresh fruits, vegetables, and nuts. Raisins, carrots, celery all taste delicious, especially after a run. Drink unsweetened fruit juices diluted with ice or water. You'll be decreasing calories and increasing essential nutrients.

Sugar No other food has been so overemphasized in our diets. Sugar contains little of real value to your body (if you are already eating a balanced diet), yet it is consumed daily in large amounts by all of us.

White, refined sugar lacks nutrient value, and, in fact, requires vitamins (especially the B vitamins) for its digestion. In effect, sugar steals vitamins from your body for its digestion, and it interferes with some enzyme activity.

One myth states that sugar increases energy. Sugar actually decreases energy over several hours because it requires energy from your body for its assimilation. Pure sugar passes quickly through the intestinal walls into your bloodstream. Some runners think this is valuable because a quick energy burst is obtained. But this immediate sudden rise in blood-sugar level is followed by a dramatic drop in levels below your body's norm, which requires the ingestion of still more sugar, and thus the cycle continues.

Excessive sugar intake is associated with cavities, heart disease, stomach and bowel disorders, and cancer. A chocolate bar contains so many carbohydrates and fats that it should be used only as emergency rations. Honey, molasses, cane syrup, and other sugar forms are just as rich as refined sugar, although they also contain traces of minerals.

Salt Sodium chloride, or salt, is found naturally in all foods, with higher concentrations in seafoods, carrots, beets, poultry, and most meats. Salt also occurs naturally in the body's fluids. It works with potassium to regulate water balance within the body, and is involved with muscle contraction and expansion, and in nerve stimulation. Salt is readily absorbed in the small intestines and stomach, and carried by the blood to the kidneys where it is filtered out and returned to the blood as needed. Water in the human body is maintained with a precise level of salinity.

Obviously, deficiencies of salt are extremely uncommon. Most Americans take in on the average 3 to 7 grams a day, while the National Research Council recommends a daily sodium intake of just 1 gram per kilogram of water consumed daily. Too much salt may be harmful. In excess, it may cause potassium to be lost in the urine. Also, sodium retained in the body holds onto water, placing an extra load on the heart. A large salt intake is also related to high blood pressure, and other forms of cardiovascular and kidney disease.

High-sodium foods include smoked fish and meat, pickles, artichokes, sauerkraut, spinach, and frozen vegetables processed with salt. Fresh vegetables are generally low in salt, as are fresh fruits. Junk foods like salted popcorn, potato chips, snack chips, and pretzels contain high levels of salt. So, too, do organ, canned, and kosher meats; bacon, olives, commercial salad dressings; cashews and macadamia nuts—which are also high in cholesterol.

Sea salt and coarse rock salt differ only in the amount of impurities in the product, not in the amount of salt itself. Going easy on salt is simple: Take the salt shaker off the dining room table.

Smoking   This is a major crime against your lungs, heart, digestive system—and family. Smoking is a killer habit.

As we detailed in the previous chapter, one cigarette contains five hundred known poisons. When a smoker inhales a cigarette, his or her heart rate quickens, blood pressure rises, the peripheral blood vessels contract, and the skin temperature drops. Nicotine and carbon monoxide in tobacco cause heart and artery disease. Tar collects in pulmonary passages, causing emphysema and cancer of the lungs. Smokers have a marked tendency to exhibit irregular heart rhythms, and run the risk of sudden death. In fact, the life expectancy of a fifty-year-old who has smoked a pack of cigarettes daily for thirty years is reduced by 8.5 years—almost a decade. Many runners have quit smoking.

Atalanta's Maddy Harmeling gave up smoking two packs a day as she became a more competitive runner. At the age of 38, she won the 1984 Jacksonville Marathon in 2:47:21 and qualified for the 1984 USA Olympic Marathon trials, where she ran 2:44:32.

FOODS TO ENJOY

All runners need foods from the four basic food groups:

- *Grains/Cereals.* Bread, cereals, flour, baked goods.
- *Milk/Cheese.* Milk, cheese, yogurt, and other milk products. Be sure to drink low-fat or skim milk to eliminate high-fat intake.
- *High Protein Foods.* Meat, fish, eggs, poultry, legumes, nuts.
- *Vegetables/Fruits.* Dark green and deep yellow vegetables, citrus fruits.

These should give us our basic nutrients: carbohydrates, proteins, fats, minerals, and vitamins, as well as water (or other fluids like vegetable and fruit juices). Our bodies require more than 40 nutrients, found in water, carbohydrates, fat, protein, minerals, vitamins.

Carbohydrates

These are the energy foods. They supply the primary energy for all body functions and muscle exertion, and they assist in digestion and the assimilation of other foods. Carbohydrates regulate protein and fat metabolism. Fats, for example, require carbohydrates for their breakdown within the liver.

The principal carbohydrates are starches such as bread, cakes, potatoes, and sugar foods such as candies, preserves, syrups, or soft drinks. The starches require prolonged enzyme action before becoming simple sugar (glucose) for digestion. The simple sugars, like those found in honey and fruit, are easily digested and turned into quick energy. Cellulose, also a carbohydrate, is found in the skins of fruits and vegetables, and is largely indigestible although it contributes bulk for intestinal action and aids elimination.

Therefore, carbohydrates offer two sources of energy for runners. As snacks, the sugars and starches provide an almost instant energy burst because of the sudden rise in the blood sugar level from the glucose. But that level drops again just as suddenly, creating a craving for more sweet food and possibly fatigue, dizziness, nervousness, or headache. As stored energy, over a period of time, carbohydrates can gradually "feed" glucose to the exercising body. During vigorous exercise, such as running, those fat reserves are reconverted to glucose and burned as body fuel.

Complex carbohydrates, like grains, dried beans, peas, nuts, and seeds, offer a nutritious energy source. They contain vitamins, minerals, proteins, and B-vitamins that help metabolize carbohydrates for fuel.

In addition, carbohydrates, by passing quickly through the digestive process, are easier to assimilate than other nutrients. They also provide a significant water supply when broken down, which is a benefit during hot weather.

On the other hand, carbohydrates are not essential for the sedentary person. The body can provide the carbohydrates for normal metabolism from stored fat. The National Research Council lists no specific daily requirements for carbohydrates because they are found naturally in the body as amino acids and the glycerol component of fats. All of us should be aware of research that shows that overuse of carbohydrates may contribute to atherosclerosis or bowel cancer.

Proteins

These body builders help bone and tissue grow and repair. They are a major building material for muscles, blood, skin, hair, nails, and the internal organs including the heart and brain. They aid in the formation of hormones that control growth, sexual development, and the rate of metabolism, and they control the balance of acids and alkalines in the blood and regulate the body's water balance. Proteins form enzymes necessary for basic life functions, and antibodies that fight foreign substances in the body. Unused proteins are converted by the liver and stored as fat in body tissue.

Proteins are essential for energy, but how essential is still open to debate. During times of stress, as when running, the body needs to consume extra protein to rebuild or replace wornout tissues. But does this mean that eating more meats, which provide complete proteins, is beneficial? Some doctors and runners claim that energy comes from mixing carbohydrates and fats, not proteins.

The American Research Council's Food and Nutrition Board recommends 70 grams of protein every day for most adults. Many doctors feel this is too high, and recommend 35 grams, but most

Americans now eat 118 grams daily, much of it in the form of concentrated protein in meats. The National Research Council suggests eating .42 grams of protein daily for every kilogram of body weight (to find kilograms, divide your body weight by 2.2; to find your protein amount, multiply by .42).

Most proteins contain a high level of fats, and some doctors now argue that eating a lot of meat is unhealthy. It takes too long for meat to pass through our digestive system, and the meat begins to decay. This, and other factors, may indicate why Americans, and other high meat eaters, are so subject to cancer of the colon. Vegetable proteins can be as nutritious as animal proteins. In raw form, fruits and vegetables are excellent sources. You can get your protein requirements from nuts, beans, whole grains and cereals, egg whites, milk, cheese, and some vegetables. For example, potatoes contain 2 percent protein of high quality. If you wish to avoid the high cholesterol levels of muscle meats, or are inclined toward vegetarianism, try shifting your diet toward nuts and grains. Whatever proteins you prefer, try cutting meat consumption way back, at least to the level of gram-per-body-weight recommended.

Fats

This nutrient contains good news and bad news. First the good news. Fats are the most concentrated source of energy in our diet. They may contain 2.5 times the number of calories, when oxidized, than carbohydrates or proteins, although they break down more slowly. One gram of fat yields about 9 calories.

Fats include butter, oils for salads and cooking, bacon fat, cream, egg yolk, avocados, and whole milk.

Fats aid in the absorption of the fat-soluble vitamins A, D, E, and K. Fat deposits surround, protect, and hold in place organs such as the kidneys, heart, and liver. A layer of fat insulates the body from the environment, and preserves body heat. Fats also prolong digestion by slowing down the stomach's secretions of hydrochloric acid.

And now the bad news.

In 1977, Americans ate a record average of 56 pounds of fats in butter, margarine, cooking oils, shortening, lard, salad dressing, and other fatty products. That doesn't include "invisible" fats eaten in foods like meat, cheese, milk, eggs, poultry, fish, grain products, even fruits and vegetables. Consumption of all fats is rising sharply, despite growing understanding that many fats and too much fat in our diets may be unhealthy.

Broadly, there are two types of fats: saturated and unsaturated. The saturated (with the exception of coconut oil) come largely from animal meats. The unsaturated, including the polyunsaturated, come from vegetables, and nut or seed sources such as corn, sunflowers, olives.

Saturated fats contain cholesterol. Doctors believe that we also manufacture cholesterol in the liver, adrenal cortex of the brain, skin, intestines, and testes. It is synthesized by the body and aids in the normal process of metabolism and it is necessary for the production of certain enzymes and endocrine secretions. It is found in all the cells of the body, but especially the liver, kidneys, brain, and pancreas.

Triglycerides, as we noted in the last chapter, are formed in the breakdown of carbohydrates, and are probably just as dangerous to your health as cholesterol. Refined sugar is easily converted into triglycerides. Alcohol provides us with triglycerides and supplies empty calories and adds fat.

All fats get broken down in the small intestine. They contribute to high triglyceride and cholesterol levels, which can be killers. Without repeating the information of the last chapter, let's remember that these fats are the leading causes of atherosclerosis, or hardening of the arteries, and the clogging of the coronary arteries and the arteries going to the brain.

The average American diet is almost 45 percent fats. The National Research Council sets no recommended daily allowance for fats, but nutritionists suggest cutting fats down to 20 percent of our diets, which means cutting down or eliminating some of our tastier—though high in cholesterol—foods, such as spareribs, hamburgers, hot dogs, roast duck and goose, French fries, sausages, sweet potatoes, and caviar. Some meats are higher than others: organ and glandular meats, hearts, kidneys, liver, and sweetbreads all have high cholesterol contents; the highest is found in brains. Stay away from lobster; crab meat contains less cholesterol, shrimp less than crab, scallops less than shrimp. Trim all visible fat from steak. Also avoid all cold luncheon meats, all dairy ice creams (use ice milk instead), rich salad dressings, creamy soups, the yolks of eggs.

If this section leaves you feeling that there's no fun left, remember: cholesterol deficiency is unlikely to occur since the substance is stored naturally throughout your body; exercise stimulates the release of this natural, stored cholesterol, which (we forgot to tell you) is vital to the development of your sex hormones.

Minerals

These basic chemicals are found in the soil and picked up by plants. We get our minerals by eating plants, or animals that have eaten plants. Minerals, therefore, exist in most foods and in the body; 17 are essential to human mental and physical well-being. They control heartbeat and the contraction of all muscles; they are constituents of the bones, teeth, soft tissues, muscles, blood and nerve cells; and are essential in maintaining the bodily processes, strengthening skeletal structures and the vigor of the heart, brain, and nervous system. Minerals aid in warding off fatigue and cramps, and they maintain the body's delicate water balance. The following six minerals are of special interest to runners.

Iron   Present in every living cell, iron combines with protein to make hemoglobin to transport oxygen in the blood from lungs to tissues. Iron builds up the quality of the blood and aids resistance to disease and stress. It also helps form myoglobin, found only in muscle tissues, which also transports oxygen to the muscle cells and benefits muscle contraction. The Food and Nutrition Board says that women need twice as much iron as men, and from the age of thirteen through the late forties should ingest 18 milligrams per day, while men need only 10. Best sources: liver; then oysters, heart, lean meats, tongue, leafy green vegetables, dried fruits.

Calcium This is the body's most abundant mineral. It works with phosphorus to build and maintain teeth and bones. It promotes the heart muscle and regulates heart rhythm (with magnesium), as well as the acid-alkali content of the blood. It assists in muscle growth and contraction, nerve transmission, and the passage of nutrients in and out of cell walls. Best sources: milk and dairy products, bone meal, oranges, eggs.

Phosphorus This mineral often works with calcium. It plays a role in almost every chemical reaction within the body, helping the body use carbohydrates, fats, and proteins for growth, cell repair, and energy. It stimulates the heart and muscle contractions. It also helps tooth development, kidney function, and nerve impulse transfers. Foods rich in proteins are also rich in phosphorus. Best sources: lean meats, fish, chicken, eggs, whole grains, seeds, nuts.

Sodium Sodium aids fluid balance in blood vessels, arteries, veins, and capillaries, intestinal fluids surrounding the cells, and bones. With potassium, sodium regulates the body's water balance, the acid-alkali combination in the blood, muscle contraction and expansion, nerve stimulation. It also keeps blood minerals soluble, preventing them from buildinig up as deposits in the bloodstream. It improves the health of the blood, purges carbon dioxide from the body, aids digestion. Sodium also helps produce the hydrochloric acid in the stomach. Best sources: seafoods, poultry, meats, carrots, beets, and kelp; but sodium is found in all foods.

Potassium Assists sodium in the ways mentioned above. It also aids in the conversion of glucose to glycogen, which is then stored in the liver. It helps with cell metabolism, enzyme reactions; it stimulates the kidneys to eliminate body wastes, and it nourishes the muscles. Best sources: green leafy vegetables, oranges, whole grains, sunflower seeds, mint leaves, potatoes (especially the peelings), bananas, cantaloupes, apricots, plus the juices of oranges, grapefruits, and prunes.

Magnesium   This mineral stimulates the essential metabolic processes by activating enzymes that break down carbohydrates and amino acids. It aids neuromuscular contractions and regulates the body's acid-alkaline balance. Magnesium helps the body absorb other minerals, and the C, E, and B-complex vitamins. It helps bone growth and heart and nerve functionings. It may also help regulate the body temperature. Sufficient amounts of magnesium are vital to the conversion of blood sugar into energy. Best sources: fresh green vegetables, unmilled wheat germ, soybeans, figs, corn, apples, oil-rich seeds and nuts.

Vitamins

Natural vitamins are found in plants and animals as organic food substances. Because our bodies cannot synthesize vitamins (with a few exceptions), we must supply them with our diet or with supplements. Basically, vitamins are components of enzymes; they are not a direct source of energy, nor do our bodies require increased vitamins during exercise. Vitamins only act on nutrients, and therefore massive amounts of vitamins will not protect against a diet deficient in essential nutrients. Vitamins help to regulate the metabolism of our bodies, to convert fat and carbohydrates into energy, and to form bones and tissues. There are about 20 active vitamins in human nutrition, but we will discuss only a few of the most important ones: A, the B-complex, C, D, E.

Vitamin A   Little is known of this vitamin's specific influence upon physical performance, although it is added to a lot of foods. It does aid in the growth and repair of body tissues, and it promotes strong teeth and bones and the formation of rich blood, and helps maintain good eyesight. It reduces our susceptibility to infection by protecting the mucous membrane of the mouth, nose, throat, and lungs. It also protects the lining of the digestive tract, the kidneys and bladder, and it promotes the secretion of gastric juices necessary for the proper digestion of proteins. Best sources: fish-liver oil, carrots, and green leafy vegetables such as beet greens, spinach, and broccoli.

Vitamin B-complex   The B-complex vitamins, of which there are thirteen, provide the body with energy by converting carbohydrates into glucose. They are also essential to the metabolism of fats and proteins. They may be the single most important factor in the health and normal functioning of our nervous system. The value of the B vitamins is long and impressive. They aid in easing postoperative nausea and vomiting resulting from anesthesia, with heart abnormalities, barbiturate overdoses, migraine headaches. Yet the B vitamins are lacking in many American diets. All of the B vitamins—except B-17—are found naturally in liver and whole-grain cereals, but brewer's yeast is the richest natural source of the B vitamins.

Vitamin B-1 (*Thiamine*), by its link to carbohydrate metabolism and lactic acid utilization, increases a runner's caloric use during endurance performance. A high carbohydrate diet requires more B-1 than most diets, and exercising athletes on a high-carbo loading should take at least 2 milligrams daily. It is vital for the breakdown of carbohydrates into glucose, which is oxidized by the body to produce energy. It is also known as the "morale vitamin," because of its relationship to a healthy nervous system and positive mental attitude. Thiamine is also thought to help prevent the buildup of fatty deposits on the arterial walls. Best food sources: brewer's yeast, seeds, wheat germ, nuts, blackstrap molasses, germ and bran of wheat, husk of rice. The portion of all grains usually milled away to give the grain a lighter color and finer texture contain vitamin B-1.

Vitamin B-2 (Riboflavin) works with enzymes to break down carbohydrates, fats, and proteins. Perhaps most important to runners, riboflavin aids cell respiration. It works with enzymes in using cell oxygen, and it also helps with good vision, hair, nails, and skin. B-2 is not stored in the body, and therefore must be supplied regularly in the diet. Best food sources: liver, tongue and other organ meats; richest source is brewer's yeast.

Vitamin B-6 (Pyridoxine) is important to the runner because it facilitates the release of glycogen for energy from the liver and muscles. It also helps maintain the balance of sodium and potassium in body fluids, assists in the production of antibodies and red blood cells, and aids in digestion by helping produce hydrochloric acid and magnesium. Best food sources: meats and whole grains.

Niacin also assists the enzymes in breaking down and using fats, carbohydrates, and proteins. It is effective in improving circulation and in reducing cholesterol in the blood. It is present in most foods, but best food sources include: lean meats, poultry, fish, peanuts, and brewer's yeast.

Vitamin B-12 is the only one in the B-complex that contains vital mineral elements. It cannot be made synthetically, but must be grown in bacteria or molds. Like other vitamins, it is essential to the normal metabolism of carbohydrates, fats, and proteins. It is of value to the runner in that it provides some long-term relief for fatigue, and is an anti-anemic. Best food sources: liver, kidney, fish, and dairy products.

Vitamin C (Ascorbic Acid)   A controversial vitamin, its use has been linked to everything from preventing colds to preventing cancer. Maybe Dr. Linus Pauling, who advocates vitamin C for cold prevention, is right, and maybe not. I do know other doctors who take it to ward off colds, and a lot of people—runners and nonrunners alike—swear that vitamin C protects them against illness and injury, and speeds recovery.

Man, apes, and guinea pigs are the only creatures that need

this vitamin. It prevents and relieves scurvy, and is necessary for the connective tissue in the skin, ligaments, and bones. It also facilitates the formation of connective scar tissue, helping to heal wounds and burns, and it aids in the forming of red blood cells. Some medical studies indicate that vitamin C fights bacterial infection, and reduces the impact on the body of some allergy-producing substances. Others believe that the lack of vitamin C may be a cause of stroke begun by breaks in the capillary walls where clots form.

Vitamin C takes two to three hours to be absorbed, and most of the vitamin not used by the body is passed out within four hours by urine and perspiration. Under stress, the vitamin passes through the body faster. Ascorbic acid is readily absorbed from the gastrointestinal tract into the bloodstream. The body's ability to absorb C is reduced by smoking, high fever, inhalation of DDT. Drinking excessive amounts of water also depletes the body's vitamin C, and cooking in copper utensils destroys the vitamin C in foods.

Some medical authorities believe that vitamin C is important under all stressful circumstances, from illness to competitive running. Tissues require more vitamin C during vigorous exercise. The sex glands, too, develop a greater need for vitamin C with increased exercise; if you're overdoing it, they will draw vitamin C from other tissues, causing a depletion.

Runners should take plenty of vitamin C. The recommended daily dosage is 500 milligrams a day. I take 1 gram a day (1,000 mg), or 2 to 3 grams when a cold is coming on.

The best food sources include most fruits and vegetables. Natural vitamin C supplements are prepared from rose hips, acerola cherries, green peppers, and citrus fruits. Vitamin C in natural form, some doctors feel, is superior to that in synthetic.

Vitamin D This is a comparatively unknown vitamin that aids both in the absorption of calcium from the intestinal tract and in the breakdown and assimilation of phosphorus, required for bone formation. Without it, bones and teeth will not calcify properly. It is also valuable in maintaining a stable nervous system, a normal and strong heartbeat, and normal blood clotting. It helps in fighting fatigue. Best food sources: fish-liver oils.

Vitamin E This vitamin plays an essential role in muscular performance, especially the cardiac and skeletal muscles. It increases the endurance and strength of these muscles by letting them function with less oxygen. By causing dilation of the blood vessels, it helps increase the flow of blood to the heart. It inhibits formation of blood clots, aids in bringing nourishment to cells, strengthens the capillary walls, protects red blood cells from destruction by poisons like hydrogen peroxide in the blood. In an ointment, vitamin E promotes healing and lessens the formation of scars. It helps regulate menstrual flow. It also protects against many environmental poisons in air, water, and food, and especially protects the lungs and other tissues from damage by polluted air. Runners may appreciate this effect. Dr. Gabe Mirkin, former medical advisor to *The Runner* magazine (now medical editor of *Runner's World*), recommends 200 milligrams the day before competition, but only then. Some doctors and nutritionists believe that E has a role in increasing male and female fertility, and in restoring male potency. Best food sources: raw seeds, nuts, soybeans, wheat germ oil.

A good diet will supply all the essential vitamins and minerals. Since most of us don't follow a perfect diet, we recommend a daily multivitamin, 500 milligrams to one gram of vitamin C, and some vitamin B-complex. Most vitamins are harmless, even in excess; the body passes out what it doesn't need in urine. Some vitamins, such as A, D, and K, in high concentrations can cause toxic side effects.

19 EAT, DRINK, RUN, RACE →

Runners don't need a special diet, just a healthy one based on sound nutrition. A runner's dietary needs aren't very different from those of other healthy people, although the high-mileage runner may need to consume more calories and carbohydrates. Runners training in hot weather will need to make some important adjustments to preserve the body's fluid and mineral balance. Some changes in diet may also be advisable during the final days before a marathon.

What we eat depends on many things, but we should concentrate on more complex carbohydrates: fruits, vegetables, and grains. According to Dr. David Costill, director of the Ball State University Human Performance Laboratory, the best diet for the average person who runs 20 to 30 miles a week should contain 50 percent carbohydrates, 30 percent fat, and 20 percent protein. The runner who puts in more than 70 miles a week needs more than 1,000 additional calories a day. This should include 70 percent carbohydrates, 20 percent fat, and 10 percent protein.

FASTING AND VEGETARIANISM

Some runners argue for fasting and against eating meat. They believe fasting cleanses and detoxifies the body, and prepares its metabolism for the stress of long distance running after its glycogen supplies are low. In a *Runner's World* survey, some 13 percent of the distance runners said that they fasted regularly for one to three days at a time, on water and juices. Other runners sometimes fast for up to two weeks, drinking only water or fruit and/or vegetable juices. They do this to condition their bodies to live off their own resources.

Fasting has its dangers, however. It should be done only after consulting your doctor, and then only in moderation. When fasting, blood acidity may be abnormal, adversely affecting muscle and body organs. Excessive amounts of minerals may be lost, and glycogen reduced below safe levels. Fasting before a marathon is the opposite of carbohydrate loading. We don't recommend it for the average runner.

Vegetarianism is a complex issue. Some vegetarians eat no meat, believing that it contains impurities and hinders digestion. Others are ovo-lacto vegetarians and exclude all flesh foods: meats, poultry, fish. But they do eat eggs, milk, and cheese.

A major cutback in all meats would probably be a sound idea for every American, runner or nonrunner. Studies show that vegetarians are leaner, and have lower cholesterol levels and lower incidence of heart disease than their meat-eating friends. Nonmeat sources of protein are easily found (nuts, soybeans, whole grains, etc.). Vegetarians have sometimes gone in too heavily for exotic diets that ignore some elementary essentials, especially the minerals and vitamins.

EATING FOR RUNNING

What is a good runner's diet? Basically, we have found the balanced diet best. Too much emphasis upon one aspect—carbohydrates over proteins, for example—can cause as harmful an imbalance as the present average American diet heavy on meats and fried foods. We also make the following suggestions:

- Cut out all white sugar (and all brown, "raw," and "kleen-raw" sugars, which are merely disguises). Use honey (but very moderately) and fresh fruits for sweeteners.
- Eat only 100 percent whole-wheat products. "Unbleached

white flour" is almost as bad for you as ordinary white flour; it can gum up your stomach and intestines.
- Cook vegetables lightly. The Chinese have developed this to a culinary marvel. Eat raw salads together with cooked vegetables. Try a little lemon juice on them for flavor (and vitamins).
- Eat little beef or pork. The more of these meats you can cut out of your diet, the better. Substitute fish and chicken (cutting away the underlayer of fat in chicken). Try eating more vegetable proteins and whole grains; try complementary proteins like rice and beans, peanut butter and legumes. They are low in cost and cholesterol.
- Cut out all soft drinks, all hard liquor. Be moderate with beer and wine. Drink more water, and add vegetable and fresh fruit juices. Use little coffee, and drink herbal teas.
- Eat only when hungry, and eat less than you need. Wheat germ, yogurt, brewer's yeast, desiccated liver (if you can stand it), and vitamin C are good daily.
- Avoid all junk foods and prepared, processed foods. Read all food labels, and avoid chemical additives.

Eat wisely—and you will run well.

Glycogen is a stored carbohydrate made from simple sugar. It is stored in the muscles and liver, and serves as the body's basic fuel by converting to sugar for the bloodstream when you need more energy. Carbohydrates create glycogen, which aids endurance. The average runner may store enough glycogen to last about 20 miles—the point at which you "hit the wall" by running out of energy.

In the late 1960s, Swedish exercise physiologist Eric Hultman developed the idea of manipulating the diet of runners to increase their glycogen stores. He developed a seven-day diet that worked this way:

1. Seven days before the race, go for a long run of two or three hours to help deplete glycogen stores in your muscles.

2. For the next three days, eat a high protein and fat diet that is low in carbohydrates. This will deplete your glycogen stores further. Regular running during this period will also burn more glycogen.

3. For the last three days before a race, reverse the diet. Now "load" carbohydrates and cut back on your running to store up glycogen in your muscles.

The Hultman diet is based on tests performed on athletes who followed this regimen. The theory is that performances improve because depleted muscles soak up more glycogen during the loading period. The athlete would then increase glycogen stores by perhaps as much as 100 to 300 percent.

The carbo-loading technique was first popularized by the dominant marathon runner of the 1960s—Great Britain's Ron Hill—and became the craze of the 1970s as the number of average men and women marathon runners increased dramatically. Dr. Paul Milvy reported that the average marathon time for those who followed this diet for the 1977 New York City Marathon was four minutes faster than the average for those runners who didn't use it, based on a sample of 2,000 runners.

The diet seems to work better for the average runner than for the faster runner. Dr. David Costill, writing in *The Runner*, said: "The difference between elite and average marathoners is that even if both started out with the same amount of glycogen, the elite marathoner would spare it by burning a higher ratio of fat. Although more oxygen is required to burn fat, the highly developed oxygen transport system of the elite runner allows this. Furthermore, he moves more economically, which means that he uses less oxygen to accomplish the same task. The average runner, on the other hand, depletes his glycogen supply sooner and doesn't have as efficient an oxygen transport system to burn fat. That's why hitting the wall is so devastating and why carbohydrate loading is more important for the average runner than for the elite runner."

We do not, however, recommend the depletion phase of the traditional carbo-loading schedule. It is too taxing physically and psychologically. The runner usually becomes very irritable, depressed, and tired. During the long-distance race, runners who have gone through the depletion phase have reported leg cramps, diarrhea, and fatigue. The phase may also place a strain on your kidneys. The system is unpredictable and may make you susceptible to colds and flu, and result in loss of sleep.

Never try this system for your first marathon, despite Dr. Costill's suggestion that carbo-loading benefits average runners most. Try the marathon distance and stress first; after you understand this race, having run it once or twice, you might want to try depleting and loading up. Even veteran runners should not try carbohydrate depleting more than twice a year. Experiment with it for a low-key race or a long training run before trying it for a major race.

Here is the system we recommend:

- Stick to your normal diet until three days before a long-distance race or marathon.
- During these three days, load up on carbohydrates (but don't overeat). The key is to increase the *percentage* of carbohydrates in your diet. Drink extra water to help convert the carbos to glycogen.
- Rest, with minimal running, during these three days to build up energy supplies.

Don't worry about skipping the depletion phase. Dr. Costill finds that runners who carbo-load but don't deplete have about the same amounts of stored glycogen as runners who go through the depletion phase. Also, there is no advantage in terms of building glycogen reserves for nonmarathon events. If you are running less than the marathon distance, continue with your normal diet.

Dr. Costill suggests eating both simple and complex carbohydrates; some nutritionists discourage eating the former. Liquid carbohydrate supplements may help runners with digestive problems. Also, studies show that some liquid supplements may increase glycogen storage faster than the normal heaping plates of pasta.

Reminder: Carbohydrate depletion is not recommended for novices; carbohydrate loading is not necessary for races of less than 30K.

Eating the Night Before a Marathon

Eat a high carbohydrate meal the night before your marathon. Spaghetti, macaroni, and noodles are good. Steamed or boiled rice is fine (fried rice contains too much oil), and potatoes without butter or sour cream will help (no French fries!). The best sources are starchy vegetables like yams, squash, carrots, peas, and beans, lentils, breads (with whole wheat flour), rolls, crackers. You might like to try hot oatmeal; some runners load up on pancakes or waffles.

This is an important meal. You should eat about 6 p.m. when preparing for a morning race the next day. Salads, green leafy vegetables, and fruits are also good. A light snack around ten o'clock, or more carbohydrates will help: some runners eat a candy bar or cookies, or bananas, oranges, or apples.

Select carefully where you eat the night before. Make reservations, or if dining out at the prerace feed, get there early. Don't upset your stomach by standing in line, and don't attend that spaghetti feast for the prerace masses if the scene is too exciting. Don't eat anything you are not familiar with. A meal at home or in your hotel room may be the best option.

Eating on Race Day, or Before Your Daily Run

Don't eat anything you haven't eaten before a previous race. You cannot eat your way to a better time—both the miles and the glycogen are in place. Don't be unpleasantly surprised.

Digestion generally requires three to five hours. That should be the length of time between your last food and the start of the race. The actual time digestion takes depends on when you eat, what you eat, and your emotional state. You should enter competition with an empty colon and stomach.

If you eat on marathon morning, your meal should be high in carbohydrates, low in sugar, fat, and protein. It should ward off hunger pangs and be easily digestible. You may eat toast, or even pancakes (watch out for the butter and syrup), and drink coffee, tea, or juice. The basic rule: Experiment before your training workouts to find what you can eat and tolerate before long runs.

Watch your starting time. Eat no later than three to five hours before it. Don't be absurd about this: If the race starts at eight a.m., don't set your alarm for four just to get up and eat. It would be better to sleep, and skip the meal. A 10 a.m. race allows you to eat lightly around six or seven, while a noon start, as for the Boston Marathon, leaves plenty of time for you to eat and digest your food. If you have any difficulties, take only fluids before running in the morning. Avoid sugar: it may cause a low blood sugar level during your run.

While eating before a marathon may help you store a little more energy, eating before short races is only needed for psychological reasons—to make you "feel" more comfortable. I recommend that if you must eat, have something light, such as toast and coffee or juice, two to three hours before running. You may be able to eat a little more food, and within two to three hours before your daily run. Only you and your digestive system can decide through experience what is best for you. I need at least three hours to digest food even before a short run or I'll have to make several pit stops.

Runners concerned with prerace diets often ignore this concern after a long run or race. But what you eat and drink for several days afterwards may affect your recovery. Proper eating continues your training, in effect, and may help minimize injury and illness while putting you back on your normal training and racing routine sooner. Eat a balanced diet to make certain you replace all lost minerals. After a marathon, be sure to eat more carbohydrates to replace lost glycogen.

DRINKING FOR RUNNING

Every runner must drink enough fluids. Prevention of dehydration and heat stress is more important than carbohydrate replacement, especially on hot days. You can die from heat stroke during a run, but not from hunger.

On the average, your body requires about six glasses of fluid daily. You will get some fluids from the foods you eat. When you exercise, you need additional fluids, at least two or three quarts daily, and half of this should be water. Drink water before and during your meals. There is little danger of consuming too much; any excess is flushed away by your kidneys. (Remember that fluids help prevent dehydration during carbohydrate loading.)

Water is the principal component of our cells, urine, sweat, and blood. It is an inexpensive, almost perfect beverage. Runners, however, drink other fluids, too. Coffee and beer are two popular, and controversial, examples.

Coffee   Caffeine is a drug. Excessive intake may cause irregular heart beats, hyperactivity, anxiety, sleeplessness, or stomach spasms, or aggravate conditions like ulcers, gout, or high blood pressure. Coffee contains caffeine, and the drug is also added to foods, beverages (the colas), and over-the-counter drugs. Adverse effects may result from drinking four or five cups of brewed coffee daily, 10 to 12 cups of instant coffee, or fifteen 12-ounce servings of caffeinated soft drinks. According to the American Council on Science and Health, some 11 million Americans consume this much caffeine daily.

Beer   A lot of runners drink a lot of beer, and argue (often loudly) that it helps them. Dr. Peter Wood, of the Stanford University Disease Prevention Program, discovered that runners outdrink nonrunners by two to one. We're still trying to determine if that's six packs or pitchers.

A quart of beer supplies about 450 calories, and contains about the same number of carbohydrates as a quarter pound of bread. But it goes down much faster, and replenishes depleted energy reserves quickly. Beer also contains B-complex vitamins and other nutrients.

One beer, however, lowers heat tolerance for as long as three days. Alcohol also promotes urination, and therefore may help create dehydration.

We do not recommend drinking a lot of beer. One or two in the evening may help you relax, especially the night before a race. A postrace, or postworkout, beer is metabolized quickly and will replace lost fluids and minerals, and help you relax. Whoever heard of a runners' party without beer?

Drinking Before Running and Racing

Whatever you drink—water or juice—before your runs, drink more of it in hot weather. Some runners swear that caffeine consumed before a workout or race improves their running and times, but the evidence is inconclusive. These runners drink a cup of unsweetened tea or coffee or swallow two caffeine pills about an hour before a race or workout. The theory is that caffeine releases fatty acids into the bloodstream as fuel, thus slowing the use of muscle glycogen and the onset of fatigue. Dr. Costill's research indicates that caffeine may increase the ability to perform physical work by as much as 16 percent in some people. But, as mentioned, others may have a negative reaction. Also, caffeine may produce nervousness or anxiety before a race, or diarrhea. It may increase heat production, which could be dangerous on a hot day.

If you want to see what caffeine does for, or to, you, drink one to three cups of coffee or tea before a long training run. Don't experiment on race day. We prefer that you improve your race times by following the training guidelines in this book and *The Competitive Runner's Handbook*, rather than experimenting with a potentially harmful drug.

Dr. Costill has also determined that sugared beverages taken a few hours before exercising may prematurely exhaust runners. Avoid sugared drinks for one to three hours before a run or race. You may have a reaction that will temporarily lower your blood sugar, leaving you with less energy.

Drink very little one and a half hours to half an hour before a race. It takes almost that long for your body to eliminate excess fluids through urination. If you drink during this time span, you may have to urinate at the starting line or just after the race begins. The American College of Sports Medicine recommends that runners drink 13 to 17 ounces of fluids 10 to 15 minutes before racing or running long distances. Your kidneys usually shut down when you start running, so last-minute fluid intake will remain in your body. In a sense, you are "fluid loading." This extra fluid will be immediately available, and help prevent dehydration and overheating.

Look for water stations at the starting area, or bring your own. Water is the safest bet before a race or long run. Avoid fruit juices, sweetened athletic drinks, alcoholic beverages—anything you aren't used to consuming.

Drinking on the Run

In warm or hot weather, whether racing or taking even short training runs, you should always drink on the run. There are at least three basic reasons for this:

1. During your run, your body temperature rises as fluids are depleted. This loss dehydrates your body, which can cause damage to your circulatory system. Fluid intake is especially important on hot days to avoid dehydration and cool your body.

2. Important minerals and chemicals called electrolytes (sodium, potassium, magnesium) are lost through perspiration, and need to be replaced. Electrolyte depletion may cause fatigue or leg cramps, or upset your body's water bal-

ance. Fluids containing these minerals can be ingested before and during the race or long run.

3. Glucose (used for energy) lost during the run can be replaced by sugar solutions, especially late in a long run.

During prolonged exercise, the body loses fluids more rapidly than they can be replaced through the stomach. Drink more than you think necessary, especially on hot days. Don't depend on your thirst: You could be down one to two quarts of fluids before your mouth even feels thirsty. Drink as much as you can without upsetting your stomach—a further reason for sticking to water. Generally, a weight loss of two percent or more in one's body weight affects performance. A loss of five to six percent affects health. A weight loss of five to seven pounds during long runs is not uncommon. A runner may lose about three to four pounds per hour during a marathon, but he or she can absorb only about 1.8 pounds of water from the stomach during the same period. Obviously, no matter how much you drink, you will not keep up with the weight loss from sweating during a long run. You will dehydrate twice as fast as you can replace fluids during the run, and you will finish dehydrated. This is why it is essential that you drink immediately before, during, and after your long run.

During your runs, dehydration, heat generated by the workout, and warm air temperatures combine to increase your body temperature. Your normal body temperature is 98.6° F. During a long run on a hot day, it may rise to 106° F., which can be dangerous if prolonged. It is critical to hold down this temperature by replacing lost fluids. Dr. Costill has shown that rectal temperatures in runners are two degrees (F.) cooler when the runners drink fluids during a two-hour run than when they do not.

Start drinking about 10 to 15 minutes before the start of your run. Then, drink about every 15 minutes during the run on hot days, somewhat less often on cool days. Your body can absorb about six ounces of fluid every 15 to 20 minutes. Therefore, you should take a full cup of fluid every two or three miles. Remember: It takes up to 20 minutes for the fluid to be absorbed; do not wait until you feel hot and thirsty—by then it will be too late. Fluids taken during the last two or three miles will aid in your postrun recovery.

Many runners carry their fluids with them in plastic bottles. Jack Shepherd, during his runs in Vermont, tucks a canteen along the road in the weeds. On the way back, he takes a break and a drink of cold water. You may want to design your training route to include drinking fountains or places where cold water is available. Or, if you are fortunate, perhaps friends will wait along the roadside during long runs, and hand you plastic squeeze bottles of your favorite road-tested beverage.

Fluid replacement is critical in short distances or races, too. Even over a distance like 5K, the slower runner should drink fluids. Faster runners will finish before any fluids are absorbed. Prerun or prerace fluid intake for short distances is still important for all runners. As a rule of thumb, if you run for more than 30 minutes, drink fluids during the run.

Fluids are essential for you during short or long runs, on hot days or on cold. Running raises your body temperature, even when nonrunners are wearing fur coats, and depletes fluids. Never think that not drinking, especially during training runs, is a way to toughen up. It is not.

Drinking during a race can be tricky. Beginner racers may think they have to grab a cup of liquid at the water stations and throw it down quickly as they run. This is difficult to do, and hard on your stomach; it may spoil your rhythm more than stopping. Other runners will try to carry the drink and sip it. The easiest way to drink on the run is to carry a plastic squeeze bottle with a nozzle. You control your intake, and you don't spill. But you do need someone to hand the bottle to you, and take it back.

During a race, beginner and intermediate racers should stop at the water stations, take a cup of liquid, making sure it is water, and drink it while walking. You will lose less time than if you try to gulp on the run. You'll also get more liquid inside you.

Race directors will tell you before the race starts where the water stations are located—at which mile marks and on which side of the road. Some races, such as the New York City Marathon, offer water on one side and an athletic drink on the other. Unless you've previously road-tested the athletic drink, and prefer it, stick to water. Take a minute, when you get a cup, to look and be certain you're at the right station and holding the right beverage. *Never* experiment with a drink during a race.

Also, don't skip a water station. Drink a little along the way. Research shows that time lost drinking is more than made up in performance by the average long-distance runner. He or she doesn't slow down from dehydration or overheating. When in doubt, be cautious: Drink on the run.

What to Drink on the Run

Should you drink water, juice, soda, beer, or commercial athletic beverages during your runs? Some runners concoct their own drinks. For most of us, however, water is best. Here are some other options available to runners:

Special Athletic Drinks   All commercially prepared drinks for runners are designed to replace lost fluids, electrolytes, and glycogen. These beverages—like ERG, Gatorade, Body Punch—make a lot of claims, and have ranks of supporters. They argue that when we sweat, we lose more than water. We need to replace electrolytes and minerals such as sodium, potassium, magnesium, calcium, and phosphorus. Athletic drinks are mostly water, with salt, potassium, and sugars.

Despite advertising claims for these drinks, and their use by athletic teams and in marathons, they are not all they claim to be. *Medical Times* tested three popular brands, and found that their salt content caused potassium loss, which could be dangerous. Potassium in these beverages was less than half that found in whole milk or orange juice—or even a can of beer! Dr. Costill's research indicates that, because the loss of electrolytes is so small during our runs, we may not need a special beverage to replace them. Orange juice, tomato juice, whole milk, and other more healthful drinks will replace all lost minerals and electrolytes.

Sugared Drinks Some runners and competitive cyclists drink sugared fluids—athletic drinks, soda, and other beverages. The cyclists claim that these drinks eliminate "bonking"—running out of liver glycogen—which may cause hypoglycemia, confusion, and dizziness.

Runners, however, are concerned with muscle—not liver— glycogen loss. The impact of sugars on runners is ambiguous. Some studies indicate that sugar taken during long runs enters the bloodstream and is used by your muscles to delay the consumption of stored glycogen, thus prolonging endurance. Other studies, however, show that glycogen previously stored in your muscles determines the onset of fatigue, not the circulating glucose (sugar) in your bloodstream.

Sugar may help you feel less fatigued, especially if you are not a highly trained runner. Dr. Joan Ullyot argues that blood sugar doesn't do anything for your muscles. But your brain needs sugar, "and if your mind perceives that the blood sugar is low, you are going to feel fatigued whether or not you have plenty of fuel." The ability to maintain blood sugar level comes with running: Trained marathoners tested during a marathon showed very high blood sugar levels. Thus, the average runner and the novice may need sugar during a long run or a race more than the well-trained runner. Sugar intake, however, delays the absorption of fluids.

The American College of Sports Medicine advises race sponsors to mix fluids and small amounts of sugar—less than 2.5 grams glucose per 100 ml. water—to help replace lost glucose. Some runners drink colas during long runs or races. The cola should be de-carbonated and diluted with water. Others drink half water, half race fluid, which they dilute to lessen the chances of an upset stomach. Some runners take sugared iced tea, which gives them water, sugar, and a "boost" of caffeine.

What you drink depends on:

Your Preference and Needs   Sugared drinks, beverages high in citric acid or caffeine, and athletic drinks may all upset your stomach. They may also benefit you. Experiment during your long runs, and during low-key races. Note in your runner's diary what you drank, how long you ran, and what the impact of those two facts was on your system. Choose a drink based on your own experience with it. Don't drink what other runners tell you is good.

Heat   Some of us run better in the heat than others. All of us need fluid during all our runs, regardless of how hot or how cold it is. Water is absorbed 50 percent faster than a sugared solution, which means water works quicker to prevent dehydration or overheating. Anything mixed with water delays its absorption. On a hot day, your best bet is water: it's more important to get fluids quickly into your system than to replace lost chemicals or minerals. Cold water is absorbed faster than warm fluids. Cold drinks—contrary to the old myth—will not cause cramps. The ideal fluid temperature for absorption is 40°F.

Distance   Under ten miles, water is all you need. Beyond that distance, you may want to experiment during your training runs with other beverages to replace lost electrolytes and sugar.

Drinking After the Run

Replace fluids by drinking after every workout and race. Studies indicate that sweating during exercise may produce an 8 percent loss of body weight and a 13 to 14 percent reduction in body water. A marathoner may lose 1 to 1.5 gallons of fluids. This loss is not permanent, since it is a loss of fluids, not fat.

Weigh yourself before and after each workout, and record it in your diary, to see how much fluid weight you are losing. Replace this lost body weight by drinking plenty of fluids after your runs. You should drink a pint of fluids for every pound of weight loss, and continue drinking for 24 to 48 hours to adequately rehydrate your system.

Start replacing fluids immediately after you finish running. Cold drinks in hot weather will help bring down your body temperature as well as replace lost fluids. Studies show that runners who drink two cups of ice water absorb half of it in 20 minutes—twice the amount of those who drink warm water. In cold weather, also drink cold water to replace lost fluids, and then add something warm to prevent chill—hot chocolate, tea, coffee, or soup.

Continue drinking fluids throughout the day. You should drink until you have clear urine. Dark urine is a symptom of, among other things, dehydration. Watch your body weight for the 24 hours after a long run to be sure you are replacing lost fluids.

Don't risk chronic dehydration by consuming too little fluid after running. This will lower your tolerance to fatigue, reduce your ability to sweat properly, elevate your rectal temperature, and increase stress on your circulatory system. The best way to guard against chronic dehydration, says Dr. Costill, is to check your weight each morning before breakfast. "If you note a two or three pound decrease in body weight from morning to morning, efforts should be made to increase your fluid intake. You need not worry about drinking too much fluid, because your kidneys will unload the excess water in a matter of hours." According to Dr. Edward Colt, there is increasing evidence of chronic dehydration among runners during long runs or marathons. Dr. Colt is seeing a sixfold increase in kidney stones among marathon runners. Kidney stones occur much more frequently in people who are dehydrated. Susceptibility to urinary-tract infections is another result.

What to drink after a long run or race?

The best beverage is water. Shepherd adds a couple of lemon or lime slices to a large glass of ice water. He keeps adding water and squeezing the citrus juices into the glass.

A few well-balanced meals, and several glasses of orange, pine-apple, or tomato juice will also replace most lost minerals. Soda pop has little potassium, and the expensive special athletic drinks have even less. We do not recommend coffee, wines, or liquor as fluids after running. Alcohol makes you urinate more frequently, thus causing you to lose fluids when you are trying to replenish them. Before celebrating with a postrun beer, drink several glasses of ice water, and then eat something nutritious with the beer.

20 STRESS AND TENSION

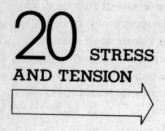

Stress is essential to life, but a cause of death. It sweetens victory, and defines defeat. It relieves boredom and helps us maintain life, resist aggression, and adapt to changing external influences. It may be pleasant or unpleasant, damaging or helpful. Its effect, especially its negative impact on our bodies, may be long-lasting, even occurring after the stressful event has passed.

Stress is everywhere in our daily lives. We may feel its characteristic signs immediately after someone's car nearly collides with our own, or both before and after an important speech, appearance, event, or business meeting.

What causes stress? Living. "Stress," says Dr. Hans Selye, director of the Institute of Experimental Medicine and Surgery and author of *Stress Without Distress* and *The Stress of Life*, "is essentially the wear and tear in the body caused by life at any one moment."

There are various kinds of stresses: emotional (from a family argument, the death of a loved one); environmental (from excessive heat or cold); and physiological (caused by an outpouring of the steroid hormones from the adrenal glands, which are extremely sensitive indicators of stress). There may also be perceived stress: How we see an event may make it more stressful than it inherently is.

Drs. Thomas H. Holmes and Richard H. Rahe, psychiatrists

at the University of Washington Medical School, attempted in the late 1970s to list stressful events and their impacts on us. They interviewed 394 men and women and asked them to rank—using marriage as equivalent to 50 units on their scale—a series of life events. From this they devised a "social adjustment scale" of stressful events. After compiling their scale, Drs. Holmes and Rahe found that stressful events have specific physiological characteristics. Their scale places death of a spouse as the most stressful event we experience. Corroborating this, the doctors discovered that widows and widowers are 10 times more likely to die within the first year after the death of their husbands or wives than all other people in their age group. Divorce, the next most stressful event, had a similar effect. The doctors found that divorced men and women, in the year following their divorce, had an illness rate 12 times higher than married people. Divorce now strikes more than one third of all marriages, and is especially prevalent among compulsive long-distance male runners.

What does this mean to us? Changes in our lives, whether good or bad, cause stress. And stress itself, whether good or bad, may impair the way we live, work, and feel. Stress changes us physically, and may cause a variety of medical ills, some imagined, and some very real, painful, even lethal. Each period of stress, Dr. Selye says, especially from frustrating, unsuccessful struggles, leaves some irreversible chemical scars. When we become burdened beyond our stress tolerance, we may become ill, or develop emotional illnesses, or suffer the physical breakdown of athletes. The list of diseases from negative stress is long, and uncontested: high blood pressure, mental depression, insomnia, impotence, viral infections, asthma attacks, ulcers, migraines, rashes, overeating, various heart diseases and arrhythmias. "The relationship of stress and behavior to cardiovascular conditions is well-documented," says Dr. David Jenkins, professor of preventive medicine and community health at the University of Texas in Galveston. "What is not as widely known is that, through its ability to depress the body's immune system, stress probably also influences the development of cancer."

What actually happens to a human being under stress? Imagine that you are facing a deadline. The boss comes in and tells you that what you've done so far is awful, that you'd better get the job finished, in good shape, on time. This may cause stress; your body prepares for action. The stressor excites your hypothalamus (a brain region near the base of the skull) which produces a substance that stimulates the pituitary gland to discharge the hormone ACTH (adrenocorticotrophic hormone) into the blood. ACTH induces the central, cortical portion of the adrenal glands. Signals begin rushing out to all parts of your body. Adrenaline pours into your bloodstream. The adrenaline increases your heart rate, sometimes to a rapid pounding. Your blood pressure rises quickly. The heart demands more oxygen, and there is an increase in respiration. (Obviously, if you smoke during stressful situations the constriction of blood vessels caused by the ingredients of the cigarette add additional, sometimes fatal, physiological stress to your heart.)

Now your heart is pounding, your blood pressure is up, your palms, armpits, stomach, or back may be sweating. Blood sugar provides emergency rations for your muscles. You and your body are ready to act. Too often in our society, however, instead of taking action or fleeing—the fight-or-flight reaction of our ancestors—we merely sit and seethe.

Research in the early 1900s by Dr. Walter B. Cannon at the Harvard Medical School showed that animals used this physiological change to act. When a wild animal fought or ran, it consumed this energy; its muscles later relaxed, its heartbeat slowed and returned to normal, its blood pressure dropped, and its breathing steadied.

The repeated suppression of this natural sequence puts an unnatural strain on our bodies. Fewer than five percent of American workers have jobs that keep them active, such as farming; with the electronic, computer age, that figure is dropping. Our lives create stress, and our failure to respond to that stress with physical action is the primary cause of tension. Too many Americans lead lives without regular exercise; underexercised muscles never get a chance to work out tension. The constant imbalance between stress and the lack of exercise underlies hypokinetic disease. The results are tension, injury, illness.

The impact of stress upon our bodies is measurable. Some people may vomit or get diarrhea; others will suffer from psychosomatic diseases, such as migraine headaches, which can be extremely painful. Our emotions also affect our muscles; and our muscles reflect our emotional problems. Repeated tensing of the muscles results in loss in length of contracture. When a shortened muscle is forced to stretch, it cannot. It may react by going into a spasm, or by tearing. Muscle tension also causes other problems, such as back pain.

According to Dr. Hans Kraus, the internationally known back specialist, back pain occurs because Americans are underexercised and overtense. Our muscles, Dr. Kraus believes, are tensing for action and not being used for anything all day long. Lower back muscles are prime targets of stress, as are, less frequently, the legs, thighs, and arms. Our underexercised and overirritated lives are especially bad for our children, who are even less active than their parents. They watch a lot of television, and as they sit before the screen they are both tense and motionless. Their predicament—tension and inaction—almost symbolizes our daily lives. Not surprisingly, Dr. Kraus has found that 60 percent of American children cannot perform the six basic Kraus-Weber tests that measure minimal physical fitness.

Headaches, too, may be caused by tension in the occipital muscles in the back of the head, and the frontalis muscles in the forehead. Neck pain may be caused by tensing of the trapezius muscles, which reach down to cover the shoulder blades, and the rhomboid muscles. The result of such tension is a series of common ailments: tension headaches, aching stiff necks, lower back pain. The latter, in fact, is epidemic. In Chapter 16, we discuss this problem and suggest exercises for it. The YMCA also offers classes to help people relieve lower back pain. This program was developed by Alexander Melleby and Dr. Kraus. They have found, as other researchers have, that lower back pain is rarely caused by organic disease, but by muscles that are weak or tense, or both. Obviously, regular exercising would alleviate much of the problem.

Tension also works on our bodies in ways that we are just now coming to understand. In a well-known study about heart disease and behavior patterns, Drs. Meyer Friedman and Ray H. Rosenman of Mount Sinai Hospital in San Francisco examined some 3,500 men during a four-year span. They broadly divided the behavior patterns they found into two types: Type A and Type B. The Type A man was aggressive, ambitious, and success oriented. He talked fast and was always on the run to meet deadlines; he competed against everyone and himself. The Type B man was calmer, working at his own pace, and under little self-imposed stress.

Type A runners are easily recognized. They carry their tensions visibly during a workout, running with tight face muscles, tight and high shoulders, and a short, choppy stride. Very often, this type of runner will power by you going up a hill, and you will pass him on the downhill as you open your stride and glide along. The Type A runner, I've observed, is often a successful man (or woman) who works hard and believes that he or she has to run hard. They run, in part, as an escape from self-imposed pressures. They are usually too busy to warm up, stretch, and begin running slowly before beating their bodies into the hard, paved roads. They also think cooling down is for other runners, and risk serious injury by foregoing that series of exercises, too. Tight calves and hamstrings as well as back pain are often the penalty they pay for running this way.

Not surprisingly, Drs. Friedman and Rosenman found the Type A man to have 2.5 times more heart attacks than the Type B. They also discovered that, among other things, emotional stress and nervous tension play a relevant role in coronary heart disease. John Hunter described coronary disease, and later suffered from it: "I am at the mercy of any fool who can aggravate me." The Type A man is also good at aggravating others.

These kinds of stresses cause diseases, from peptic ulcers to high blood pressure to mental illness. Stress and tension and their symptoms can be greatly relieved, if not eliminated altogether, by learning to relax and by exercising regularly. As the next chapter details, jogging and running (or other forms of aerobic exercise) have been shown scientifically to ease tension and stress while improving one's self-image and confidence. Research also shows that running enhances creativity and eliminates depression. A conference at the New York Academy of Sciences during the mid-1970s concluded that long-distance runners benefited not only physically, but were also more independent and emotionally stable and less anxiety-prone than their nonexercising counterparts.

Dr. William Glasser, author of *Positive Addiction,* suggests that running one mile three times a week results in increased self-confidence and greater imaginative powers. In his work, Dr. Glasser reports that the lonely runner, like the lone meditator, drains off tensions and releases negative emotions. Few runners can run and worry. As we shall see, since Dr. Glasser's work in the early 1970s, further scientific research has proven that running or other aerobic exercises releases hormones and chemical substances that contribute to our sense of well-being, creativity, and even decision-making abilities.

Stress, of course, damages us not only physically, but also mentally. Further research since the early 1980s shows that running itself can create two debilitating stresses: physical and mental.

The person exposed to physical stress from running throws up defenses to it. If the stress comes in small quantities and regularly, the body may adapt to it. But if the physical stresses are too heavy and too repetitive, the body cannot cope, and exhaustion, ailments, or injuries may result. The trick is to learn to relax and stretch, and to train enough to build, but not to injure. Tom Osler, a former national 50-mile champion, lists some danger signs that might indicate our physical stress burden is becoming excessive:

1. Mild leg soreness.
2. Lowered general resistance (sniffles, headaches, fever blisters).
3. A washed-out feeling, or an "I-don't-care" attitude.
4. Poor coordination (general clumsiness, tripping, poor auto driving).
5. A hangover from your previous run.

Where Dr. Glasser talks of a positive addiction to running, other medical researchers in the early 1980s identified what they called negative addiction to running. These researchers identified a category of long-distance runner who put in more than 70 miles a week, and whose life was characterized by a loss of perspective about running. These runners put running ahead of their vocational, social, and personal lives; they abused their bodies and ran even when severely injured; they could not stop running without experiencing "withdrawal symptoms." They became like alcoholics: Running was so important that they did it despite all obstacles, even when told it might seriously impair their health.

Instead of relieving stress, running for some men and women adds to it. They make running obligatory, not optional and fun. While running can relieve stress; running may also manifest our stresses. The obligatory runner is no longer free not to run: he sets his lifestyle to achieve a self-identity that always eludes him. Running is not unique to obsession. Other elements of our lives may take on ritualistic patterns: religion, working, courting, grooming. But we must remember that, as Amby Burfoot writes, running is a valueless activity. Although the results of running may have great value—less stress, for one—we must understand our reasons for running, and control them.

Running can become too all-encompassing; it can become our primary reason for living. The runner who puts everything into racing or training or simply running a lot is perhaps psychologically wounded. He or she is missing the point. Running should be fun; it should balance your life, make you more fit, less sedentary. It should bring you new friends, new goals, a fresh sense of who you are and where you are going. It should not damage your career, family, or love life; it should not make you into something you are not meant to be. Runners think that because they are running they are automatically physically and mentally healthy. Yet we all agree that physical injury is part of running. So, too, is mental injury; running will not save us from mental stresses. One of the better New York City runners jumped out a window to his death not long ago. A forty-five-year-old British executive died from an overdose of aspirin. In his suicide note, he said that life was not worth living because he couldn't run after a knee injury.

What all runners need more than anything is balance. We need to control our stresses—even the stress from exercise—by doing several things. Hans Selye offers five important steps:

1. Identify the various stages of life, wonder about the type of person you are and the type of person you wish to be, set realistic goals, distinguish between healthy and unhealthy ambition (which is never satisfied).
2. Maintain a broad network of family and friends with whom you share interests, work, ambitions, and fun.
3. Engage in regular exercise in a gentle manner; this confers physical and psychological/emotional benefits, and provides diversity.
4. Vary your routines, create hobbies, take vacations to enjoy life, not to recover from it.
5. Continue your self-education and pursue further studies;

work to have compassion for others and for yourself. "The more we vary our actions," says Dr. Selye, "the less any part suffers from attrition." The ultimate goal is to keep our muscles, organs, and brains healthy and active.

We cannot—and Dr. Selye and others argue that we should not—avoid stress. Stress is part of life, a natural by-product of all our activities. What we must avoid is allowing stress to make us sick, weaken our resistance to disease, or kill us. We need to control the stresses we face. Here are some enjoyable possibilities.

RELAXATION

The ability to relax improves with training. Medical studies show that relaxation exercises can reduce tension and distress. Most importantly, they reduce high blood pressure and heart rates resulting from stress, as well as muscle tension. They also help to "break" muscle tension which frequently causes injury. Further, relaxing prior to exercising helps stretch tense muscles; a relaxed muscle stretches more easily. Third, relaxation exercises reduce muscle strain and soreness after workouts.

"The link between exercise and tension reduction," says Dr. William Morgan of the University of Wisconsin, "is so clear that it is no longer even questioned by researchers." But what if you can't exercise? Here are some good methods to alleviate stress and to relax.

- If stress is not inherent in an event, but in how you perceive that event, modify your perceptions and reduce your stress.
- Express your anger.
- Choose your fights. "Flee" by fantasizing, taking short walks, going away for a weekend. Talk to a friend. Give in once in a while instead of insisting that you are always right.
- Organize your time. Identify time-wasters and try to eliminate them or modify them. Pace yourself (here is a direct lesson from running). Stick to a plan.
- Learn mini, at-your-desk relaxation exercises. Tighten all

the muscles in your body, starting with your head and neck and going down to your toes. Slowly, let your body go limp from head to feet. Or, relax by imagining yourself in a relaxing environment like the beach or at a tropical waterfall.

- Breathe slower. Dr. Jenny Steinmetz, a California psychologist who specializes in stress management, has her clients take a seven-second inhale and an eight-second exhale to relax. Do four of those each minute, for two minutes. If you have trouble counting seconds, try Dr. Steinmetz' clever trick: Say a three-syllable word to equal one second. For example, one-el-e-phant, two-el-e-phant, and so forth.

Two of the best forms of relaxation are meditation and yoga. These can be done regularly, and also before and after running. Experiments show that during meditation there is a marked decrease in the body's oxygen consumption, respiratory rate, and heart rate. Studies at Harvard University indicate that by meditating some people can dramatically lower their blood pressure. As we will see in the next chapter, meditation before, during, and after a run is reaping a wide variety of benefits for its adherents.

There are several well-known methods of relaxing and meditating. We describe here a few that runners have tried with success.

Autogenic Training

Devised by Dr. H. H. Smith, a German neurologist, these six mental exercises should be practiced several times a day until you can elicit them at will.

In a quiet room, lie down, close your eyes, and:

1. Focus on a feeling of heaviness in the limbs.
2. Focus on the sensation of warmth in your limbs.
3. Concentrate on your heart and its slow beat.
4. Focus on controlled breathing.
5. Concentrate on feelings of coolness on your forehead.
6. Concentrate on total relaxation of the whole body.

Progressive Relaxation

After twenty years of investigation, Dr. Edmund Jacobson published a book about relieving skeletal muscle contraction, which he believed caused or aggravated anxiety and related diseases. The idea is to lie on your bed or the floor, assume a passive mental state, and calm "uncontrollable" tensions by relaxing controllable muscles. For every minute that you keep larger muscles relaxed, other smaller ones let go as well. Even tiny contractions of the muscles are avoided to achieve deep relaxation.

Transcendental Meditation

One of the most widely practiced forms of meditation, TM became popular in the 1960s when the Beatles, Mia Farrow, and others practiced it. TM is a controversial form of meditation requiring lessons at a qualified TM center, and a huge fee.

The Relaxation Response

Sometimes called the poor man's TM, or (more often) "a terrific aspirin," this popular meditative technique employs the traditional four components of meditation coupled with some reassuring medical findings about reduced blood pressure. It was devised by Dr. Herbert Benson of the Harvard Medical School. The four components:

1. Find a quiet environment that will help you concentrate.
2. Employ a mental device to shift your mind from the external, stress-filled world to your inner, peaceful world. Such a stimulus may be a sound, word, or phrase repeated silently or aloud; or an object. "Mind wandering" is a major obstacle here, but an accepted one.
3. Assume a passive attitude. This includes not worrying about your mind wandering, or about how well you are performing.
4. Be comfortable. Some people sit in the cross-legged "lotus" position. Shift around. Dr. Benson warns, however,

that "if you are lying down, there is a tendency to fall asleep."

Relaxation is simply stillness, quiet, a word or sound repeated; you are awake and in control. You may be still, or on your run. You may want to link the two: Start with meditation, stretching, and then go on your run, repeating your sound or word through the entire process. (This is detailed in the next chapter.)

Runners at Harvard's Thorndike Medical Laboratory developed, with Dr. Benson, a variation on those four meditative components. Shepherd has tried them and thinks they're fantastic and beneficial.

- Sit quietly in a comfortable position, close your eyes, and deeply relax all your muscles. One method Shepherd uses is the yoga massage: Begin by gently rubbing your head, and move slowly to every part of your body including fingers and toes. Keep your muscles deeply relaxed.
- Breathe through your nose. Try some yogic breathing here: In one nostril and out, then in the same nostril, but out the other (block the first with a finger), then in that nostril but out the first. Continue for several minutes, alternating nostrils. Then, as you breathe out, silently say the word "one." Continue for 15 to 20 minutes. You may open your eyes to check the time, but don't use an alarm. When you finish, sit quietly for several minutes, first with your eyes closed and later with your eyes open.
- Maintain a passive attitude. Permit relaxation to occur at its own pace. Ignore all distracting thoughts. Continue repeating the word "one" (or any other soothing word). Do not worry about whether or not you are achieving a deep level of relaxation.

Yoga

After you have been running for about a year, you may want to experiment with different warm-up and cool-down exercises.

Yoga may appeal to you, and you may wish to incorporate some of the exercises here into your stretching routines.

Yoga is widely used among athletic teams. In baseball, the Kansas City Royals, St. Louis Cardinals, Philadelphia Phillies, and California Angels practice it. In football, the New England Patriots, Pittsburgh Steelers, Denver Broncos, New York Giants, and other teams teach yoga for stretching and relaxation. Among the many college teams, Georgia Tech's Bulldogs have employed the well-known Arden Zinn to instruct them in yoga. Jean-Claude Killy, the skier, and his French teammates practiced yoga 30 minutes a day in training for the Olympics and the European championships. Their coach, Honoré Bonnet, said: "The purpose is to liberate the mind and relax the body."

This is also why runners try yoga. The stretching is gentle, smooth, nonpainful, and achieved over a period of time. It is a good answer to a lack of flexibility. "Stretching by bobbing or bouncing," writes Dr. Herbert de Vries, the U.S.C. physiologist, "invokes the stretch reflex which actually opposes the desired stretching."

It is difficult for a book to teach yoga, since it is a spiritual as well as physical exercise, but there are yoga positions that may benefit runners. Here are several we like. Most of them will be difficult to perform at first, but with consistent, unforced practice, they can be mastered.

The Plough (Halasana)   On your back, arms forward on the ground, slowly lift your legs and inhale; raise your hips and back and bring your legs all the way over your head until your toes touch the floor behind you. Bring legs slowly back to floor, and rise into a sitting position. Then slowly lie back down.

Variations: In the Plough, stretch your legs as far apart as possible. Or, bring your knees down to your ears.

Forward Bend (Paschimothanasana)   Sitting on the ground, back straight, legs together straight out in front of you, raise your arms as high overhead as possible, stretching your spine upward. Inhale deeply, exhale and lean forward catching your toes (if possible). A supple runner or reincarnate can hook his fingers around his big toe, and bring his head to his knees, elbows on the floor.

Knee Stretch (Bhadrasana)   Sit, and press soles of feet firmly together. Place hands on knees, and gently push them to the floor. Pull heels as close to your crotch as possible, clasp toes, and bend forward until your head touches (or almost touches) the floor.

Deep Lunge (Sirangusthasana)   Stand, legs wide apart, hands clasped behind back. Bend your left knee, and lean forward over it, trunk bending and head pressing down. Try to bring your forehead all the way down to your toes. Hold for half a minute and repeat to the other side.

Forward Bend (Padahasthasana)   Stand, inhale and raise your arms high overhead, arching slightly to the rear. Slowly bend down, exhale, legs straight, bring hands to heels and head to knees. Hold for several seconds. Inhale while straightening.

Variation: Clasp hands behind back, bend from waist, bring head down slowly to one knee and then the other, stretching sideways.

Try sitting in the lotus position: Bend right leg and place the foot on left thigh; draw the ankle in toward the groin. Fold the left leg over it onto other thigh. Keep back straight. Place hands, palm out, on knees.

If you are troubled with back problems, don't try doing the Cobra or the Bow. These, and some other yoga positions, may be harmful to your back and aggravate sciatic discomfort.

Try some of these yoga positions as substitutes for your regular stretching. (But remember to do the full amount of stretching exercises.) One reason we emphasize varying warm-up and cool-down exercises is that they are so important we don't want them to become boring or repetitious. Substituting yoga is fun. Remember to continue the deep breathing, and to breathe with the yoga exercises, too.

So, run after warming up with meditation, relaxation (or yoga), and stretching. Run loose, because running is vital to your emotional as well as physical health.

21 RUNNING INSIDE YOUR HEAD

John Donahue is forty-three years old, and works for a contractor in Rochester, New York. He runs five miles almost every day. Like a lot of other runners who have gotten into shape and run regularly, Donahue began running to lose weight, but he continues because of its psychological benefits. "After about 35 or 40 minutes," he said, "it seems as if all sorts of tension are relieved. It's almost like floating. . . . I am more mentally alert after I run. Things are more noticeable, clearer—imagine lots of cobwebs that you have just cleared away. Problems can be sorted out a lot easier."

Dr. George Sheehan, the cardiologist, long-distance runner, and philosopher, talks about a "third wind" and his "peak experience" when he is "completely at peace with things" and becomes "quite creative, almost poetical" while running.

Dick Traum, the New York businessman who runs with an artificial leg, says: "I really enjoy the opportunity to organize my thoughts away from business interruptions. Sometimes I just 'tune out' for hours and release tension. It takes about half an hour to completely unwind, at which time I feel very high, as if I were running without any effort whatsoever."

Running also helped Mary Beth Byrne, a financial librarian in New York City, to find the time to consider a change in her career, and to sort through her attitudes toward her work. "Running helped me find more satisfaction in my work," she said. "It

gave me the courage and the strength to make several major decisions. I found new challenges at work and am happy that it is not
more demanding than it is because now I have time to run a lot. If
I had made the career change I had been contemplating, I would
have had very little time for running.

"I have found that running allows me to think of positive
things, and to solve problems. I can think things through on the
run and later I can make a better decision. Sometimes I just go
blank. I get great freedom—sometimes just looking at the trees
and scenery, and not thinking about anything at all. It has been a
very personal thing for me, allowing me to be more optimistic.
The act of running combines body and mind in a way that is very
satisfying."

Joe Henderson calls the experience "meditation on the
move." And it is. If you are running more than five miles a day,
more than four days a week, you may have experienced it: the flow
of movement, the second wind, the creativity, the euphoria, the
"third wind," and even a meditative high. Dr. Sheehan calls running at this level "the opening of the creative side of your brain."
It doesn't always happen, but when it does, he says, "I seem to see
the way things really are. I am in the Kingdom."

Are runners crazy? Since the beginning of the "running
boom" in the early 1970s, magazines, newspapers, television, and
books have all extolled the psychological and emotional benefits
of vigorous exercise. Far more important, since the late 1970s,
medical scientists have been corroborating what runners have
known all along: That exercise makes us feel good.

Dr. Thaddeus Kostrubala started running to strengthen his
heart and to lose 60 pounds. As he got into shape, he realized that
not only was his body becoming firmer, but his mind was sharper
and more creative as well. A psychiatrist in San Diego, Dr. Kostrubala began treating some patients suffering mild forms of emotional disease with therapy that included jogging. His patients
began running for as long as an hour a day, three days a week, fol-

lowed by group therapy. He has already returned a paranoid schizophrenic to school, and helped a heroin addict kick his habit. "I've never experienced this kind of success in psychotherapy before," he says.

Dr. John H. Greist, a University of Wisconsin-Madison psychiatrist, studied the effect of jogging on clinically depressed patients. During a ten-week running program for eight patients, six found relief from depression by walking, jogging, or running two to seven times a week, both alone and in groups. Most recovered from their depressed state, says Dr. Greist, within three weeks of running, and have maintained the recovery. After a year, Dr. Greist reported, ". . . most patients who were treated with running have become regular runners and remain symptom-free."

Dr. Herbert de Vries, a physiologist from Los Angeles, tested patients suffering from severe anxiety and tension. One group was given tranquilizers. The others went on regular vigorous walks. Dr. de Vries found that those taking the 15-minute walks on a regular basis were calmer; that is, the exercise had a greater calming effect than the tranquilizers. In more recent studies, Dr. de Vries reports that rhythmic exercises such as walking, running, cycling, and even bench stepping from five to 30 minutes at 30 to 60 percent maximum intensity will elicit a calming, tranquilizer effect.

There is now hard scientific evidence for these reports. Running and other aerobic exercise causes some potent chemicals and hormones to be released in the body. Researchers at Penn State Medical School found elevated levels of dopamine and other "natural opiates" in the blood of runners who had just finished running a marathon. Dopamine may be partly responsible for the anti-depressant effect of running.

Other neuroscientists and cell biologists have isolated opiates called endorphins that echo the actions of heroin and opium. Beta-endorphin, only discovered in 1975, originates in the pituitary gland, and appears to be released by fatigue brought on by strenuous exercise. Beta-endorphin is a painkiller that prevents the transmission of pain. With the endorphins are the enkephalins, which exist in the brain and spinal cord. They travel to receptor sites and act as messengers or neurotransmitters; they also block the perception of pain by intercepting pain messages being re-layed to the brain. These "natural opiates" may to some degree explain a runner's "addiction" to exercise, since the exercise re-leases chemicals and hormones that create in the body a state of painless well-being.

Dr. Malcolm Carruthers and his British medical team have also found that men and women who exercise vigorously release greater levels of the hormone norepinephrine. This hormone, Dr. Carruthers reports, is "the chemical basis for happy feelings," and just 15 minutes of vigorous exercise "doubles the body's level of this hormone, destroying depression—and the effect is long lasting."

What do these physiological changes mean to the average runner? For one thing, we may be calmer, less depressed, even better able to make important decisions. The University of Flor-ida researchers determined that men and women who perform regular aerobic exercise have lower levels of anxiety and fewer medical complaints. A study at the Sunflower Mental Health Center in Kansas found that 92 percent of all runners reported improved problem-solving abilities when running than when not running. A Purdue University research team agreed that aerobic exercise improves problem-solving abilities, and added that it also enhances skills in forming strategies to solve complex problems. Psychologists at York University in Toronto have concluded that marathon runners have significantly less anger, depression, and confusion than the population at large. And Dr. William Glasser believes that running puts us in touch with our right-side brain function—the creative side.

Clearly, running and other forms of vigorous exercise allow us to discover our bodies and our selves. Such exercise also has an immediate and long-term effect on our self-esteem. Several studies show that runners have high self-esteem—whether this is caused by the release of hormones or improved self-image remains unclear. Studies with alcoholics show that running as little as one mile a day for 20 days is sufficient to raise their self-esteem. Consistent aerobic exercise raises psychological benefits, including self-sufficiency and resolve; it lowers levels of anxiety and depression.

Running and aerobic exercise works because improvements come quickly, and build. Even a little jogging creates men and women who, studies show, are conscientious, more trusting, more imaginative, a bit more introverted, forthright, dominant, resourceful, and happier than nonexercisers. Running may even raise our IQs through increased oxygen supply to the brain. Tests also show that:

- Runners have developed a sense of success and mastery over a particular task, and their environment.
- Runners find that they can change themselves for the better in terms of health, body image, self-confidence, and self-acceptance.
- A runner's sense of confidence flows into other areas where he or she also experiences success.
- Running is seen as a positive activity that replaces negative or neurotic behavior and habits.

What does this "running high" feel like? How can we bring it about?

From both physiological and emotional sources, long slow aerobic running can, as Dr. Kostrubala writes, "produce an altered state of consciousness. A non-ordinary avenue of perception does seem to open up." The experience is often like a dream, but remembered by the runner and there to be considered, and sought again. Dr. Kostrubala, himself a marathon runner, is very clear about what he thinks we runners are experiencing. "The slow long distance runner experiences a part of his unconscious." His or her running also achieves "an altered state of consciousness that can be called a kind of Western meditation."

Dr. Kostrubala, in *The Physician and Sportsmedicine* magazine, writes that during "the first 20 or 30 minutes [of a run] you feel rotten, fatigued, shot down. Some in depression will actually cry. The draining feeling is emotional, not physical. That sense of depression disappears in 30 minutes. . . .

"Almost as consistent is the 'runner's high' that occurs 30 to 40 minutes after starting. It's a distinct euphoria with feelings of excitement and enthusiasm. This is why most of our group runners supplement the dosage with independent running.

"I call the period of 40 to 60 minutes the 'altered state of consciousness' that must be similar to the catalytic experience of drugs or religion that allows us to alter our lives from within. It's an opening to the unconscious. . . .

"The thought process is altered. Problems become irrelevant or annoying, and are let go. And, like some inner consultation, a random jumble of ideas flashes through the field of consciousness."

There is, of course, the need to "listen to your body." Dr. Kostrubala, and other doctors, recommend that if running doesn't feel good after 30 minutes, you may want to stop. There are usually distinctive stages in running inside your head. The first 30 minutes may make you ask, "What the hell am I doing here?" Mild euphoria may start after 30 minutes. Tensions may drain away. You may be lulled by the rhythm of your steps or your breathing. Ideas may flash in and out of your mind from the periphery of your consciousness. After an hour, a form of meditation, in which colors and thought patterns will flow through your awareness, may take affect. Your mind may become sharp and clear.

There are many ways to achieve this condition; not all involve running. For example, Lynn McCutcheon, a sports psychologist in Virginia, found that both runners and weightlifters reported an exercise high. He suggests that "getting high" may be an experience common to a variety of strenuous sports.

Joe Henderson, author of *The Long-Run Solution*, suggests five steps that are good general rules for vigorous exercise as well as reaching a meditative state during running. First, he says, start your run without an end in sight. It will take 20 to 30 minutes to pick up the flow, and by then you'll know how much you can do. Second, if the run goes badly, stop and try again tomorrow. Remember, any running is better than none at all: "Even a trickle of running adds something to the pool of fitness." Third, let your pace find itself. You will usually run along the edge between comfort and discomfort. Fourth, run for yourself; don't look ahead or behind you. And fifth, run for today; don't compete with yesterday or tomorrow. Take pleasure in being less than the best.

There are several things that will inhibit or facilitate "penetration into one's inner world" while running. On the negative side:

- Competition, or the obsession with running miles.
- New surroundings that distract you. Some runners argue that new surroundings take your mind off your run during those first often uncomfortable 30 minutes.
- Other people and the yakkety-yakking of group runs; valuable for fun and sociability, group runs are out if you wish to reach a meditative state.
- Conversation, with someone else or with yourself, will misdirect your concentration; some runners like to talk to themselves to pass through stages of their runs. Don't talk, either to yourself or others.

By avoiding these four circumstances during a run, and by running at a steady, nontiring pace, and letting your mind spin free, with ideas flowing through it like water down a mountain stream, you can encourage the meditative state.

Dr. Leonard Reich, a New York City psychologist and runner, says, "I tell my friends cryptically that I try not to think about anything. In fact, I concentrate on clearing my mind of all thoughts so as to become receptive to the activity in which I am engaged. I call this 'meditative running.' " The first step, Dr. Reich suggests, is to "focus oneself in the present, to become aware of the here and now. This means to be receptive, to open awareness to all internal and external stimuli, to allow all the forces in the immediate situation to have equal attention."

Some runners sit and chant a mantra—a repeated word or sound—and then run. Others relax, begin running, and meditate on their steady breathing or the sound of their feet. Dick Buerkle, an Olympic distance runner, hears a steady beat as he runs, and sometimes the beat takes the form of a song with his feet pounding out the rhythm. He also likes to tie bells on his runnings shoes for a meditative sound. Other runners perform math computations, and still others seek meditative trances, almost becoming hypnotized like the Tibetans who run for 24 hours at a speed of 7 minutes per mile in a trance state achieved by meditation.

There are several ways of entering such a meditative state. Try these out, and you may find one that works for you. Dr. Kostrubala, for example, suggests an "inner-directed attention" on parts of your body: legs, back, feet, even your sweating and your breathing. Chant a phrase or childhood prayer like "Matthew, Mark, Luke, and John, bless this bed I lie upon." Or, count your footsteps, or repeat numbers like a mantra by counting one through 100, or, says the running psychiatrist, "just count until you're silly with numbers."

Bud Winter, a sports psychologist at San Jose State, suggests creating a state that is the opposite of tension. Keep unused muscles relaxed, and remember the chant of the long-distance runners: "Let the meat hang on the bones." Set your mind by making up a short phrase that expresses the attitude you want to carry as you run. Repeat the slogan or phrase over and over. Winter suggests "Calm," as in "caaaaallllllmmmmmmm."

The following are some methods you might want to try for

reaching meditation on the run. Since I believe that running should be fun, I've included some wild ideas.

Sit quietly and alone near your running path. Close your eyes, or focus them on the ground immediately before you. Concentrate on your breathing. Count your breaths: Count ten exhalations; start over and count ten more. Do this for about 15 minutes. As you feel yourself relax, start "imagery"—the technique for becoming proficient in any sport. Visualize yourself running well. Vividly picture yourself running the way you've always wanted to run: relaxed, smooth, powerful, easy. Create visual sensations of yourself. Rise slowly, and start walking. Focus on your feet hitting the ground. Listen to your breathing. Focus on your body. Begin a slow shuffle, and then a slow run. Bring the meditative state into your running by counting breaths or steps, or by repeating prayers, a mantra, or numbers. After 30 minutes of running, let your mind wander free. Let ideas, fantasies, colors, smells flow through you. Be receptive, open to internal and external stimuli. And, as Dr. Reich urges, "make your body rhythm so graceful that it enters the rhythm of the universe."

Another run, for men and women in good condition, might follow this pattern: Meditate alone in a field until ready to run. Stand, keeping your eyes half-closed, run slowly, and accelerate to surge. Open your eyes as you increase your speed. Then slow down, and return to a meditative position; rise, and run again.

The latter method is utilized by several West Coast runners who have added meditation between sets of runs or before and after each workout.

We know, from medical studies, that one of the most inhibiting factors in muscular activity is the production of lactic acid in the blood. Lactic acid escapes from the muscles to the bloodstream when the oxygen supply is inadequate. *Scientific American* published medical reports that show that 10 minutes of meditation may reduce lactic acid in the blood equal to the reduction caused by 8 hours of sleep. Meditation before running, therefore, could have a profound effect on muscle strength. (For some standard meditation techniques, see Chapter 20.)

Mike Spino of the Esalen Institute, and James Hickman, a San Francisco research psychologist, have devised several mental exercises that are both meditative and helpful in preparing runners for running. One of the best is called a "witness meditation," which is designed to move you from a sitting into a running meditation.

First, you assume the standard Zen sitting posture, fingers curled, the left hand in your right palm, thumbs touching gently. Place your hands in your lap, and close your eyes. Breathe deeply into your abdomen. Proceed gently and slowly, and relax. Inhale deeply, filling the cavity, and as you exhale, release tension. After two minutes or so, switch and breathe deeply into the upper chest and lungs. Fill the upper chest. Exhale slowly and relax. Inhale and exhale in long draws, relaxed and rhythmical. After another two minutes, combine the two: inhale, filling your abdomen first and then your chest. Exhale from the chest and then the abdomen. Inhale, filling the abdomen and then chest; exhale from the chest and then the abdomen.

Spino and Hickman suggest that you next "visualize a light about the size of a halo directly over your head," and while inhaling slowly "draw light from this halo into the body." This "light" should relax and calm you. As the light fades from sight, you have "a personal energy source."

If this is too much for you, move to the next step from the rhythmical breathing: the "Zen walk." This helps you carry "the contemplative state of awareness into movement." Walk around in a circle, slowly making contact with the ground, first with your heel and then toe and then gradually increasing to a faster walk. Stop, look at a spot on the ground, "breathe into the spot." Now, "picture yourself as a primordial person," begin shuffling at a slow pace and then, in a "state of concentrated awareness," slowly begin running. Here, you might incorporate Dr. Kostrubala's ideas for meditating on the move.

This exercise with all these separate steps and ideas won't appeal to some runners, but my co-author Jack Shepherd thinks we all ought to have at least one crazy run every week. Mine is what I call an "Animal Run." I'll just run like a wild animal, full of speed and fury, with abandon, often alone, although sometimes with a fellow animal who takes turns pushing the pace. These runs strengthen my body and sharpen my mind. I think "guts" all the way through the run, and fantasize about my memories of one of my greatest heroes—Steve Prefontaine. I can still see him running beyond his limits on mental stamina alone with his agony mask hiding his joy for exceeding his threshold of pain, and when I play "animal" I pretend I'm as tough as he.

I believe a sense of euphoria comes with three types of runs: the meditative high from running alone at a reflective pace; the competition high of running fast at the edge of our physical limits; and the "high" of running with friends, of fellowship.

We are just beginning to understand the relationship between running and meditation. The so-called "primitive" peoples may be our ultimate teachers. The Tarahumara Indians in northern Mexico live in the mountains and run slowly from house to house, village to village. During workdays, groups may jog 30 miles or more, and on weekends, 150 miles.

Australian aborigines track kangaroo by slowly jogging with them until the animals are exhausted. The famous Bushmen hunters of the Kalahari Desert in Africa jog after eland for distances of more than 20 miles, and remain fresh. A group of Hopi Indians traditionally ran 10 miles before dawn to their fields, worked all day, and ran 10 miles home. It is not surprising that some of these—such as the Hopi—were meditative people. None counted miles, aerobic points, or time per mile. They ran out of desire, or the need to obtain food; it was part of their lives.

Now that running is part of your life, expand it. There are many ways, at many levels, to achieve meditation on the move.

For me, Dr. Sheehan sums it up best: "For every runner who tours the world running marathons, there are thousands who run to hear the leaves and listen to rain and look to the day when it all is suddenly as easy as a bird in flight. For them, sport is not a test but a therapy, not a trial but a reward, not a question but an answer."

22 RUNNERS MAKE BETTER LOVERS

⟶

It was a foggy, romantic morning. More than 10,000 men and women, some in costume, crowded around the starting line for the annual Bay-to-Breakers Race in San Francisco. Most of them stayed warm by jogging in place, performing stretching exercises, or running back and forth short distances across the starting line. The prerace tension and excitement—this is more a race for fun and show than prizes—raised spirits and hopes. A festive feeling mingled with the fog and runners.

At the starting gun, a great mass of runners surged forward, and each began finding his or her pace. One runner, settling into his run, found himself behind an especially lovely woman whose stride matched his own. She glanced at him, he at her, and silently they paced each other for the first few miles. Finally, using an opening line he had tried elsewhere, he asked: "What's a nice girl like you doing in a place like this?"

"Who says I'm nice?" she replied with a mischievous smile. He pulled closer, took her elbow, and the two of them veered off into the fog-shrouded park.

Do runners make better lovers? The evidence, while still more subjective than scientific, will bring a smile to the faces of runners averaging below 70 miles per week. Marathoners may frown—or disagree. Runners, like other people who exercise regularly, feel and look better. They develop firm, lean bodies. Along with pride in your body comes a self-confidence that often carries over into your work and leisure. Sam McConnell, at the age of seventy-seven, runs 6 miles a day. "Running stimulates all aspects of health—physical and sexual," he says. "Most people over fifty don't have much sex, but running is a great contributor to the drive. I feel better today sexually than I did twenty years ago, and I attribute this to running."

Runners are endurance athletes who are conditioned to pace themselves to superior performances. They participate in an activity that values endurance, versatility, flexibility, overcoming obstacles (such as minor aches, pains, and other discomforts), the shared experience, the ability to perform in any weather or climate (indoors or out), and, of course, distance over time. Runners are also often more sensitive to the changes in their bodies, and from their training habits, know what it is to defer gratification. Persistence, durability, and taking pleasure in each step toward a distant rewarding goal also characterizes runners.

Consider the story of another running friend of mine, a member of the New York Road Runners Club. He had recently bedded a young woman runner, and they had quickly decided—quick being a month—that runners do indeed make better lovers. To prove their point, so to speak, they made an agreeable pact: "The bet," my friend told me, "was that I could get an erection and make love within 30 minutes after finishing a marathon. I was certain that marathon runners have extraordinary sexual prowess."

Eagerly, she accepted his bet, and the week of the New York Marathon, the two laid out, as it were, their plans. By agreement, they abstained for two days before the race, and when he approached the starting line, it was with a more-than-usual eagerness to finish. At the gun, he jumped ahead to a fast pace, and maintained it with unusual vigor. The dreaded "Wall" at 20 miles came and went, and he was still running brilliantly. "In fact," he said later, "I finished in my fastest time and didn't even think about the normal aches and pains we usually suffer in the closing stages of a marathon. I even carried a contented smile over the last three miles. And I not only won my bet, the payoff also removed every trace of my usual postrace stiffness."

Any controversy about sex and running, however, usually focuses on prerace, not postrace activity. Many runners at every level have found that one of the surprising and healthful side effects of running is a general improvement in their sexual activity. Sex, after all, is a physical act; some call it the perfect exercise. Whatever, sex is a beautiful gift. Running, rowing, cycling, swimming, even vigorous walking are positive acts toward self-improvement that often result in taut muscles, narrow hips, thinner thighs, better body tone. In short, exercise makes us feel good about ourselves.

Sedentary men and women, studies have shown, are often afraid to be too active. They fear they might get hurt, or have a heart attack. They are under stress that they have no means to alleviate. Fear and stress make all of us tired. Fear and stress also inhibit, if not end, sexual drive and performance, which of course leads to more stress and fear, which in turn further inhibits the sexual drive, and so forth. Sedentary men and women may worry about their bodies. They are less flexible; when they engage in sexual intercourse their hearts race and their blood pressures increase. The sex act itself may be difficult and scary. "A person who has good physical fitness," says Dr. William Masters, the sex researcher, "invariably functions more effectively sexually than a person in poor shape. Sexual function is a physiologic process and every physiologic process works better in a good state of general health than in a poor one."

Physical activity works in two major ways to improve our sexual lives: it gives us confidence while toning and strengthening our bodies, and it is a superb outlet for emotional stresses. With new muscle tone, cardiovascular improvement, and flexibility, and less stress—in short, feeling good—we are ready, even eager to be more sexually active. We gain confidence and lose timidity.

Take, for example, the study by Dr. James R. White, Ph.D., of the University of California at San Diego. Dr. White put a group of 115 men (average age 44) through a nine-month exercise program, which included running, stretching, and calisthenics for about an hour a day, five days a week. At the end of the nine months, the runners reported more "major sexual fantasies," and that they engaged in more kissing and caressing of loved ones. Sexual intercourse also increased significantly, from 2.29 to 3.1 times per week—although how one makes love 2.29 times remained unclear. Dr. White also reported that while exercise did not create extramarital sex, those who had previously had extramarital sex now also engaged in it more often. The results of this study are similar to those from a study done by Dr. Lewis E. Graham, a Stanford University psychologist, on 81 middle-aged male university employees. "The more miles the exercisers run," Dr. Graham concluded, "the more satisfied their partners became with their sexual relations."

Sexual bliss, however, is not proportionate to miles in the bank. The White study, for example, also reported that seven men in the test group who were marathon runners reported a decrease in sexual desire and activity. As a 43-year-old Michigan man who runs 70 miles a week told *The Runner* magazine survey: "My sex drive lessens when running heavy depletion runs, peaking for a race. The body, it seems, has only so much energy."

Dr. Marvin Gewirtz, a New York City social psychologist and health researcher, whose talks include "Sex and the Long Distance Runner," points to a high number of divorced runners and joggers. He cites one study that warns of "problems of commitment and sexual satisfaction" when running reaches the level of 70 miles a week or more. At that point, the runner becomes obsessed with only one aspect of his or her life—mileage. "Running within bounds poses no threat to a marriage," says Dr. Gewirtz. "Runners who are not exhausting themselves are in much better shape and have much more stamina. Obviously that's going to pay off in bed as well as on the track."

Dr. Gabe Mirkin, a Washington, D.C., physican and runner, cites a survey of New York City Marathon runners that indicates that divorce occurs 3.5 times as frequently among marathon runners as among the population at large. Joan Paylo, a nonrunner, wrote about her marathon-obsessed ex-husband: "Do runners really do it better? If you can catch them in between soaking their swollen feet, taping their muscles and tallying up their mileage. Though he won a pair of running shoes and some trophies that winter, he lost me."

There are three types of running marriages: where both the husband and wife run; where the husband runs and the wife doesn't; where the wife runs and husband doesn't. The best relationship—in or out of marriage—is where both partners run, but perhaps not together. They have a shared interest, and a shared vigor, that may strengthen their bond. In addition to a marathon obsession, trouble occurs in a relationship where the woman runs and the man doesn't. The woman gains body awareness and self-confidence, and may view disapprovingly her sedentary and probably overweight husband. He, on the other hand, now finds that he must keep up with an athletic, healthful, confident woman who is spending more time exercising and less time pampering him.

A normal pattern of running, however, can contribute to a better sex life. "Sex is a physical activity that can be quite strenuous," Dr. Ronald Lawrence told *The Runner* magazine, "and with running, strength increases. There is a cardiovascular improvement and a resulting ability to perform better sexually." While we feel more confident and our bodies take on a firmer muscle tone, there are other concrete measurements of running's benefits. Dr. J. R. Sutton and colleagues at the Gavin Institute of Medical Research, St. Vincent's Hospital, Sydney, Australia, demonstrated that physical exercises may increase testosterone levels in male athletes. Among several things, his studies found that in men of average level of fitness, testosterone levels began to rise after ten minutes on a stationary bicycle. Testosterone levels reached their peak at 20 minutes of exercise.

What does this mean? For one thing, the hormone testosterone influences the male sex drive. Further, other studies show that exercising muscles need more testosterone to help store energy in the form of glycogen. The hormone may also increase carbohydrate metabolism in the muscles of exercising males. But production of this hormone depends on an increased blood flow around the testes; conversely, decreased blood flow means descreased testosterone output. Exercise increases blood flow. More exercise, therefore, means greater output of testosterone, which in turn increases male sex drive. There may indeed be some truth to the T-shirt that reads: "Runners Keep It Up Longer."

And what about women? Less research has been done on women's exercise and sexual drives, but early studies also indicate an increase in certain sex-drive hormones with vigorous exercise of longer than 20 minutes. *The Runner* survey revealed that women are more likely than men to ascribe sexual benefits to running. They feel that running has increased their self-confidence and sexual vigor. "Running has enhanced every area of my life, not only appearance and sex," a thirty-six-year-old teacher from Indiana told *The Runner*. "I'm a more dynamic teacher, a more assertive woman, a less depressed person than before."

Sex also begins in the head. Attitudes about yourself and the opposite sex are crucial, and with low self-esteem you will be slow to get involved. Obviously, one major benefit of exercise is improved self-image. This may come from the sense of discipline, from hormonal changes in both men and women, or even from changes in the brain from better blood circulation or transmission of nerve impulses. Another benefit, also not clearly understood, is that running simply makes you feel good. Sixty percent of all Americans suffer from some sort of depression. Studies now show that anxiety levels and depression drop off sharply with vigorous exercise. And anxiety is the biggest problem with sex; when you're not depressed, you're more in tune with your life and its partners.

One of the most persistent questions concerning sex and exercise is: Should I abstain from sex the day before a race? In *The Runner* survey, 90 percent of their respondents said they made love before racing. According to all surveys, that's a wise practice.

Dr. Craig Sharp, chief medical advisor for the British team at the 1972 Olympics, has been researching the sex-performance myth for a long time, "mainly because of the bad advice people have been getting." Some athletes, says Dr. Sharp, "upset their personal lives on non-physiological advice given for either puritanical reasons or through old wives' tales."

Dr. Sharp writes: "I can find no factual evidence either in scientific literature or in discussion with many athletes and sportsmen of world class that sexual activity in moderation up to and including the night before a match has any detrimental effect on the sport in question."

Indeed, there are stories of world class runners having sex, or masturbating, almost immediately before races in which they set records. Dr. Sharp notes the case of an Olympic middle-distance runner who set a world record an hour after making love, and that of the British miler who broke four minutes shortly after having sex. For the rest of us, having sex the evening before a big race may be relaxing, and let us get a good night's sleep. But beware! Remember Casey Stengel's warning about his athletes: "It isn't the sex that wrecks these guys, it's staying up all night looking for it."

The actual sex act takes fewer calories and less time than a good set of warm-up calisthenics. Studies indicate that sexual intercourse on the average lasts nine minutes and will cause the aggressive person to burn 250 calories an hour. That's only 40 calories, or about the same energy used walking up two flights of stairs. That shouldn't trouble any conditioned runner's competitive level. In fact, you have more to fear from overtraining than from sexual gymnastics before a race. "When you're overtrained you lose your sexual desires," says Dr. George Sheehan. "Staleness is a total neurohormonal metabolic exhaustion, and it's reflected in all activities—creative, sexual, spiritual."

Sex is a good activity, though neither aerobic nor a big calorie burner. Still, as Dr. Abraham I. Friedman advises: "Next time you're hungry reach for your mate instead of your plate."

One of the most convincing answers to the question "Do Runners make better lovers?" came one evening from a grey-haired man I interviewed in the Eliot Lounge after the Boston Marathon.

"I hear you're doing a book about running," he said, "and you've got a chapter on sex."

"Yup," I replied, and smiled.

"Well, for what it's worth, I started running when my wife died ten years ago. I was retired and had lots of time. And I was bored. I live in a retirement village, and I hate checkers and shuffleboard. So I started running. I qualified for Boston about five years ago, and I run about 60 miles a week."

At this point, I put down my beer. I was becoming most impressed with this old guy.

"Only problem is, the old ladies won't let me alone. There are damn few men my age around anyway, and one who runs 10 miles a day and keeps himself in shape is in high demand." He smiled, and chuckled. "I started wearing my old wedding ring, but that only cut down the number by a few. I find that I just can't say no. I really like young girls in their late fifties, early sixties. And when my body says yes so easily, why should my head say no?"

I agreed, and we both laughed.

"Young man," he said conspiratorially, "let me tell you something. I'm getting more now than I did when I was forty or fifty years younger."

We laughed again.

"Hey," I asked him, "how old are you anyway?"

"Me? I'm seventy-two."

Now that's something to look forward to.

PACE CHART
(1–4 miles)

Mile	2-Mile	3-Mile	4-Mile
7:00	14:00	21:00	28:00
7:10	14:20	21:30	28:40
7:20	14:40	22:00	29:20
7:30	15:00	22:30	30:00
7:40	15:20	23:00	30:40
7:50	15:40	23:30	31:20
8:00	16:00	24:00	32:00
8:10	16:20	24:30	32:40
8:20	16:40	25:00	33:20
8:30	17:00	25:30	34:00
8:40	17:20	26:00	34:40
8:50	17:40	26:30	35:20
9:00	18:00	27:00	36:00
9:10	18:20	27:30	36:40
9:20	18:40	28:00	37:20
9:30	19:00	28:30	38:00
9:40	19:20	29:00	38:40
9:50	19:40	29:30	39:20
10:00	20:00	30:00	40:00
10:10	20:20	30:30	40:40
10:20	20:40	31:00	41:20
10:30	21:00	31:30	42:00
10:40	21:20	32:00	42:40
10:50	21:40	32:30	43:20
11:00	22:00	33:00	44:00
11:10	22:20	33:30	44:40
11:20	22:40	34:00	45:20
11:30	23:00	34:30	46:00
11:40	23:20	35:00	46:40
11:50	23:40	35:30	47:20
12:00	24:00	36:00	48:00

PACE CHART
(5-Mile/10-Mile/Half-Marathon)

PACE CHART
(5K/10K/Marathon)

5-Mile	10-Mile	Half-Marathon	5K	10K	Marathon
35:00	1:10:00	1:31:42	21:45	43:30	3:03:32
35:50	1:11:40	1:33:53	22:16	44:32	3:07:54
36:40	1:13:20	1:36:04	22:47	45:34	3:12:16
37:30	1:15:00	1:38:15	23:18	46:36	3:16:39
38:20	1:16:40	1:40:26	23:49	47:38	3:21:01
39:10	1:18:20	1:42:37	24:20	48:40	3:25:23
40:00	1:20:00	1:44:48	24:51	49:43	3:29:45
40:50	1:21:40	1:46:59	25:22	50:45	3:34:07
41:40	1:23:20	1:49:10	25:53	51:47	3:38:29
42:30	1:25:00	1:51:21	26:24	52:49	3:42:52
43:20	1:26:40	1:53:32	26:56	53:51	3:47:14
44:10	1:28:20	1:55:43	27:27	54:53	3:51:46
45:00	1:30:00	1:57:54	27:58	55:55	3:55:58
45:50	1:31:40	2:00:11	28:29	56:58	4:00:22
46:40	1:33:20	2:02:22	29:00	58:00	4:04:44
47:30	1:35:00	2:04:33	29:31	59:02	4:09:06
48:20	1:36:40	2:06:44	30:02	60:05	4:13:28
49:10	1:38:20	2:08:55	30:33	61:07	4:17:50
50:00	1:40:00	2:11:07	31:05	62:09	4:22:13
50:50	1:41:40	2:13:16	31:36	63:12	4:26:32
51:40	1:43:20	2:15:25	32:07	64:14	4:30:50
52:30	1:45:00	2:17:33	32:38	65:16	4:35:06
53:20	1:46:40	2:19:44	33:09	66:18	4:39:28
54:10	1:48:20	2:21:55	33:40	67:20	4:43:50
55:00	1:50:00	2:24:05	34:11	68:22	4:48:12
55:50	1:51:40	2:26:15	34:42	69:24	4:52:30
56:40	1:53:20	2:28:26	35:13	70:26	4:56:52
57:30	1:55:00	2:30:39	35:44	71:28	5:01:18
58:20	1:56:40	2:32:50	36:15	72:30	5:05:40
59:10	1:58:20	2:35:01	36:46	73:32	5:10:02
60:00	2:00:00	2:37:12	37:17	74:34	5:14:24

Note: Times are averaged and rounded off—they are not exact to the second.

RECOMMENDED READING

Fitness/Training

Anderson, Bob. *Stretching.* Bolinas, Cal.: Shelter Publications, 1980.

Cooper, Dr. Kenneth. *The Aerobics Program for Total Well-Being.* New York: M. Evans and Co., 1982.

Cooper, Dr. Kenneth. *The Aerobics Way.* New York: M. Evans and Co., 1977, and Bantam Books, 1978.

Friedberg, Ardy. *Weight Training for Runners.* New York: Fireside Books, 1981.

Glover, Bob, and Schuder, Pete. *The Competitive Runner's Handbook.* New York: Penguin Books, 1983.

Melleby, Alexander. *The Y's Way to a Healthy Back.* New York: New Century Publishers, 1982.

Myers, Clayton. *The Official YMCA Physical Fitness Handbook.* New York: Popular Library, 1975.

Roth, Peter. *Running U.S.A.: The Complete Guide to Running in 125 American Cities.* New York: Aardvark, 1979.

Sheehan, George. *Running and Being.* New York: Simon and Schuster, 1978.

Nutrition

Brody, Jane. *Jane Brody's Nutrition.* New York: W. W. Norton, 1981.

Clark, Nancy. *The Athlete's Kitchen.* Boston: CBI Publishing Co., 1981.

Pritikin, Nathan. *The Pritikin Program for Diet and Exercise.* New York: Grosset & Dunlap, 1979.

Wood, Dr. Peter. *The California Diet and Exercise Program.* Mountain View, Cal.: Anderson World Books, 1983.

Physiology

Astrand, Per-Olaf and Rodahl, Kaare. *Textbook of Work Physiology.* New York: McGraw-Hill, 1977.

Costill, David. *A Scientific Approach to Distance Running.* Los Altos, Cal.: Track and Field News, 1979.

de Vries, Herbert. *Physiology of Exercise for Physical Education and Athletes.* Dubuque, Iowa: William C. Brown Co., 1974.

Psychology/Stress

Friedman, Meyer, and Rosenman, Ray. *Type A Behavior and Your Heart.* New York: Alfred A. Knopf, 1974.

Glasser, William. *Positive Addiction.* New York: Harper and Row, 1976.

Kostrubala, Thaddeus. *The Joy of Running.* New York: Lippincott, 1976.

McCutcheon, Lynn. *Psychology for the Runner.* Occoquan, Va.: Forefront Publishing, 1983.

Sachs, Michael, and Sacks, Michael. *Psychology of Running.* Champaign, Ill.: Human Kinetics Publishing, 1982.

Seyle, Hans. *Stress Without Distress.* New York: J. B. Lippincott, 1974.

Sports Medicine

Glover, Bob, and Weisenfeld, Dr. Murray. *The Injured Runner's Training Handbook.* New York: Penguin Books, 1984.

Kraus, Dr. Hans. *The Cause, Prevention and Treatment of Backache, Stress and Tension.* New York: Pocket Books, 1969.

Mirkin, Dr. Gabe, and Marshal Hoffman, *The Sportsmedicine Book.* Boston: Little, Brown, 1978.

Weisenfeld, Dr. Murray. *The Runner's Repair Manual.* New York: St. Martin's Press, 1980.

Women

Averbuch, Gloria. *The Woman Runner.* New York: Simon & Schuster, 1984.

Lance, Kathryn, *Getting Strong.* New York: Bobbs-Merrill, 1978.

Lance, Kathryn. *Running for Health and Beauty.* New York: Bobbs-Merrill, 1977.

Ullyot, Dr. Joan. *Running Free.* New York: G. P. Putnam's Sons, 1980.

Ullyot, Dr. Joan. *Women's Running.* Mountain View, Cal.: World Publications, 1976.

Running Publications
National Masters News
P.O. Box 2372
Van Nuys, CA 91404

New York Running News
International Running Center
9 East 89th Street
New York, New York 10028

The Runner
One Park Avenue
New York, New York 10016

Runner's World
P.O. Box 366
Mountain View, CA 94040

Running Times
14416 Jefferson Davis Highway
Suite 20
Woodbridge, VA 22191

RUNNING ORGANIZATIONS
The Achilles Track Club
Richard Traum
Personnelmetrics
1001 Avenue of the Americas
New York, NY 10018
For the physically disabled.

American Running & Fitness Association
2420 K Street, NW
Washington, DC 20037
Formerly called the National Jogging Association, this membership organization (over 35,000) promotes running and fitness.

The Athletics Congress (TAC)
P.O. Box 120
Indianapolis, IN 46206
The national governing body for track and road racing. All competitors racing internationally or in national events sanctioned by TAC are expected to be members.

The New York Road Runners Club
The International Running Center
9 East 89th Street
New York, NY 10028
Conducts hundreds of races, classes, and clinics for all levels of runners. Membership (over 25,000) includes subscription to *New York Running News.* Building is home of a very complete running library.

Road Runners Club of America
Sanford Schmidt
732 Linden Place
Alton, IL 62002
The most active organization in the road-racing field, with over 200 member clubs—mostly small, local groups.

Robert H. Glover and Associates, Inc.
4 East 75th Street
New York, NY 10021
(212) 787-7480
Corporate fitness consultants; running classes of all levels from beginner runner to advanced competitor; personalized running consultations by appointment.

INDEX